Art and Intimacy

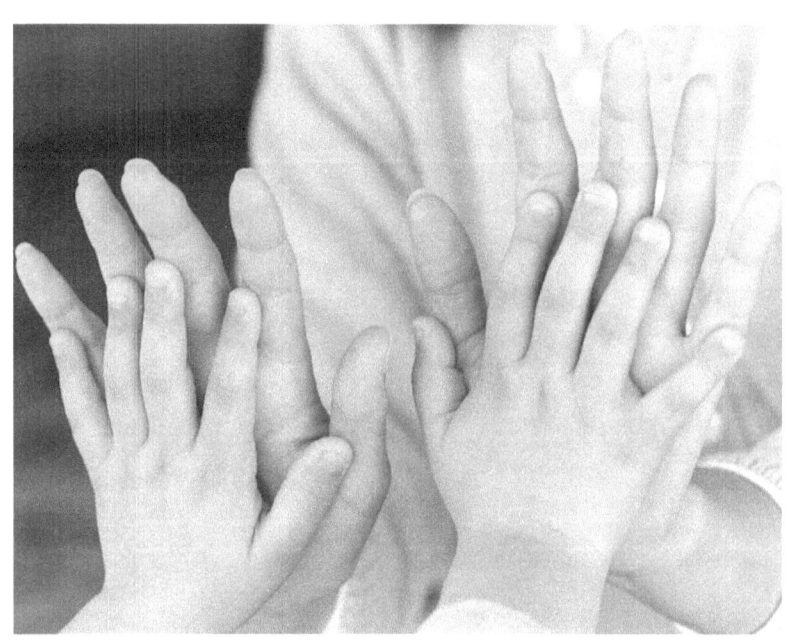

ARTand *Intimacy*

How the Arts Began

Ellen Dissanayake

A McLELLAN BOOK

UNIVERSITY OF WASHINGTON PRESS
SEATTLE AND LONDON

This book is published with the assistance of a grant from the McLellan Endowed Series Fund, established through the generosity of Mary McCleary McLellan and Mary McLellan Williams.

Library of Congress Cataloging-in-Publication Data
Dissanayake, Ellen.
  Art and Intimacy : how the arts began / Ellen Dissanayake.
    p.   cm.
  "A McLellan book."
  Includes bibliographical references and index.
  ISBN 978-0-295-99196-2 (pbk. : alk. paper)
    1. Arts and society.   2. Intimacy (Psychology)   I. Title.
NX180.S6D58   2000
701'.15—dc21   99-37639
                                                                          CIP

The paper used in this publication meets the minimum requirements of American National Standard for Information Sciences—Permanence of Paper for Printed Library Materials, ANSI Z39.48-1984.

Frontispiece photograph by Elizabeth Leeor.

Cover art: *Maternité*, by Jacques Villon, c. 1943. Oil on canvas, 57⅜ × 38 in. Courtesy of the Patrick and Beatrice Haggerty Museum of Art, Marquette University, Milwaukee, Wisconsin. Gift of Mr. and Mrs. Ira Haupt, 62.7

For Joel Schiff,
leaf by niggle

Contents

Illustrations

Preface

PROSPECTIVE READERS WHO pick up a book called "Art and Intimacy" might well wonder what is in store. Both words have intrinsic appeal—at least for many. At the same time, "art" is notoriously vague, with multiple meanings and associations. And "intimacy" may seem to be either a tease (with its euphemistic suggestion of *sexual* intimacy) or a turn-off (with its overtones from popular psychology's manuals for "improving relationships"). What could these two broad and imprecise subjects have to do with one another.

Quite a lot. In the pages that follow I unite the notions of intimacy as love (in its sense of close affiliation or relationship as well as sexual intimacy) with art (in the sense of "the arts") by showing that biologically—that is, in human evolution—they are fundamentally related. While it is hardly possible in a short summary to make a rather complex, book-length argument plausible (otherwise, why write the book?), I will here briefly state the premise. The biological phenomenon of love is originally manifested—expressed and exchanged—by means of emotionally meaningful "rhythms and modes" that are jointly created and sustained by mothers and their infants in ritualized, evolved interactions. From these rudimentary and unlikely beginnings grow adult expressions of love, both sexual and generally affiliative, *and the arts.* That is to say, in their origins in ourselves and in our species, love and art are, I suggest, inherently related.

Such a claim may intrigue, delight, dismay, or activate the nonsense-detectors of prospective readers. Some people will prefer, with good reason, to leave love and art unanalyzed. But almost everyone else has something to say about them. While poets may be inclined to wax rhapsodic about love and art, positivists treat both as fictions or illusions, tricks of our minds that cannot bear much reality. Art and love may be exalted as divine gifts or reduced to male competition and brain chemicals.

Notwithstanding the perils that await one who wishes to add to the existing myriad views on love and art—nor discounting the inordinately high kitsch-potential of invoking mothers and babies—I have tried in the following pages to develop a reasoned and plausible view that will be acceptable to both the tender- and the tough-minded, that is, to poets and positivists alike.

Having said this much, I defer until the introduction any further description of the varied strands that make up my argument and its implications. But I should comment on other of the book's features, apart from its many-splendored subject matter, that may seem to depart somewhat from standard academic studies.

To begin with, my approach is highly interdisciplinary. Although I have tried to write for nonspecialists, I have drawn upon ideas and findings from a greater number of academic fields than is customary: ethology, evolutionary psychology and sociobiology, evolutionary theory, infant psychology, developmental psychology, neuroscience, cognitive science, cognitive archaeology, physical and cultural anthropology, art history and theory, aesthetics, and cultural history.

Although interdisciplinary studies are routinely praised as good things, as a congenital interdisciplinarian I have found that this approval is frequently more professed than real. It is painful for someone who has over decades mastered an esoteric field to watch a novice presumptuously pick and choose blossoms from this patch and that and arrange them into a strange new bouquet. My justification is that from the synthesis of these disparate ideas and findings comes a coherent and fruitful account that is reinforced from several perspectives. Also, one can see new possibilities as well as dangerous pitfalls when looking at established gardens of theory from outside their boundaries.

It is not difficult, however, to understand why many scholars avoid interdisciplinary studies, since *intra*disciplinary matters in any one field can be so factional and often fractious. Within the field of evolutionary theory alone there are long-standing, well-developed, complex, and sometimes contentious discourses about the processes, mechanisms, and details of such things as intraspecific competition and cooperation, the relationship between ultimate and proximate levels of selection, the relationship between ontogeny and phylogeny, levels of selection (gene, individual, and group), sexual selection theory, and the nature of human nature. Anthropology, too, is riven by differences of opinion about the relationship between nature and culture, the definition and extent of culture, cultural relativism versus what used to be called "the psychological unity of mankind," and even the relevance of biology to an understanding of human behavior. Within neuroscience there are many shades of opinion about, for instance, the psychobiological nature and psychological function of emotion and its relationship to cognition.

When these specialist arguments are directly relevant to my general theme, I engage with them, but elsewhere, where it matters less, I have chosen not to burden the text or nonspecialist readers with their subtleties and complexities. When my interpretations of certain academic matters and findings differ from the most prominent views, I have tried to show, either in the text or in the notes, that I am familiar with their proponents' counterclaims. I apologize if specialists in a particular field, or partisans of particular arguments, feel that I have misleadingly presented complex arguments as if they were settled or straightforward, just as I apologize if they are periodically bored with descriptions of what to them seems elementary and uncontroversial. In some cases I have chosen not to mention at all some well-known views on the subjects I treat—for example, Freud's ideas about love and infancy or Winnicott's about art and infancy, interesting as these may be—because they were framed outside (and I believe could be profitably subsumed under) the more embracing view of evolutionary psychology.

Another important way in which my study differs from many other works of academic scholarship is that my thesis of the joint origin of love and art is not only theoretical but also has practical or tangible implications for the way we live today. It is not from an irresistible dilettantism that I partake of so many fields but because when synthesized these various studies show, from numerous perspectives, how the psychobiological mechanisms shared by love and art—what I call rhythms and modes—evolved as natural ways to satisfy essential human needs that today are frequently neglected. If this biological argument is sound, then it follows that for us as individuals and as a society it is important to begin taking the arts seriously (see chapter 6).

These two differences from traditional works of scholarship—an extreme interdisciplinism and the advancing of a "message"—are responsible for yet another departure, having to do with citing others' work. In academic books, notes and references are customary because they establish that authors have adequate knowledge of their subject and can provide sources for their claims. Like all scholars, I have made extensive use of the work of others, whose names appear in the text, notes, and index and as some three hundred citations in the reference list.

However, as in my choice not to describe every tangential specialized controversy, it was neither practicable nor, indeed, possible to cite every authority who contributed to every idea or theme in my argument. Such omissions are in part because over a long life I have become indebted to many intellectual predecessors in ways of which I am not even aware. In other cases I have enlisted well-established information that needed no defense—not to pass these ideas off as my own or to suggest that I am the first person to advance them, but to support my argument about rhythms and modes in human emotional life and to supplement my message about taking the arts seriously.

Thus specialist scholars should probably be advised that once I have set up my academic argument, which is original, in the introduction and chapter 1, using conventional citations, I go on in the remaining chapters sometimes to rely on generally accepted, even self-evident, observations and ideas from psychology and anthropology without conscientiously crediting their original or present-day proponents. As it is, many readers will probably feel that I have too many rather than too few citations.

These unreferenced assertions should be largely uncontroversial—they are what we all know, at least once it is pointed out. I enlist them to make clear that we live in an environment very different from the one in which we were evolved to live. It seems to me that this is one of the most important things for us to realize about ourselves today. Knowing where we came from is intrinsic to knowing what we are, collectively as a species and individually as we each try to lead satisfying and worthwhile lives. The manifold subject areas I have utilized together provide a good grounding for understanding human nature in this sense.

My Darwinian, or biosocial, perspective is what E. O. Wilson (1998) has recently called "consilience," a point of view that unifies the biological and the cultural. It embraces the perspectives that students of human behavior have traditionally used: the social or "human" sciences of history, economics, anthropology, psychology, and sociology. And it incorporates the arts and religion into human evolutionary discourse.

Insights from biosocial or evolutionary psychology are sometimes belittled—especially by those meeting them for the first time—for "stating the obvious," for "saying what everyone already knows": babies are cute, chocolate truffles taste good, people want to feel appreciated, we all need and enjoy the giving and receiving of love.

Evolutionary psychology restates such common sense observations and well-established ideas in anthropology and psychology but then goes on to show that the obvious has become the way it is for good evolutionary reasons. It is not the "answers" or "conclusions" but the explanations that are insightful and novel. When I say things such as people need to "belong," to have a sense of "meaning," and to feel "competent" in their lives, I do not mean to suggest that I consider these to be original, pathbreaking insights. What is original, I believe, is the way in which these obvious needs are subsumed within my overarching scheme of the bioevolutionary importance and primary interrelatedness of love and art, which itself leads to implications about taking the arts seriously—not for their own sake but because they evolved as intrinsic to human existence.

And this seems to me a message worth arguing in a convincing, well-supported way. For although individual artists today certainly may be serious about their work, neither the aesthetic theories of philosophers in their ivory towers nor the common sense of men and women on the street provides good reasons for taking the arts seriously. Chapter 6 is an extended argument for what the arts could contribute to our lives today. The appendix presents a "naturalistic" aesthetics and indicates how aesthetic experience might be reconceptualized within a biosocial framework.

My consilient view has meant stepping somewhat outside the frame of evolutionary psychology in order to consider psychological needs and emotional responses not only as "mechanisms" that prompt us to do what was adaptive hundreds of thousands of years ago but also as felt indications of value that suggest how and why our lives can and should be more humanly fulfilling. To take the arts seriously is to rediscover routes to belonging, meaning, and competence in a world where for many these are no longer part of the human birthright.

Although my study is different from many others in the ways just described, it resembles every other work of scholarship in its indebtedness to the work and collegiality of countless others, past and present. I would like particularly to mention some of these people, realizing that I cannot possibly acknowledge all who have aided, inspired, or taught me over the years.

Dr. Colwyn Trevarthen, now Emeritus Professor of Child Psychology and Psychobiology at the University of Edinburgh, helped me find much of what I needed to know about mothers and babies. My fourteen months in Scotland were made possible by a fellowship at the Institute for Advanced Studies in the Humanities at Edinburgh University, where the director, Professor Peter Jones, and Mrs. Anthea Taylor were unfailingly welcoming and helpful. Aline Dunlop's kindness in making available to me her flat in the center of the Old Town helped to ensure that my stay in Edinburgh will remain in my mind and heart as the acme of scholarly bliss.

Friends and colleagues have read early versions, sections, or all of the manuscript and made invaluable suggestions. I would like to thank, in alphabetical order, Power Boothe, Joseph Carroll, Wendy Eisner, Ted Melnechuk, Edwina Norton, Robert Storey, and Colwyn Trevarthen. My great and good friend from New York, Joel Schiff, has shared my thoughts and interests for well over a decade and contributed more than anyone to their development and to whatever inner fortitude or faith is required to keep working for years on a project whose course and final destination were by no means straightforward. I should say that I have not always followed his (or others') suggestions, and no one else should be held accountable for my idiosyncratic interpretations.

Sections of several chapters began or were developed as articles in *American Craft, Surface Design Journal,* and *Philosophy and Literature.* Other parts grew out of various talks I was invited to give to academic and other audiences. These talks gave me the opportunity to apply my ideas to fields as disparate as ceramics and dance, glass art and biomusicology, printmaking and comparative literature, art education and archaeology, art therapy and the visual art avant-garde, as well as to evolutionary psychology and its subfield of bioaesthetics.

Writing a complex work of scholarship requires time (that is, economic freedom) and access to libraries. In addition to expressing my gratitude for the fellowship in Edinburgh, I must thank my parents, Margaret and Fritz Franzen, for providing what amounted to a writer's colony grant for two years in tranquil, sympathetic, demand-free surroundings at their home on Discovery Bay in Port Townsend, Washington. During this time, the Jefferson County Library managed to locate dozens of arcane works that I requested through interlibrary loan and delivered them to me by bookmobile on Wednesday mornings at Cape George Firehall. In 1997 the College of Fine Arts at Ball State University provided a most warm and welcome academic home in Indiana, where I was that year's Emens Distinguished Professor.

Once again I am delighted to publish a work with the University of Washington Press, whose attention to my books, both before and after publication, has been all a writer could ask for. In these days of cut-rate book production and short-term book promotion, I am a fortunate author indeed.

Art and Intimacy

Introduction

LOVE AND ART

IN ALDOUS HUXLEY's early novel *Antic Hay*, Theodore Gombril, Jr., attends a concert of chamber music and hears a performance of Mozart's String Quintet in G Minor. Although he is deeply moved by the music, Gombril suffers from the same temperamental disposition as Huxley himself and many of his male characters: a hypersensitivity to the rude incongruities between the ideal and the real. Watching the individual performers take their bows, Gombril notes the first violinist's undisguised vanity, his weary "poached eyes" and disdainful smile. A second player is beady-eyed, potbellied, and bald; the next one, "monolithic and grim." The others sweat and posture, or twitch nervously. How strange and ironic, Gombril reflects, that from these "ridiculous," worldly, flawed creatures can emerge such divine, transfiguring sounds. Looking at them, who would believe it?

Those with unflinching Huxleyan minds might also sometimes consider their own less-than-perfect selves and souls and those of their lovers, which nevertheless sometimes transcend these imperfections—as the chamber musicians did—and create together in the act of physical love something divine and transfiguring. How miraculous that our mortal bodies in these inelegant actions should become the instruments for a composition of sensations that, at their best, awaken us to—or immerse us in—a reality transformed beyond anything imaginable in ordinary life.

For most of us, love and art are our closest encounters with perfection, experiences that may be likened to ideas of heaven and bliss. "How pure the passion," thinks Gombril as he listens to the Mozart slow movement, "how unaffected, clear and without clot or pretension. . . . Blessed are the pure in heart, for they shall see God. Pure and unsullied; pure and unmixed, unadulterated" (p. 206).

Both love and art have the power to grasp us utterly and transport us from ordinary sweating, flailing, imperfect "reality" to an indescribable realm where we know and seem known by the sensibility of another, united in a continuing present, our usual isolation momentarily effaced. And in such states, we recognize that *this* is the reality, and ordinary reality is only an illusion.

Such experiences are "emotional," yet suffused with a kind of bodily knowing that can be described, if at all, only inadequately by analogy with other mingled modes of being—movement, sensation, transformations. Here, for example, is Gombril's (Huxley's) partial description of the Mozart quintet's slow movement:

> The instruments come together and part again. Long silver threads hang aerially over a murmur of waters; in the midst of muffled sobbing a cry. The fountains blow their architecture of slender pillars and from basin to basin the waves fall; from basin to basin, and every fall makes somehow possible a higher leaping of the jet, and at the last fall the mounting column springs up into the sunlight and from water the music has modulated up into a rainbow. Blessed are the pure in heart, for they shall see God; they shall make God visible too, to other eyes. (p. 206)

And here are his words for the introduction to the final movement:

> Blood beats in the ears. Beat, beat, beat. A slow drum in the darkness, beating in the ears of one who lies wakeful with fever, with the sickness of too much misery. It beats unceasingly, in the ears, in the mind itself. Body and mind are indivisible and in the spirit blood painfully throbs. Sad thoughts droop through the mind. A small pure light comes swaying down through the darkness, comes to rest, resigning itself to the obscurity of its misfortune. There is resignation, but blood still beats in the ears. Blood still painfully beats, though the mind has acquiesced. And then, suddenly, the mind exerts itself, throws off the fever of too much

suffering and laughing, commands the body to dance. The introduction . . . comes to its suspended, throbbing close. (pp. 206–7)

Comings together and partings, murmurs, a cry in the midst of sobbing, silver threads ("architecture") of water rising and falling, leaping and springing, sunlight and water somehow becoming rainbow. Or amid the slow beating of blood, a pure light sways in the darkness. In love and art our responses partake of many modes simultaneously, as well as successive tides of rhythms. The most "spiritual" art is felt viscerally; the most bodily love is idealized. Subterranean and empyrean are conjoined.

In art and love, senses and modes of feeling intertwine. The sounds of music are felt as if they were touch: warm, cool, sharp, flat, soft, heavy, light, piercing, brittle. Or they are colored—velvety green, sky blue, silver. They seem to rise, dissolve, shift, and change like things we see, or they unroll like strands and skeins and filaments. Like a shaft of light they illuminate; like a sudden fin they emerge from an undifferentiated sea.

Touches and movements of bodily love suggest space—depth and height, expansion and contraction, rising and falling, swirling, sinking. Love also has its rhythms, not only material but temporal momentum, weight, and fullness. In the temporal experience of art, as of love, we seem to travel through rooms or landscapes of ever changing shape in a charged, expanding present. In both we are immersed in longing, which wakens, anticipates, then swallows the space between significances where nothing is. Love and art sound intimacies, find harmony in deepest immediacy. And in talking or writing about both love and art, we—I speak for myself—recognize the inadequacies, and the edge of embarrassment, in our powers of description.

Perhaps only an obtuse killjoy would then want to ask where such powerful feelings come from, and why. Cast up on the further shores of the revelations of art or love, I find myself as bemused as Gombril: astonished that our mortal frame should know something of this nature and that another mortal (artist or beloved) should have conceived and shared—made possible—this journey, the felt conjoinment, the sense of equipoise that it could happen no other way. The expanded sense of being. But whence—and why?

I am of course aware that not all experiences of art, or of love for that matter, are as momentous or transfiguring as those just described. The "art" and "intimacy" (love) of my title acquire force and value from their rare

and sublime embodiments, but they are meant also to apply to lesser incarnations. In the pages that follow, I explore the bodily origins and inter-
connections of the felt rhythms and modes of love and art, tracing them
to what may appear to be inconsequential or even unlikely psychobiological beginnings in the earliest months of individual infancy and in the
pre-Paleolithic infancy of the human species. I show that human newborns
come into the world with sensitivities and capacities that predispose them
to join in emotional communion with others. I then argue that these same
sensitivities and capacities, which arose as instruments of survival in our
remote hominid past, are later used and elaborated in the rhythms and
modes of adult love and art.[1]

I choose the words "rhythm" and "mode" as general terms for the admittedly indescribable—literally unverbalizable—sense of intermingled
movement and sensory overlapping that characterizes infant experiences,
as it also characterizes subsequent experiences of love and art. (After all,
the word "infant" means, literally, "unable to speak," and as my efforts to
describe them reveal, experiences of love and art are also intrinsically
nonverbal.) Yet several senses of these words connote fairly well what I
wish to convey of the ineffable tides or undertows of such experiences.

"Rhythm" derives originally from the Greek word *rhein*, "to flow."
Among its dictionary meanings that I adopt for my purposes here are "an
ordered, recurrent alternation of strong and weak elements in the flow of
sound and silence in speech [or music]"; a "movement or fluctuation
marked by the regular recurrence or natural flow of related elements"; "a
regularly recurrent quantitative change in a variable biological process";
and "the effect created by the elements in [a structured event] that relate
to the temporal development of the action."[2] That is, I mean to suggest
movement in time and the sense of forward flow of sound and nonsound,
both "natural" (or biological) and humanly organized in performances of
love or art.

"Mode" comes from the Latin word for "measure" and thus also
suggests rhythm and an arrangement of something. My meaning here,
however, includes other connotations that have to do with *manner*, or
mode-of-being—that is, a particular form (modality) or variety of sensation and expression—and with style, manifestation, and emotional state
and their intermodal or crossmodal associations and expressions. "Mode"
is also associated with *mood* and with sensation.[3]

Rhythm has to do with an *unfolding in time*, the patterned course of
an experience; modes are *qualities* of that experience—its sense of swift-

ness, solidity, opening, closing, speed, forcefulness, fullness, barrenness, lightness, and so forth, on a dynamic scale of moreness and lessness. One might say that rhythms are something like verbs, whereas modes are like adjectives, except the two usually interpenetrate, coalesce with other senses (sight, sound, touch, smell, taste, balance), and change from moment to moment. The words "rhythm" and "mode" are meant to be polyvalent, then, suggestive of states of being and states of feeling.

Instilled as part of our biological nature, the rhythms and modes of infancy demonstrate and develop the psychological capacities that predispose humans to mutuality—the sharing of emotional states in patterned sequences with others. In the close early interactions between infants and their caretakers are the prototypes for what will become our later experiences of love, allegiance, art, and other forms of self-transcendence.

In the first chapter I describe how rhythms and modes became, during human evolution, a means of coordinating and expressing emotional states of *mutuality* between mothers and infants, eventually becoming the basis for "enculturation" and participation in everyday life—that is, *belonging* to a social group (chapter 2), finding a sense of life *meaning* (chapter 3), developing *competence* for life (chapter 4), and eventually engaging in the *elaborating* of experience that we now call the arts (chapter 5).

In other words, preverbal rhythms and modes of infancy do not only underlie our ability to engage intimately with others. Additionally, in the early history of our species, expressed as rudiments of the arts (for example, moving together in synchrony, matching vocalizations and gestures, handling or manipulating the physical world), they facilitated the acquisition of the human cultural way of life. The complex societies of today are very different from societies living in ancestral environments (or even recent traditional societies), and acquisition of life knowledge and competence often is gained by means of intellectual abilities more than with rhythmic-modal sensitivities. Implications of this shift in how humans acquire culture are addressed in chapter 6.

AN UNORTHODOX VIEW OF HUMAN NATURE

Because this is a book about love and art, it is also about human nature: what we are "really like" under the veils of our genders, ethnicities, religions, ways of life—that is, the various wrappings of our cultures.[4] To say that humans have a nature that underlies culture is to accept that humans are a species which, like other animals, has evolved. Such a position, that of evolutionary (or biosocial) psychology, recognizes that humans have evolved *to require culture*—they cannot exist in a cultureless or culture-free state—and that they are born with common, cross-culturally recognizable predispositions ("needs") to acquire culture.

My thesis begins with the assumption that it is in the inborn capacity and need for (1) *mutuality* between mother and infant (the prototype for intimacy or love) that four other essential human capacities and psychological imperatives are enfolded or embedded and gradually, in their time, emerge. Mother-infant mutuality contains and influences the capacities for (2) *belonging to* (and acceptance by) a social group, (3) *finding and making meaning*, (4) acquiring a sense of *competence through handling and making*, and (5) *elaborating* these meanings and competencies as a way of expressing or acknowledging their vital importance.

It is my overall contention that in our species' development of culture, as in our own individual development from birth to maturity, the rhythms and modes of love and art have been critical, inasmuch as they have affected these five psychosocial needs or propensities. My view of human nature emphasizes evolved mechanisms (called here "rhythms and modes") for mutuality and sociality, a position that departs considerably from that of either the general public or the scientific establishment (whose views on this subject tend to be surprisingly similar).

In common parlance the phrase "human nature" is usually invoked with a rueful shake of the head to comment on some lapse that involves one or more of the seven deadly sins: gluttony, lust, sloth, pride, anger, envy, and greed. "It's only human nature" to be selfish or lazy, to lie, cheat, or steal if you can get away with it.

Similarly, human evolutionary studies have tended to think of human nature as being composed not of psychological or emotional *needs* that arise from a primary capacity for mutuality but rather of competitive behavioral *strategies* that serve an underlying selfishness.[5] Evolutionary psychologists emphasize the pervasiveness in all animals, including humans, of these inherent strategies or tactics to acquire or invest in various limited but desirable resources such as high-quality mates and other material or social goods—high status, good reputation, abundant food and possessions. "Success" is defined in such studies by better and longer survivorship and better and more numerous descendants, achieved as a consequence of individual differences of ability in competitive strategies and tactics.

In this view, love and art, like altruism and cooperation, are themselves strategies or tactics that some individuals can employ competitively, in the right circumstances, more successfully than others. For example, mothers and offspring are shown to have conflicting interests (Trivers 1974), as at weaning, and to use deception—such as infant fussing or maternal feigned indifference—to get their way. Babies may try to obtain as much care and attention as possible, more than their mothers are able to give, and mothers themselves are motivated, whether they consciously know it or not, to maximize their reproductive success by raising the greatest number of healthy children, not just their present infant, to maturity (Daly and Wilson 1995).[6] Although this is an established way to view the matter, it contributes to a misleadingly one-sided view of humans. If we regard altruism as *only* a strategy for competition, we will be blind to instances when it is not performed for competitive reasons or is not deceptive. An assumption of simple conflicts of interest is not the only way to interpret infant and parental behaviors.

Indeed, a number of recent psychological studies of early interactions between mothers and infants, to be described in chapter 1, modify this sweeping assumption of pervasive selfishness. Evolutionary science has yet to recognize and take account of their implications. The studies establish unequivocally the extent to which mutuality between mother and infant, and its influence upon other consequent or related psychological needs, developed over hundreds of thousands of years of human evolution as a crucial motivating force that enabled our ancestors to survive in the earliest human "life-style"—that of small bands of foragers and hunters on the African savannah.

The foraging-hunting way of life of our hominid ancestors required not only resourceful, competitive individuals but also strongly bonded social groups that could work together with confidence and loyalty, convinced of the efficacy of their joint actions. The usual view of humans as selfish, cooperating only so they could advance their own interests, cannot account for the resilience and responsivity of the skeins of mutuality.

It takes a saint or a Pollyanna to claim that humans are not selfish or lazy or that they do not lie, cheat, and steal. They manifestly do, more than most of us are comfortable admitting. Like other animals, humans can be shown to possess a strong (and undeniable) underlying self-interest and impetus for self-preservation. Yet despite the ignoble record of individual and collective human nastiness, what are we to make of the fact that the earliest ability of human infants—who cannot yet use objects, hold themselves upright, or even look about them with a balanced head—is to engage in emotional communion with others? Each of us is born with a mind—senses and emotions—that moves us to seek and engage in intimacy with others before we do anything else.

By going more deeply into the matter, we can look at the truism "it's only human nature" another way—in terms not of original sin(s) as much as original sensitivities. If mutuality and its associated needs were not *evolved characteristics* of human nature, they would not matter: we could omit them. Like lizards, we could get along fine without intimate ongoing relationships with others, without feeling accepted by our social group, without a sense of meaning or competence in our lives, or without demonstrating our serious regard and care for what is important to us.

The fact is, however, that people manifestly have such needs, and—if their satisfaction is not forthcoming—feel humanly incomplete and impelled to seek mutuality, belonging, meaning, competence, and elaboration as best they can, frequently in aberrant ways and with maladaptive results to themselves and to their fellows. Using the scheme that I outline in these pages, I believe one can demonstrate that much human "sinfulness" and selfishness arise from the thwarting or distorting of these primary needs—which in ancestral environments were commonly met in the natural course of life—and from their consequent diversion to substitute sources of satisfaction in societies that neglect to address, acknowledge, and satisfy them.

CULTURE AND HUMAN NATURE

Nearly thirty years ago I spent a year in Sri Lanka, a small island nation in South Asia, then called Ceylon. Eventually I returned there and married a Sri Lankan, and I have lived there on and off for a total of some fifteen years. It sounds trite to say that the experience has changed my life—marriage in general does change lives. But certainly I have never again been able to look at Western ways and the things I once took for granted in quite the same way. In fact, I am always aware now that there is a different way of thinking about or doing almost anything.

Such a realization underlies the currently fashionable claims of "cultural relativism," the position that each culture is a unique entity that has its own internal consistency and integrity, even though someone from another culture may find it strange and inscrutable. From this perspective, any view of a culture (including one's own) is at best an incomplete interpretation, but almost certainly individual cultural biases will interfere with understanding the behavior and values of someone from another culture.

Without even leaving home, I think we all eventually discover something of this incommensurability of cultures when we become close to someone from another kind of family than our own—not to mention another religious background, race, or geographical area. Even the sexes, male and female, have different "cultures," so that one's view of what is right or natural will often conflict with what his or her mate considers to be right and natural.

Yet my intimate life with Sri Lankans, despite differences between us, made me the opposite of a fanatical cultural relativist: I have in fact become more impressed with the deeper human similarities that underlie cultural differences. I have become, that is, a firm advocate of a common human nature.

Living in other cultures has made me aware not only of how much we humans do not understand about each other but also of how much we nevertheless are *able* to understand. I have become more aware of the nonverbal aspects of our associations with others, the things that go unsaid because we do not know the words for them (or because there *are* no words for many things). And yet communication takes place—to a large degree by means of the "rhythms and modes" I will describe. (Mismatches of rhythms and modes may be responsible for miscommunications as well.)

Living in another culture has also made me passionately curious about human nature, that is, about how humans are alike and how and why we got that way. Recognizing a fundamental sameness under the skin—humanness—has sent me to learn about a wide diversity of subjects: about our archaeological or ancestral past; about other societies, especially premodern or traditional societies that are closer to the ancestral societies in which human nature evolved; about children, especially infants, who come into the world "uncultured" and thus have common infant behaviors; about other animals. All these subject areas give insights into where humans came from and what we share. Underlying capacities for engaging in love (or mutuality, a term I prefer because it is more descriptive and less emotionally charged) and for engaging with the arts (which I will trace to the more rudimentary impetus to elaborate) are among the many traits we share.

I use the words "love" and "art" in my chapter title because they are more accessible and recognizable than "mutuality" and "elaborating." These longer words will, however, stand for the underlying and related universal motivational schemes of what we in modern societies often mean by "love" and "art." In contemporary America (and other industrial and postindustrial societies based on market values and generally character- ized by terms such as secular, pluralistic, consumerist, specialized, indi- vidualistic, and informational), the *concepts* of love and art show only blurred outlines and traces of their originals—like a photocopy of an oft-photocopied photocopy. Yet I maintain that the need for and propensity to attain mutuality and to elaborate artfully—whether we use the words "love" and "art" or something else—are innate.

Many people are surprised to learn that "innate" does not mean "in-evitable." Most innate aptitudes in humans require fostering—a child who never hears language will not learn to speak; someone who lives in a desert will not learn to swim; women who have never been around ba-bies will not instinctively know how to care for them. Yet speaking, swimming, and mothering are all evolved ("innate") propensities— things we will normally learn to do. Mutuality with others and elaborat-ing the things that are important to us are similarly innate propensities, among many others.

Any culture (or subculture) places its individual stamp on our innate propensities, emphasizing some, devaluing others. So we have, for ex-ample, more or less peaceable and more or less aggressive societies that bring out these characteristics in their members (who, as individuals, also vary in their temperamental, behavioral, mental, and physical features and abilities). A few individuals may deliberately choose lives of celibacy, si-lence, or isolation from society. To accept that humans have a "nature" does not imply uniformity and determinism.

Because an understanding of human nature is assisted by knowing about as many different cultures as possible, I refer in the following chap-ters to a number of societies outside of Europe and North America, par-ticularly some that have (or recently had) more traditional ways of life. At the end of each chapter, I devote a section to reflecting upon some of the ways in which modern societies have diverged from what seems to have been the ancestral hunter-gatherer prototype, and what these divergences imply.

I suggest that at least some contemporary personal and social prob-lems can be understood as arising from responses to powerful evolved needs and impulses that in a Paleolithic hunter-gatherer society would have been normal and adaptive but that in complex, pluralistic modern societies are not.[7] Ancestral ways of life "selected for" (or promoted) some traits that can be maladaptive today—for example, unthinking allegiance to authority, conformity, mistrust of those considered to be outsiders. Other predispositions—making things with our hands, using our bodies for work—have atrophied through disuse and disinclination. Yet these traits, in the small homogeneous subsistence societies in which humans lived for 99.9 percent of their evolutionary history, gave a kind of security and aptitude for life that contemporary people frequently lack.

I find it ironic that instead of suffering from unavoidable disease, predation, accident, and malnutrition (in a nevertheless caring, helping, interdependent hunter-gatherer society), our modern children—most of whom have inoculations and antibiotics, safe homes, and more food than they can eat—may nonetheless suffer from parental neglect or abuse, a sense of meaninglessness, social vulgarity and violence, and general indifference from the institutions that control and direct their lives. The simple fact that suicide is the third highest cause of death in American teenage youth (and that the teen suicide rate is 95 percent higher today than it was in 1970) is evidence to me that something is awry in the way we live.[8] Adolescents in hunter-gatherer societies may undergo painful initiation ordeals and serious or fatal accidents, but they rarely, if ever, kill themselves.

In the chapters that follow, I show that mutuality and elaboration (love and art), and the mechanisms (rhythms and modes) that express and sustain them are valid, age-old, if today neglected, ways to instill a sense of belonging, meaning, and competence in people in modern societies who require more from their lives than diversion.

HOW MUTUALITY MAY HAVE ORIGINATED

Like other momentous adaptive forces, mutuality probably emerged from an unlikely antecedent—in this case, the collision course between two incompatible anatomical trends. It is well known from human evolutionary history that our hominid ancestors, unlike our ape cousins, walked upright on two legs. Bipedality required a number of corresponding anatomical changes, including alterations in the bones, muscles, and other tissues of feet, legs, and hips to enable better walking and running.

Upright walking permitted other useful adaptations: for example, it freed the hands for carrying and gesturing, and it undoubtedly contributed to changes in habitat and way of life that promoted larger brains—the second trend. Over four million years, hominid brains more than doubled in size, from around 450 cubic centimeters to 1,100 (Mithen 1996, 12).

Obviously there was a conflict at the time of childbirth between a large-brained infant and the narrow pelvis shape necessary to support an upright walker, requiring several other adaptations that would ease the risk to both mother and infant. Over time, the female pelvis changed in shape and flexibility, even becoming able to open slightly at the time of birth. For their part, babies developed a large fontanelle (or opening along the suture lines of the skull) that allowed the head bones to be temporarily compressed during the process of birth; their brain growth patterns also altered.

Yet even these adjustments were apparently not enough, for we find that over the millennia infants were born in an increasingly immature state (Morgan 1995), so that at birth their bodies would more safely and comfortably pass through the birth canal. There was obviously intense selective pressure for infant "prematurity." A truly "full-term" human pregnancy, if human infants were as mature at birth as infant apes are, would last for twenty-one months (Leakey 1994, 44) and result in a twenty-five-pound baby (Morgan 1995, citing Portmann, p. 59, and Gould, p. 60). Although human females are in the same size range as female great apes and have similar gestation lengths, their babies are much more immature at birth, although twice as large. A human infant's brain continues to grow and mature outside the womb: between birth and age four, its size triples (Mithen 1996, 192).

The adaptive anatomical and physiological changes that made these earlier births possible would have been accompanied by behavioral adaptations too. Because human infants were helpless for a far longer time after birth than infants of any other species, they required prolonged attention and care. Mothers and infants who found ways to develop and sustain intense affective bonds would have been at an advantage over mothers and infants who did not.

As primates, human ancestors were already well equipped for mutual affection. Monkeys and apes are renowned for their general sociability and for having long-lasting social bonds. But it is evident that ancestral human mothers and their physically helpless young gradually developed capabilities for social interaction that went beyond those of primate mother-infant communication and affiliation.[9]

Indeed, human mothers and infants today, in the face-to-face play that is so familiar and ordinary that we sometimes dismissively refer to it

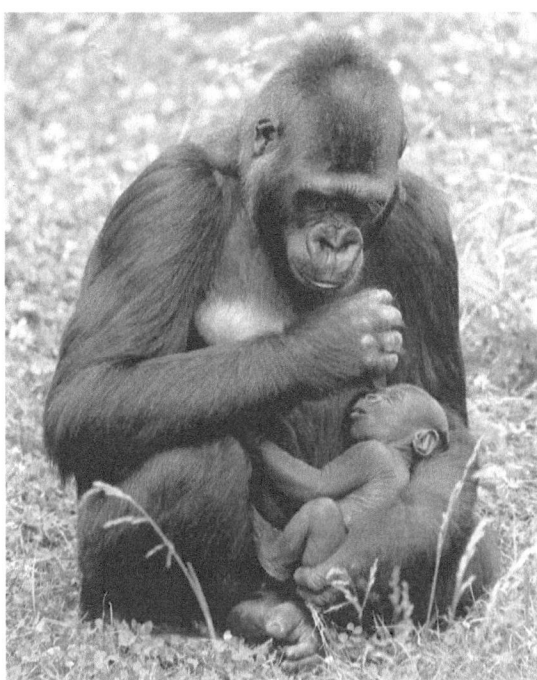

Western lowland gorilla mother and infant. Like all primates, gorillas have close mother-infant bonds. Photograph: Jessie Cohen, National Zoological Park, Smithsonian Institution.

as "baby talk," are unconsciously doing something quite specialized. Using rhythmic head and body movements, gestures, and facial expressions, as well as vocal sounds, they mutually create and maintain communicative ("protoconversational") sequences that careful analyses have shown to be exquisitely patterned over time. Some of these sequences show alternation or turn-taking, whereas others display simultaneity or synchronicity. These exchanges not only communicate emotional information but also allow for emotional state-sharing, or *attunement*. For both mother and baby (who are unaware of the complex intricacies of their duet), they are pleasurable—joyous, captivating, and fun.

I suggest that these interactions were developed during human evolution because they fostered and sustained emotional bonds ("love") between a mother and her physically helpless infant—bonds that would motivate the mother to devote the necessary care and attention to enable the infant's survival. While "instinctive" mother love seems to suffice for most mammals, it may not be enough in higher primates. Captive chimpanzee and gorilla mothers in zoos frequently have difficulty raising infants unless they have observed others of their kind caring for babies.

Mothering in humans is innately predisposed, to be sure, but like mothering in chimps and gorillas, it requires social facilitation.

Because of the requisite extremely long period of infant helplessness in humans, it seems that in addition to a mother's learning the specifics of infant care by watching other mothers and handling others' babies, it would have been an excellent fail-safe device for a baby to be perceived as being distinctly lovable. The communicative sounds, gestures, and facial expressions of primates express such fundamental motivations as affiliation, appeasement, hostility, and fear, along with ambivalence. The specifically human adaptation came when human mothers and infants, using the affiliative facial expressions, gestures, and sounds already operant in other primates, began to elaborate them in dynamic, patterned (that is, rhythmic and modal) sequences that would sustain each partner's own positive feelings while they were communicated to the other.

This *relationship*, or *emotional communion*—not simply "affiliation" or "sociability"—has become so crucial to the human project that infants are born with specialized brain pathways for seeking out and responding to just these emphasized and elaborated rhythmic and modal signals from other humans (Aitken and Trevarthen 1997; Schore 1994; Trevarthen, Kokkinaki, and Fiamenghi 1999). The most precociously mature functions of a young child's brain are those that communicate needs, feelings, and motives to other persons and lead these others to present the world to the child in precisely regulated ways (Trevarthen 1987, 108).

Somewhat older babies and toddlers spontaneously display untaught traits of sharing, sympathy, conciliation, and social participation. Yet although children also unmistakably show untaught traits of selfishness, aggression, anger, or deceit, humans do not lose their capacities for emotional attunement with others. These remain as covert rhythmic and modal signals in the subtleties of facial expressions and what is called "body language," and in the prosody of spoken language (the expressive tonal and dynamic features of speech). They comprise much of what is called "chemistry" or "vibes" in our engagements with others—the nonverbal signs of attunement. They are of course also manifested and elaborated in lovemaking with a sympathetic partner, distinguishing it unmistakably from selfish or deceitful simulations.

Where we also find and feel these primary indications of sympathetic and emotional expression—further enhanced with dynamic variety and highly affecting shape—is in experiences of the arts. Dance, music, poetic language, and other kinds of performance share many sug-

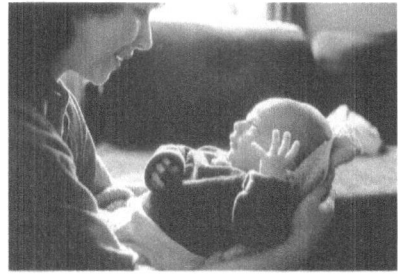
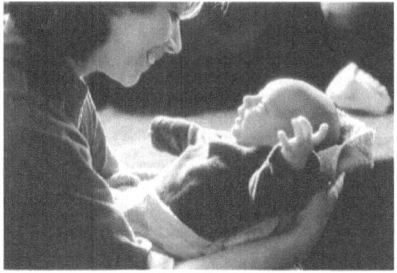

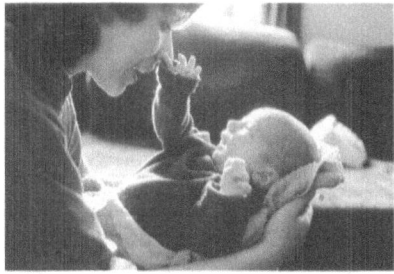

Already at three weeks, an infant orients to his mother's face and displays a surprising variety of expressive face and hand movements. Photographs: Saskia van Rees.

gestive features with mother-infant engagement. Even the static visual arts partake of these primary elements because of their overlapping analogical associations with kinetic and other sensory experiences. These features and analogies are explored in the pages that follow.

That humans have an inborn capacity for engaging in and responding to the arts may seem even more astonishing to a contemporary reader than having a native capacity for mutuality. Evolutionary scientists, like many other members of society, often seem uncomfortable with the arts, just as they seem to be uncomfortable with emotion and what cannot be verbalized.[10]

Yet what is meaningful in life is not necessarily what is, or even can be, encoded in words. It is time for nonverbal, emotional experience to be incorporated into our contemporary view of human nature along with mutuality and its personal and cultural concomitants. These are more difficult to discern and discuss than observable or verbally describable experiences and individual self-interested behavior, but they have been no less intrinsic and essential to human evolution. In chapter 6, I make the case that the arts remain the birthright of modern individuals and that even in societies that no longer take the arts seriously, they still provide avenues for belonging, meaning, competence, and an enlargement of the sense of being.

1

Mutuality

IN CONTEMPORARY NORTH AMERICA and elsewhere, the subject of love is confused and confusing. The word is used to mean everything from affection to devotion, from endearment to passion, from *caritas* to *agape*. Often, like intimacy, it refers automatically to romantic love and sex ("*love*making"). I use the words "love" and "intimacy" in this book because of their intrinsic appeal, but what I mean by both words is more usefully addressed with a less familiar (and less culturally freighted) word— "mutuality."[1]

Although mutuality sounds, at least in English, rather boringly legal or financial, other of its dictionary definitions are more instructive, as well as more inviting: "directed by each toward the other or others," "having the same feelings one for the other," "shared in common," and "characterized by intimacy."

Obviously love and mutuality are not always quite the same thing, for we can love one-sidedly or unrequitedly, at a distance, in vain, too much, not enough. In these cases, mutuality is what love desires but may well not have. We might say, as people often do, that love is a funny or crazy thing, a mystery, a sort of divine madness. Or we are told (or tell ourselves) that love is an illusion, a will-o'-the-wisp; more clinically, it is viewed as projection, narcissism, self-delusion, or nature's trick for propagating the species.

Mutuality between mother and infant, as I will describe it, is none of these things—neither one-sided, unrequited, nor an illusion, projection, or trick. It is, I suggest, the originary source of subsequent affectional, affiliative bonds—many of which we call "love"—between individuals as pairs or members of groups. Further, the same rhythmic-modal capacities and sensitivities that evolved to make possible mother-infant mutuality also create and sustain these other ties of intimacy, including adult love-making—to be distinguished from copulation as dining is distinguished from feeding, or as expressing gratitude to a game animal after one has killed it is distinguished from throwing it in the back of one's pickup.

In my view, these considered ways of accomplishing vital subsistence activities should not always be automatically reduced, as evolutionary psychologists frequently have done, to nothing but immediate satisfaction of the underlying physical need. Humans evolved with the capacity and desire to perform at least some ordinary activities in special or elaborated ways. But that is getting ahead of my story.

Because sex is an obvious biological necessity, and we are predisposed to find it of compelling interest, let us first look more closely at the standard evolutionary view of love, before expanding the discussion with the subject of mutuality.

THE SEXUAL IMPERATIVE

Especially in modern societies, romantic love is the theme of countless songs, poems, novels, films, plays, operas—testimony to its pervasive importance in our lives and to the varieties of emotional turmoil that attend falling in love, courtship, sexual desire, possession, and the bliss of union, as well as jealousy and the end of love. This preoccupation with love is not uniformly the case everywhere. Although people in many other societies certainly compose and listen to love songs and love poetry, they are frequently even more interested in tales of adventure and valor or stories with built-in object lessons about correct behavior. Young men of Nilotic cattle-keeping cultures in southern Sudan devote considerable time and originality to describing and praising the unique features of their oxen (Coote 1992).[2]

Evolutionists, of course, explain our preoccupation with love in song and story as a fundamentally sexual one—as evidence and assurance that people will reproduce. As I write this chapter, I am aware of a pair of swallows diligently fetching insects for their five babies in a nest on a little ledge under the eaves. They seem never to rest but, almost on the wing, quickly stuff one gaping beak and then swoop off again. This frenzy of activity, which so far as I can determine never ends from dawn to dusk, is the last chapter of the swallows' seasonal raison d'être: reproduction of another generation.

About a week after their arrival from South America, the pair to-gether build a nest from pellets of mud which they place in regular layers mixed with long slender grasses. They line the nest with a circular mat of grass and top it with a blanket of soft white feathers. Altogether, nest build-ing requires about a week of labor, after which the female lays her eggs. The birds alternate sitting on them and providing each other with food. The nestlings hatch after two weeks, and the parents then really go to work, collecting around nine hundred insects per day over the ensuing three weeks—a total of some twenty thousand weevils, chinch bugs, grass-hoppers, beetles, mosquitoes, and other insects (Dunning 1994, 156)—until the young ones are able to leave the nest under their own wingpower. Even then, the parents still provide food, often on the wing.

The activities of birds in spring vividly illustrate an imperative of na-ture that is true for all of life: you are here to make small copies of your-self and then (if, like the swallows, parental care is required) to do all you can to assist them to grow up healthily so that they can eventually make, in turn, small copies of their own.

Hence the importance of sex—our name for the urge that ensures that all this will happen, even if ordinary usage tends to restrict the mean-ing of the term to the physical activity of copulation. Yet for every animal, the act of mating is usually only a minute part of the whole—a means to the end of manufacturing offspring. Biologically speaking, sex (or, more accurately, reproduction) is a general behavioral category that encom-passes nearly everything the animal does.

For males, this usually includes finding a territory and defending it, as well as acquiring and displaying other resources of vigor and virility (by such means as singing, showing off, even fighting other males), in order to attract the best possible mate. Females, too, display their resources—usually signs of youth and hence health and fertility—and then, after bear-ing young, give their all to raising them. In some species there are slight variations in these roles, as when both members of the pair share in nest building and provisioning. But in all creatures of two sexes, reproduction in this broad sense makes themselves, if not the world, go around. If this were not so, there would be no new creatures every season to replace those that have grown old.

Is this true for humans? As all-absorbing as sex may be at certain periods of one's day or one's life, most people believe that they exist for reasons other than making love or even reproducing. Apart from the burdens and satisfactions of child rearing, we have work-in-the-world that provides self-fulfillment. While some of us seem to do nothing but make and spend money, and others suffer from not knowing what we are here for, a lot of us probably feel (or hope) that we make a few others' lives better or happier. We are here to learn, teach, preach, serve, befriend, build, create, defend, help the helpless, and—so far as we are able—find hope and meaning in life.

In the earliest millennia of hominid evolution, some four or five million years ago, our ancestors—like other animals—probably did not think about the meaning and purpose of life in general or of their individual lives. Like the crustaceans, lizards, and antelope that they hunted for food (or like the swallows under my eaves), our ancestors existed to stay alive and to reproduce—that is, their daily lives consisted of engaging in activities that ultimately contributed to the survival of themselves and their offspring. If ancestral humans, like other wild animals, had not given their supreme efforts to successful reproduction, you and I would not be pursuing our individual existences today.

Because we live much longer than ancestral humans, long past the age of primary childbearing, and because we are shielded by a prosperous society from the pressures of primary subsistence, we may not be particularly aware of the significance of reproductive imperatives in our lives. But an evolutionary perspective helps us to realize that even though our lives may not be principally devoted to reproduction in an obvious sense, we nevertheless frequently behave like our ancestors in ways that in the past would have enhanced our reproductive success (and may, indeed, enhance it now).

We generally choose our clothing, makeup, and hairstyles in order to make ourselves look good for others—to attract mates and allies or to compete with rivals. We work hard to acquire a nice house, car, and other possessions. We strive to improve and display our skills—our athleticism and physical fitness, our kindliness, sociability, competence, leadership, prosperity, dependability, mastery, discernment, knowledge. Although these strivings benefit others and are socially useful, they also advertise our reproductively advantageous qualities even if we have no children or are, for various reasons, imperfect parents.

For males, the reproductive imperative further means enjoying the company of healthy young women with physical and temperamental features that indicate good childbearing potential. What we call "beauty" in women usually refers to signs of youth (and even a few traits reminiscent, subliminally, of infancy): smooth, light-toned, and unblemished skin, firm flesh, glossy hair, full lips, shapely firm breasts and hips with a proportionately narrow waist, and a friendly, receptive disposition.

While some older women may be "interesting" and even have their own kind of dignified or mature beauty (and young women need not be all that "beautiful" in a Hollywood starlet sense), it is evident that, given the choice, most men prefer the company of young females to those who display signs of age (and its attendant loss of reproductive potential): wrinkled or pouchy faces, gray or faded thin hair, compressed lips, flabby, loose, blotched or darker-toned skin and flesh, a thick waist, and a "mature" (competent, assertive, or argumentative) manner. It is not simply a matter of general taste, because men do not have similar standards for their male companions. Again, this observation is not meant to imply that older women do not possess sexual attractiveness at all, but to point out that in most cases women of reproductive age tend to receive more attentive and favorable treatment from men than do older women. It does not seem fair, but there are unarguable evolutionary reasons for the bias.

Females, too, are romantically interested in young, healthy, attractive males, but unlike men, they usually require more than sex appeal before agreeing to sexual union. They look for indications that the man has "resources" (of time, money, attentiveness, and emotion) that he is willing to "invest" in the relationship. Although women may not be consciously aware of it, these are tacit signs of male willingness to stay around to help provide for any results of their mating, something that was of critical concern to their Paleolithic forebears.

Even when they are not particularly youthful or physically attractive, men with ambition, dominance, and status (social, athletic, financial, political) are usually attractive to women because they demonstrate superiority in acquiring resources that over the millennia have contributed to their mates' (and their eventual children's) reproductive success. These differences in how men and women present themselves to each other and in what they want from partners have been ascertained in numerous research studies. They are also evident from a brief perusal of the personals advertisements of any newspaper.

To be sure, men like women with status too, as trophies. But high-status women rarely mate with low-status men, whereas high-status men are quite willing to mate with low-status women and even to marry them if they are young and beautiful. Generally speaking, youth and beauty are sufficient resources for females.

While it is true that differences between males and females in both sexual behavior and sexual attitudes have declined in Western societies over the past four or five decades, there remain noteworthy differences in such things as frequency of masturbation (males do it more), timing and causes of arousal (males are aroused more quickly than females, females are aroused less by sight, which arouses men, than by touch), finding the trait of dominance attractive (females do, males do not), being willing to dissociate coitus from emotional involvement (males are, females are not), and motivation for coitus (Townsend, Kline, and Wasserman 1995, 31). For a female, the number of sexual offers she has is less important to the number of partners she will have than her expressed attitudes about her behavior, whereas for males, opportunity tends to be the major influence on number of partners, apart from what is claimed to be one's attitude (Townsend, Kline, and Wasserman 1995, 43).

Some might attribute American women's preoccupation with prospective partners' emotional investment to the ideology of rapturous romantic love that permeates the novels, popular songs, and films that many women avidly consume. One might ask, however, why—since romantic fantasy is so inescapable—it is females who patronize this stuff, whereas males generally choose adventure stories and films and read pornography more readily than romance.

Such differences in human male and female sexual attitudes and behavior are based in evolved biological differences. That is, for ancestral females, a fertile copulation required that she then invest in her offspring nine months of gestation, the perils of childbirth, two years or more of lactation, almost continuous tending of a helpless, demanding infant, and another several years of unflagging vigilance and solicitude. Her reproductive success depended not only on a healthy, vigorous mate to produce high-quality sperm that contained his healthy, vigorous qualities but also on having a *partner* who would be able to provision, defend, and otherwise care for her and the child, especially during the early weeks, months, and even years when both were most at risk. Ancestral males, on the other hand, theoretically needed to invest only their quickly replenished sperm and fifteen minutes of their time in a fertile copulation. Thus for a male there was far less need to look for anything beyond a prospective mate's youthful sexiness as a return on his physical contribution.

Of course it is *better* for a male's reproductive success if he stays around and helps the mother care for his infant. But his loss due to irresponsibility or careless mate choice is nothing like hers. (She loses not only a child but also at least a year of her life in hosting what is in fact an endoparasite, a "silent partner" that consumes a fair portion of the nourishment she takes into her body—not to mention the lengthy postponement of a child fathered by a more suitable partner.) Also, unlike the female, a male can never be absolutely sure that a child is really his. With mating success as an ultimate criterion, it pays a male to lay his sperm in other men's nests and let these men help raise the offspring with *their* resources.

This difference in costliness of reproductive investment also explains why females are often attracted to older, even less physically attractive men if they have money, fame, prestige, and power. It was Henry Kissinger who famously observed that power is the ultimate aphrodisiac. For successful male athletes, musicians, authors, artists, and politicians, groupies are legendary perquisites of achievement, a bonus that female athletes, musicians, authors, artists, and politicians are less likely to find—especially if they are portly, assertive, and fiftyish, as Kissinger was when he made his observation.

Males and females of today are not, of course, consciously assessing the childbearing or resource potential of the females and males they meet and judge. They may expressly want *not* to have children or may not be interested in a long-term association at all. But more often than not, and whether or not they act on their inclination, they will find appealing the characteristics of the opposite sex that during ancestral times afforded reproductive success. The neural circuits in their brains have been formed to respond to these signals and to elicit the appropriate behavioral response. We can and do love and desire less-than-curvaceous-juicy-willing women and men who are less-than-hunks-or-honchos. The sexy broad may be a bimbo and the hunk or honcho a jerk, so we gladly settle for less than a Perfect Ten since there are reasons other than sexual ones for choosing mates. But chances are that what turns us on in our less-than-ideal partners will be approximate or real characteristics that would have been desirable on the savannah.

A MORE EMBRACING VIEW
OF REPRODUCTIVE SUCCESS

The previous section has been something of a caricature, although its basic outlines, like those of other caricatures, depict a likeness of human reproductive behavior—even if exaggerated. But it is only a partial like-ness, not the complete story: sexual interest, choice, desire, and infatua-tion leading to copulation are only the beginning of reproductive success. Although humans, like other animals, have an interest in mate quality (vigor or other resources), in the achievement of fertile copulation, and even in the father's provisioning of the mother and young after birth, re-productive success in humans, in particular, has evolved to require some-thing more than what sufficed in other animals.

Although maternal care is vital to any mammal's reproductive out-come, in human mothers and infants an emotional relationship of mutuality—expressed, coordinated, and elaborated in interactive behav-ior—became increasingly indispensable. Oddly, as I mentioned in the in-troduction, a preponderant proportion of studies of human reproductive success overlook or are unaware of this prominent and momentous fact.

The First Relationship

Humans share with other primates a close and enduring attachment be-tween mother and child. People who have associated with monkeys and apes in the wild or in zoos and laboratories have reported the distress of both mother and baby if one is deprived of the other by death or acci-dent. Baby rhesus monkeys raised in the laboratory as orphans drink milk from a bottle attached to a wire dummy in their cage but will spend time clinging to an adjoining cloth-covered "mother" and, when frightened,

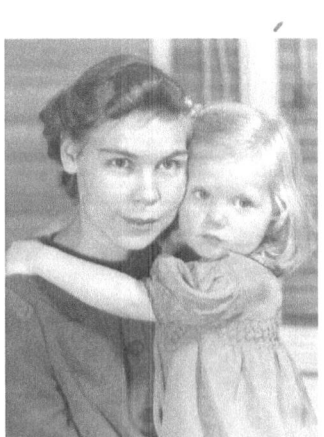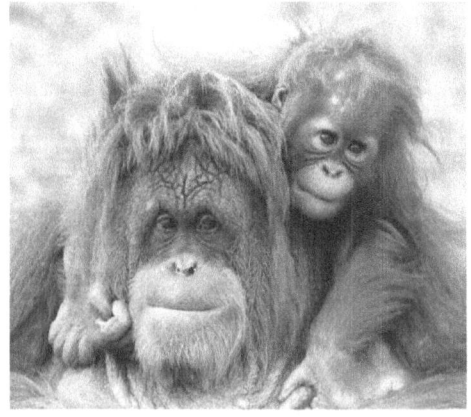

Close physical and emotional attachment characterizes the mother-infant relationship in human and nonhuman primates (here, an orangutan mother and baby). Photographs: Kirk Mears and Jessie Cohen, National Zoological Park, Smithsonian Institution.

run to it for comfort (Harlow 1958; Harlow and Zimmermann 1959). We can be sure that the earliest hominids also had intimate mother-infant bonds, which for an urgent evolutionary reason evolved to be not only closer but even richer and more versatile than those of apes and monkeys.

As I described it in the introduction, bipedalism—walking on two rather than four legs—necessitated, rather paradoxically, that human babies be born in a helpless state in order to survive. Like the young of many birds, for which the term was first devised, human infants are *altricial*, from the Latin word meaning female nourisher—implying that the young cannot feed themselves.[3] (In birds such as the swallows described earlier, both parents may feed the altricial young; in humans and other mammals, it is the mother who initially supplies nourishment in the form of milk secreted from her own body.) Altricial young who successfully induce their parent(s) to look after them will prosper; those whose parents do not feel rewarded when they regard their little one—who see a harbinger of hardship rather than a bundle of joy—will fail to thrive.

It seems only natural that living creatures find parenthood rewarding. The sight of that eager gaping beak or the smell of that warm amniotic-fluid-soaked kitten somehow inspires mother and father bird or mother cat to do what is necessary and to go on doing it as long as required. Some primates have to bolster this natural tendency by observing and thereby learning from other mothers with babies.

Early hominids obviously possessed the motivations and social reinforcements of their primate cousins, which enabled them to care for their offspring, too. And so do most of us today, who admit to undeniable satisfaction while caring for a small helpless thing—especially when it is our own. Neurotransmitters such as oxytocin are released in mothers before childbirth and with suckling, so that "maternal affect," if nothing interferes with it psychologically or physically, is a demonstrable biological reality. And apart from that, our brain circuitry has evolved to respond with tenderness and positive emotion to such signs of lovability as small size, a round head that is large in proportion to the body, big eyes, plump cheeks, downiness, softness, and other indicators of infantility—in baby animals and in pets, stuffed animals, cartoon characters, and advertising images as well as in our own kind.

Although most people take human mother love for granted, it was an important evolutionary adaptation. Until the 1960s, psychologists generally thought of it as fairly straightforward: human mothers, like other animals, had "maternal emotion," and babies—through condi-

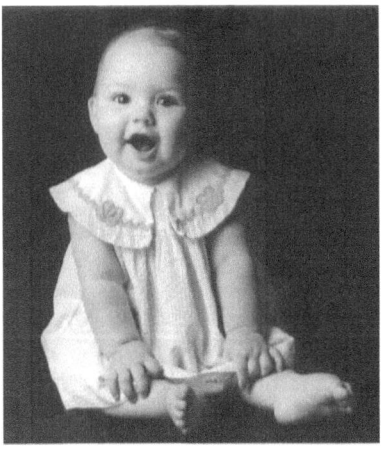

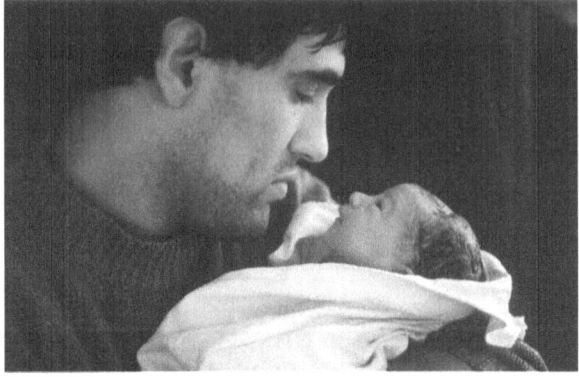

This newborn infant girl's readiness for companionship is evident in her expression. Photograph: Saskia van Rees.

Chubby cheeks, soft skin, a large head and eyes, a plump body, and a bright smile make infants instantly attractive to most adults. Photograph: Elizabeth Leeor.

tioning, like pets—gradually came to love the person who fed and looked after them.

In 1969 in England, John Bowlby, a child psychiatrist with an interest in ethology, challenged this rather simplistic idea in the first volume of a pathbreaking treatise called *Attachment and Loss*. He was acquainted with the reactions of young children who for various reasons—illness, death, wartime dispersals, abandonment—had been separated from their mothers, and he was led to propose that there is a positive need for infants to form what he called *attachment* with caretakers. By the age of about eight months, especially in circumstances of uncertainty, children in all cultures do similar things to attract and sustain their mothers' attention: they cry when separated, lift their arms to be picked up, cling to her body, stay near her, and even when playing happily look at her frequently. They do this whether or not the mother has shown them affection. In orphanages, young children often choose one staff person as a favorite, even if other individuals feed and tend them. Contrary to previous assumptions, the tendency to attach was observably separate from simple conditioning to a positive stimulus such as food or care.

Bowlby suggested that the evolutionary value of attachment was that the helpless hunter-gatherer's baby would not wander off, and when frightened or alone it would cry, reach out, move toward, or otherwise try to resume contact with a specific protective figure rather than remain vulnerable to predators or accidents.[4] Many helpless young birds and mammals have comparable behaviors.

In the years since Bowlby's formulation, research with much younger infants has enriched his pioneering work, showing quite remarkable and unexpected earlier abilities and proclivities for interaction and intimacy. These suggest that attachment—which in Bowlby's scheme appears at about the time the baby is first able to move about on its own and is concerned primarily with the infant's physical safety through "proximity seeking"—should be viewed as a late-appearing consequence of a prior, equally innate and adaptive predisposition to engage in relationship and emotional communion, over and above any need for protection.

University of Edinburgh psychologist Colwyn Trevarthen (1979, 1998) has called this predisposition *innate intersubjectivity*. He sees it as a fundamental inborn readiness of the baby to seek, respond to, and affect the mother's provision of not only physical protection and care but also emotional regulation and support—that is, her provision of companionship. Trevarthen's studies, like many others, show clearly how the mother-infant pair together engages in a mutually improvised interaction based on innate competencies and sensitivities—an interaction, sometimes called "baby talk," whose importance was for years overlooked if not altogether dismissed.[5] Long before the attachment described by Bowlby takes place, this common pastime, which falsely seems to be both trivial and inane, provides enjoyment and intimacy for both participants and significant developmental benefits for the infant.

The Complexities of Baby Talk

From the first weeks, in all cultures, human mothers (and even other adults) behave differently with infants than with adults or even older children. In most cases a mother's vocalizations to the baby and her facial expressions, gestures, and head and body movements are exaggerated—made clear and rhythmic. Babies in turn respond with corresponding sounds, expressions, and movements of their own, and over the first months a mutual multimedia ritual performance emerges and develops. Exquisitely satisfying to both participants, it inundates both mother and baby with a special pleasure that is all the more powerful because it is not just felt alone (like the interest, excitement, or joy felt while privately thinking about or watching one's baby) but is mirrored or shared.

This mother-infant interaction has been well studied in a number of different cultures over the past quarter century.[6] Its beginnings are now seen to be at birth, although as the weeks and months pass it becomes more and more a consciously improvised and improved-upon duet. All over the world people (especially mothers) talk to babies (and generalizing, often to any smaller creature) in a special vocal register: a higher, softer, breathier, singsong tone of voice. The contours—the ups and downs—of these utterances are much more labile and exaggerated than the contours of ordinary speech to other adults (Fernald 1992).

Mothers in many cultures speak to small babies as if they expect a reply: "*Too* much milk? You've had *too* much milk? Ohhhhhhh!"—even when they realize that infants cannot understand words. In some societies there is no tradition of *talking* to babies, but other rhythmically regular noises such as tongue-clicking, hissing, grunting, or lip-smacking may be used and supplemented by physical movements and exaggerated facial expressions.

While talking or making sounds, mothers rock or pat the baby as well as look at or gaze into its face. They usually smile. The things they say are structured in time, like poetry or song: if transcribed, they reveal formal segments like stanzas, often based on one theme, with variations, that has to do with the looks or actions of the baby (frequently its digestion: burps, hiccups, and poops) or something about its lovability—for example, "Mommy loves you. Yes. Yes. Did you know Mommy loves you? Yes she does. She does. She loves you."

As in this segment, the words are organized into phrases, each (whether having one or seven syllables) about three and a half to five seconds in length (Lynch et al. 1995; Turner 1985). The utterances are rhythmic and highly repetitive. At the end of one stanza, after a pause, another subject or theme may suggest itself: "You sleepy? You sleepy now? Come on, don't sleep yet. Noooo. Don't sleep yet. Come on. Come on. All right, then. All right."

At about four weeks, if not earlier, while the mother is talking in this manner, the baby will look back intently, make real eye contact, and present the mother with a deliberate smile. Its eyes will show awareness and a kind of complicity: it will be unmistakable to the mother that the infant is really responding *to her*, to her voice, her smile, her touch, her being.

No one knows when in human evolution this happened.[7] Although primates in general have specialized brain circuits dedicated to identifying and responding to others' emotional states as shown in their faces, voices, and behavior (Brothers 1992; Brothers and Ring 1992; Brothers, Ring, and Kling 1990), only humans have a social smile linked to sustained eye con-

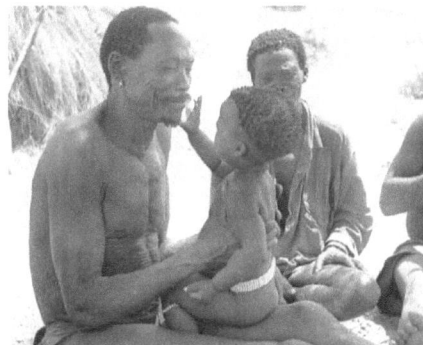

left: !Khoisan males show fond expressions to infant. Central Kalahari, southern Africa.

below: Yanomamö mother comforts formerly crying infant by talking, bringing her face close, and then rubbing noses. Upper Orinoco, Brazil. Photographs: Irenäus Eibl-Eibesfeldt.

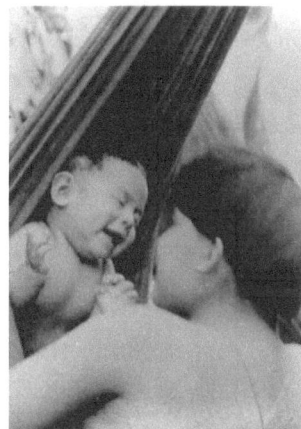
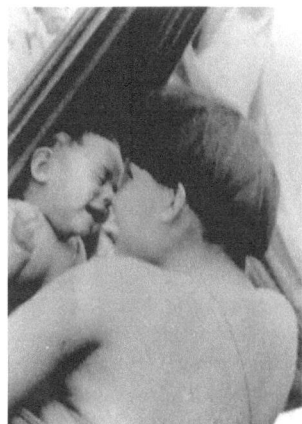

tact. Ethologists propose that the human social smile is derived from a similar expression that is used by adult apes (and presumably ancestral humans) for appeasement, as in bonobos (a kind of chimpanzee that is considered to be as closely related to humans as is the larger chimp) (de Waal 1989, 224), or for reassurance and friendly greeting, as in chimpanzees (van Hooff 1989, 138). Such signals deflect the possible hostility of someone much larger and more powerful; we still use smiles when we accidentally bump into strangers, so they will know that we are not deliberately being aggressive or threatening.

Faces, and especially eyes, are of immense importance to all primates because they indicate emotional state and thus probable intention. Special cells in the brain respond to their subtle expressive changes (Brothers 1992; Brothers and Ring 1992; Brothers, Ring, and Kling 1990). Staring into another's eyes is an especially potent signal in the animal world—it

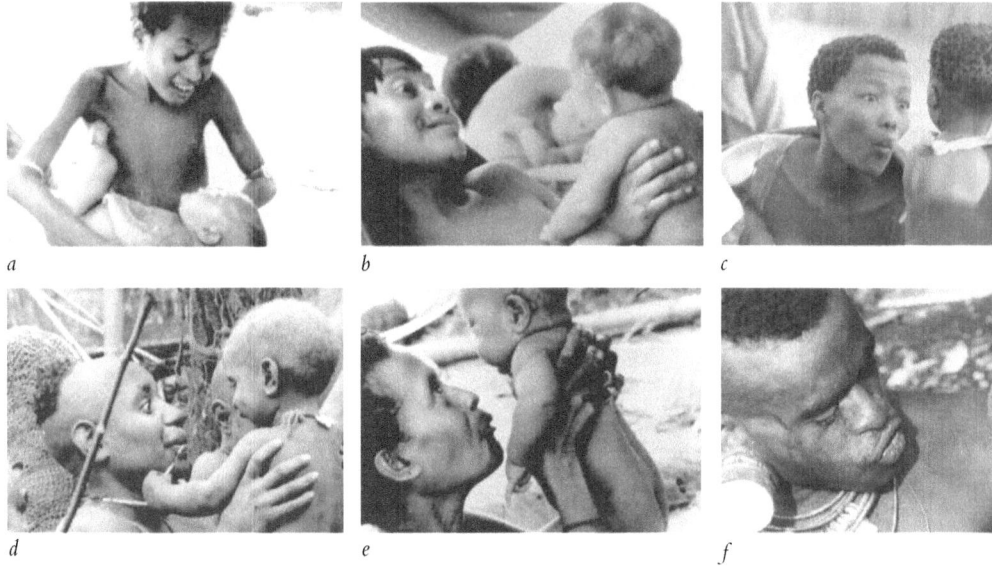

Adults in every culture make exaggerated facial expressions as they interact with infants.
Photographs : Irenäus Eibl-Eibesfeldt.

a. *Raised eyebrows. Older brother and small sister, Trobriand Islands, Papua New Guinea.*
b. *Raised eyebrows. Father and infant, Yanomamö, upper Orinoco, Brazil.*
c. *Playful grimace. Woman and infant, !ko Bushman, southern Africa.*
d. *Mock surprise with raised eyebrows. Woman and infant, Eipo, Irian Jaya.*
e. *Mother making face to attract infant's attention. Trobriand Islands, Papua New Guinea.*
f. *Father pursing lips to sulky infant. Eipo, Irian Jaya.*

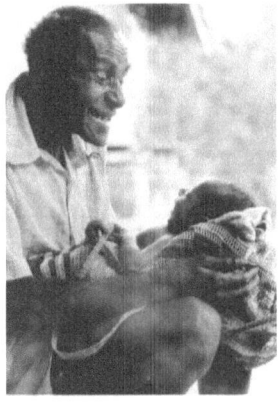

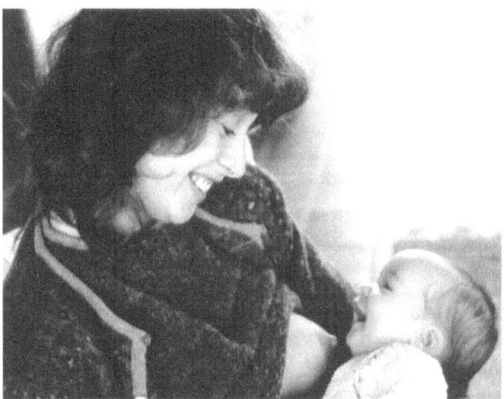

Raised eyebrows and exaggerated
smile. Grandfather and infant,
East Sepik Province, Papua
New Guinea. Photograph:
Maureen MacKenzie.

While suckling, young infants often gaze raptly at their
mother's face or, as here, stop to bestow a happy smile.
Photograph: Saskia van Rees.

normally indicates aggression and can be seen as such when two human males challenge each other in "tough guy" films. Although brief eye contact is synchronized with starting or finishing speaking (Baron-Cohen 1995, 118), in most human social situations overlong eye contact is discomfiting—with two exceptions: between lovers, when it indicates trust and surrender, and between mothers and babies. (In fact, in infants eye contact reliably triggers smiling [Baron-Cohen 1995, 42].)

With the invention of bottle-feeding, even fathers can experience the delightful intimacy of gazing into the intent and gratified eyes of a suckling baby; nursing mothers have probably experienced this intoxicating pleasure for hundreds of thousands of years. The conventional explanation for human females having enlarged breasts is male sexual selection—that is, women with protuberant breasts were preferentially selected by males as sexual partners. It seems also plausible that a rounded breast was adaptive because it permitted mothers and infants to look into each other's eyes as the baby suckled (Reynolds 1975). Babies' communion and attachment with their mothers seems at least as strong a driving selective force as male choice.[8] No nonhuman primate female has an enlarged breast: a baby is obliged, while suckling, to place its face close to the mother's chest or, at best—in those species whose teats are long and flabby—to turn and look outward. Apart from bonobos, who look into each other's eyes while copulating, no nonhuman primates show sustained eye contact except, like other animals, in contexts of threat and aggression.

Up to about eight weeks, the human mother's baby talk is primarily soothing and fondly affectionate: it provides a kind of tranquilizing regularity, like a lullaby. There may also be a tender singsong jokiness: "*Talk* to me, *talk* to me, won't you *talk* to me?" Gradually she will more insistently engage the infant's attention, attracting and sustaining it by stops and starts, moving her head closer and farther away or raising her chin and letting it drop suddenly while making an exaggerated, wide-eyed expression with pursed lips and perhaps a "tch" or tongue click. (One can observe strangers doing these things to babies of the appropriate age in supermarket checkout lines, and other public places.) Such antics generally induce the baby to respond with wriggles, kicks, and smiles. Without an expected infant response (and one's own wish to provoke it), there would be no reason to behave in this otherwise inexplicable way.[9]

Once smiles are regular and predictable, the mother-infant tango really takes off in free improvisation as the baby becomes even more spiritedly interactive. The mother may hold it in both hands facing her or may lean over the infant in its crib or on the floor or in a little seat. The word

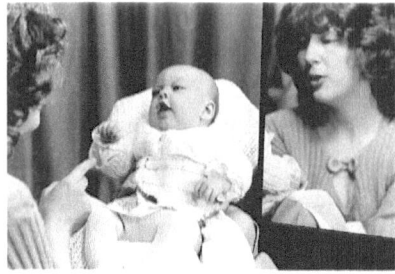

"Protoconversation" of six-week-old girl and her mother. The mother's repetitive, short utterances change in pitch, contour, and amplitude from U-shaped inviting or questioning to falling imitative answers after the infant has made a bisyllabic "coo." Note the pauses in the mother's speech as she waits for the infant to take her turn, which she does precisely on the mother's andante *beat. (Source: Trevarthen 1993.)*

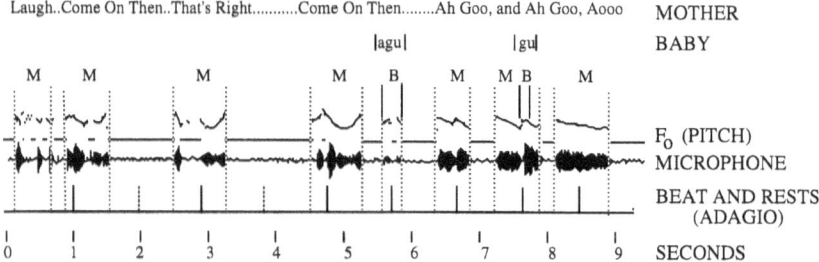

"engagement," to anyone who has watched a videotape of mother-infant interaction, is apt. There is a discernible moment when it happens: the baby's attention clicks in and the two are engaged, like the clutch in a car, off and rolling, sharing a mutual ongoing "ride."

The baby's kicks or arm movements and its smiles and coos and gurgles, even hiccups, are interwoven with the gestures, sounds, and nods or other facial movements of the mother until one or the other—usually the baby—looks away and "disengages." Perhaps it is overstimulated, whereupon the mother might begin again at a lower level of intensity. Or it is bored or fussy, so the mother tries more intently to attract or distract the baby and reengage its attention in a new bout, using a different sort of vocal contour from the ones used for a pleasantly excited infant (Papousek, Papousek, and Koester 1982).

A temporal analysis of the sounds, movements, and facial expressions of these interactive sequences reveals an amazing attunement, a synchronization of interaction.[10] Both mother and baby adjust their responses to each other within seconds or fractions of seconds, according to discernible "rules" of mutual regulation that are made up as they go along (Beebe 1986). What is particularly interesting is that small infants are not only supremely sensitive and responsive to rhythmic properties of their mothers' sounds, facial expressions, and body movements but are also able to perceive these "cross-modally."

For example, three-week-olds can perceive the similarity between bright colors and loud sounds (Lewkowicz and Turkewitz 1980). At six months babies recognize that a pulsing tone (heard) and a dotted line (seen) are alike, as are a continuous tone and an unbroken line (Wagner et al. 1981). Thus in early interactions, behaviors are not only directly mirrored or imitated but also may be *matched* by either partner in supramodal qualities such as intensity, contour, duration, or rhythm—qualities that apply to any sense modality.[11] That is to say, the loudness of a sound may be matched by a strong arm or leg movement (or vice versa); the downward contour of a head movement may be matched by a downward fall of the voice (or vice versa) (Beebe and Gerstman 1984; Eimas 1984; Marks, Hammeal, and Bornstein 1987; Stern 1985).

When a baby reaches four or five months of age, a mother (who has already improvised rhythmic nonsense games) will often add special songs to her baby-talk routine—songs improvised on the spot, traditional nursery songs, or even adult songs. But she accompanies this singing with energetic sideways wagging or up-and-down nodding head movements. Her exaggerated facial expressions (wide and sometimes rolling eyes, pursed mouth, raised eyebrows, tongue clicks, raised chin) accompany the songs or the utterances she makes between the songs (which continue to have exaggerated vocal contours, exaggerated tempo and dynamic changes,

Diagram below shows double television system (using separate rooms) for observation of conversational communication. On pages 36 and 37 is a microanalysis of one and a half minutes of protoconversation with an eight-week-old infant girl, showing the development of playful turn-taking marked by expressions of happiness. The mother teases her daughter and makes her laugh. Five seconds after the sequence begins, the baby is frightened by a piercing sound in the loudspeaker that carries the mother's voice. The mother then soothes the infant and gets her to smile and coo. At the end, the infant makes three utterances, each about three seconds in duration. (Source: Murray and Trevarthen 1985.)

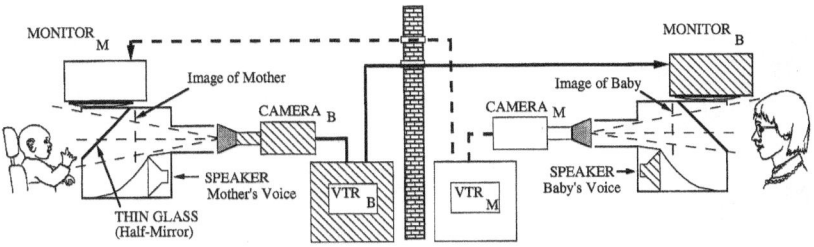

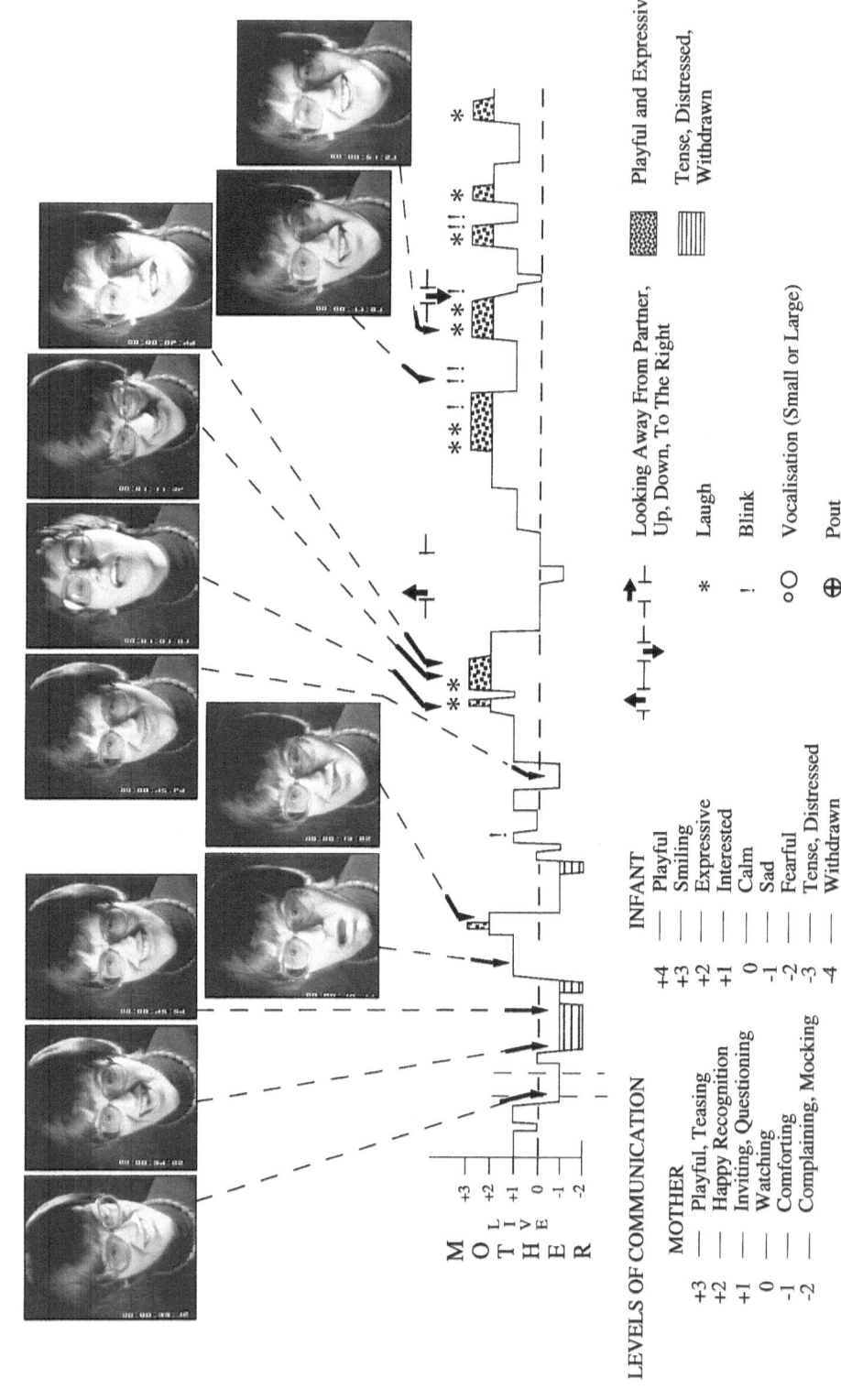

LEVELS OF COMMUNICATION

M O T H E R
L I V E L

+3
+2
+1
0
-1
-2

MOTHER
+3 — Playful, Teasing
+2 — Happy Recognition
+1 — Inviting, Questioning
0 — Watching
-1 — Comforting
-2 — Complaining, Mocking

INFANT
+4 — Playful
+3 — Smiling
+2 — Expressive
+1 — Interested
0 — Calm
-1 — Sad
-2 — Fearful
-3 — Tense, Distressed
-4 — Withdrawn

⎹━┨━┨━┨━⎸ Looking Away From Partner,
           Up, Down, To The Right

*   Laugh

!   Blink

○O   Vocalisation (Small or Large)

⊕   Pout

▓▓▓ Playful and Expressive

▥▥▥ Tense, Distressed,
     Withdrawn

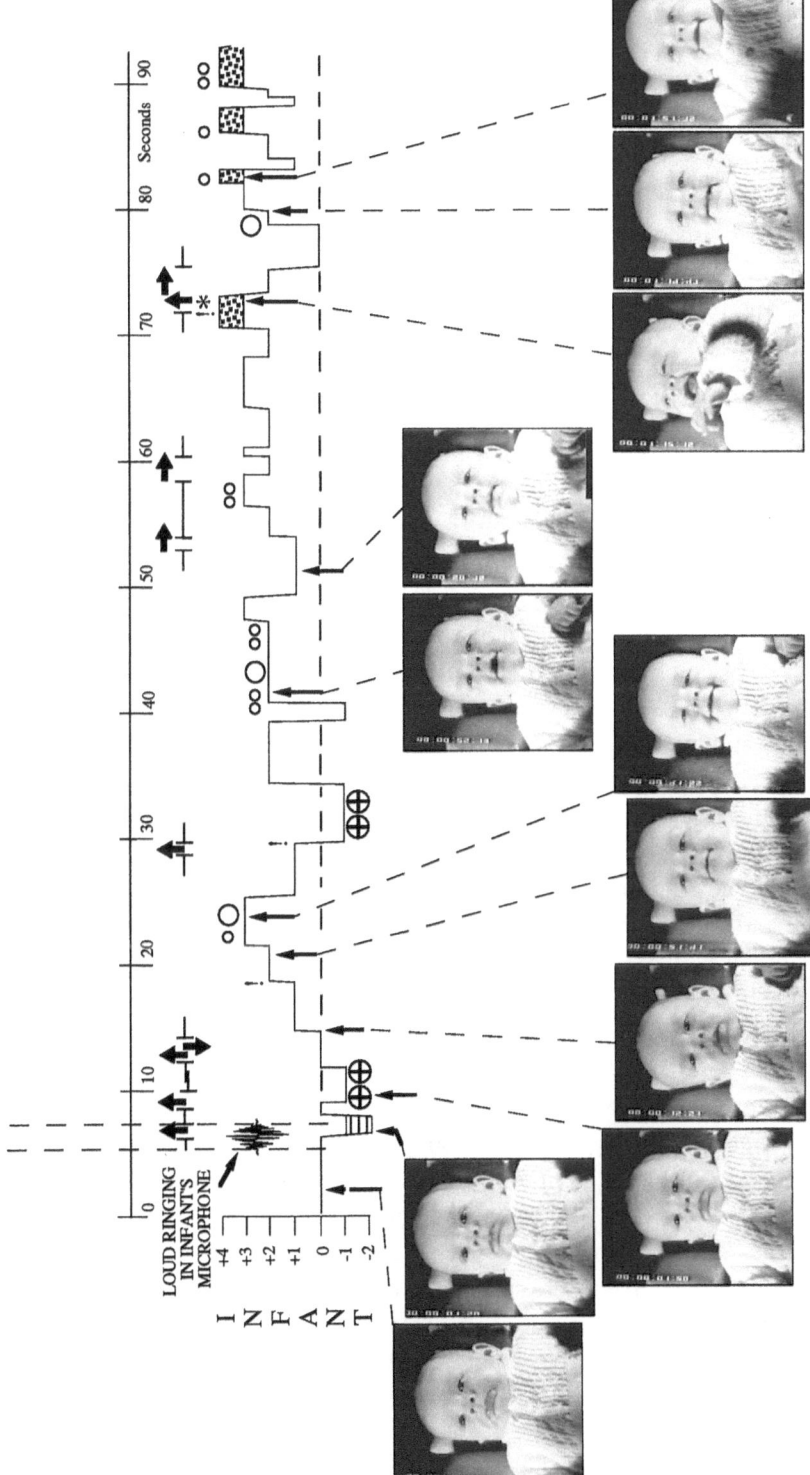

and pregnant pauses). Rather than soothing the infant, she is now deliberately and energetically entertaining it, building up to climaxes in singsong rhymes or nursery songs such as "This Little Piggy" or "Eentsy-Weentsy Spider." Six-month-old babies soon learn to anticipate the climax and wait breathlessly at the pause for the inevitable "wee-wee-wee" or tickle, and then "break up" in chortles and peals of laughter. If carried and danced with or bounced up and down, the baby will urge its parent to continue by its own rhythmic bucking and bobbing.

Interestingly, the three-and-a-half to five-second segmental length of a typical utterance in baby talk corresponds to the temporal length of a poetic line, a musical phrase, and a phrase of speech in adults (Lynch et al. 1995; Turner 1985). That infants are supremely sensitive to this universal measure and its rhythmic subdivisions in syllables and syllable clusters, and that mothers spontaneously produce it, argues that both the creation and the experience of the temporal arts of poetry, music, and dance (the movements of which accord with music) inhere in our fundamental psychobiology—our inner brain sense of rhythm and melody.

The feelings of mutuality that unite mothers and infants arise from occurrences in their brains and other bodily systems that are, of course, as unknown (and irrelevant) to them as are the complex workings of nerves and muscles when we play a musical instrument or return a tennis serve. Human brains respond to signals of special love and interest that are recognized (processed) as such by our different senses when they come to us as certain kinds of interesting facial expressions (seen), appealing vocal sounds (heard), and rhythmic bodily movements (felt). When exaggerated and patterned in time, these "signals" are maximally affecting to the infant's nervous system: that is, they are processed in the brain as "good"—"affiliative"—and are automatically translated into emotions of delight and pleasure. When shared with ("matched" or mirrored by) another, they result in states of what can be called attunement (Stern 1985), inter-*jo* resonance or "the space of we" (Nakano 1996), or, as I do here, mutuality.

Neurologists (e.g., Schore 1994, 80) describe how external indicators of internal states, such as vocal, facial, and gestural expressions of adoration and pleasure, trigger physiological arousal in both the "receiver" and the "sender," whether infant and mother or beloved and lover. Thus, producing the signal additionally generates or reinforces the emotion (Ekman 1992; Ekman, Davidson, and Friesen 1990; Ekman, Levenson, and Friesen 1983). (Such feedback effects have received popular attention from studies of hospital patients who, by consciously trying to smile and laugh,

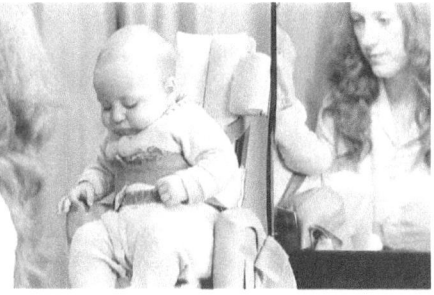
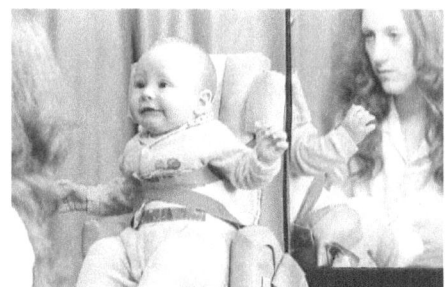
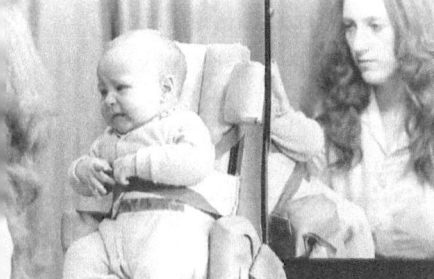
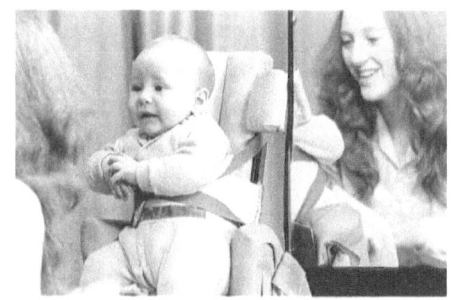
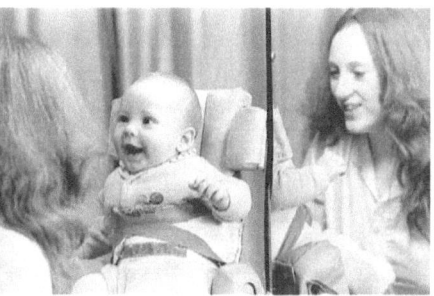

In the "still-face" experiment, the mother, as instructed, remains silent with a still face. Her sixteen-week-old infant first looks down and touches the chair. Whining and waving its hands in the air, it tries to reengage, looking imploringly at the unresponsive mother. Bringing its hands to its chest, it looks away unhappily. As the mother begins to smile and talk again, the baby looks at her face, complaining, with hands clasped. Finally, as the mother continues to talk and smile, the baby smiles back, coos, and raises its hands. The disruption is repaired. Photographs: Colwyn Trevarthen.

recover from illnesses sooner than people who are bad-tempered or gloomy [see, for example, Cousins 1979, 1983].) Simply making the facial or vocal correlate of an emotion tends to release the brain chemicals that cause people to *feel* the emotion, so we can assume that early hominid mothers who performed and even exaggerated affiliative signals to their infants would have produced in themselves more affiliative and loving feelings than if they had remained poker-faced, stiff-bodied, and silent.

In a mechanistic sense, what are produced, matched, and exchanged in early mother–infant engagements are positive emotional and motivational states of interest, pleasure, amusement, desire to establish relationship, intention to please, and intention to communicate with the other (Trevarthen 1984, 1990; Trevarthen, Kokkinaki, and Fiamenghi 1999). Matching or imitating another person's expressed states can evoke similar psychological and bodily states in oneself, thus making it possible to enter into or share the other's feeling (Beebe and Lachmann 1988; Ekman, Levenson, and Friesen 1983; Zajonc 1985). Being mirrored by another enhances one's own mood or state.

The Benefits of Baby Talk

Trevarthen likens the baby's developmental path toward mutuality and social communication to a flower's opening. Incipient receptivity to the forms of adult conversation and even adult music and poetry are in a baby's repertoire from birth, as the flower's petals and parts are folded in the bud. With the sunshine and rain of a loving, responsive adult's cooperative participation, these infant propensities enlarge, open, and spread out, gaining function and fruition.

Psychologists and others have described the specific and noteworthy benefits to infants of this kind of experience (e.g., Greenspan 1997). It contributes to the bond between mother and child, enabling the pair to adjust to each other's individual natures. A mother directs and modulates the baby's state or level of attention and arousal (for example, she may alert, soothe, praise, and please [Fernald 1992, 420]), and by offering emotional regulation and support she can also help the infant achieve self-regulation and homeostatic equilibrium (Hofer 1990). The baby learns that its behavior affects others and that others desire and even require its participation. In interacting with others besides its mother, it gains interpersonal practice in recognizing individuals and predicting their moods and behaviors from subtle changes in voice, face, and body movement.

Baby-talk interactions also provide intellectual, linguistic, and cultural practice. By anticipating what comes next in a familiar sequence, the baby "hypothesizes" or predicts when a climax will occur and experiences its fulfillment. Being able to recognize pattern in the behavior of others—what psychologists call "sequencing"—is essential to eventual social and intellectual competence, making it possible to comprehend and predict others' behavior (Greenspan 1997, 6, 67).

Hearing the mother's words in conversational interplay prepares the way for eventual spoken language, contributing to the baby's abilities of both understanding and producing meaningful sounds (Kuhl et al. 1997). The mother's face provides abundant information about what will eventually be grammar, a clue that we who have learned to speak may not be aware of unless we learn a Sign Language for deaf persons, where facial expressions are grammatically significant. Because different cultures have different baby-talk styles—more or less verbal, more or less intense—the young participant is exposed to the norms of its particular social group.

Some psychologists (e.g., Aitken and Trevarthen 1997; Schore 1994; Trevarthen and Aitken 1994) have recently proposed that the face-to-face baby-talk interaction—or, more accurately and scientifically, the motives that are active in it—provides essential, even crucial stimulation for an infant's developing brain, critically and indelibly shaping and influencing the child's intellectual, social, and emotional functioning for the rest of the lifespan. The normal development of babies in cultures where mutual gaze is discouraged would suggest that this conclusion is too sweeping. In these other cultures, however, babies are carried about continuously on their mothers' bodies amid a rich social environment in which they gain, sometimes without much face-to-face communication, similar opportunities for interacting with and adjusting to the rhythms and styles of their intimates. For example, among the Gusii of Kenya (Dixon et al. 1981), where looking directly at infants is avoided and there is little conversing with them, film analyses nevertheless reveal a high degree of matching in interactive behaviors so that a rhythmic, cyclical pattern is achieved. Motive processes can apparently be transmitted by any part of the rhythmic, cross-modal, dynamically modulated performance—not exclusively by the eyes and face.

It is interesting to note that the face and head movements used by mothers in the baby-talk ritual also occur, in unexaggerated form, in friendly nonverbal communication among adults. They serve as visual signals of a motivation for contact and affiliation. Normal (and even psychotic) persons produce these visual signals, which include "look at," "flash" (a short up-and-down movement of the eyebrows, often accompanied by a smile, which nearly always elicits a smile from the receiver), "bob" (a quick backward movement of the back of the head, which functions as a friendly invitation or encouragement, depending on the accompanying verbal meaning), "smile," and "nod" (used for maintaining contact once it is established) (Grant 1968, 1972; Schelde and Hertz 1994). (These signals can all be seen on the mother's face in the microanalysis diagram.) That small infants everywhere can easily recognize and respond to these very signals argues for their evolved importance in human communication.

Other studies indicate that certain essential behaviors in social interactions—receiving and giving praise, recognition, encouragement, comfort, smiles, and touch—serve as regulators in adults of both physiological states and moods (McGuire and Troisi 1987, 234). These same actions and intentions—coded in special facial expressions, vocal contours, and rhythms—are precisely what infants elicit from their mothers and what most mothers automatically and abundantly bestow. What is not widely appreciated is that infants recognize the positive intentions and feelings of another person through rhythmically patterned cyclical movements (of face, body, and voice) that are coordinated (in timing and intensity—that is, rhythm and mode) to their own expressive movements.

The existence of evolved mechanisms in mothers for spontaneously producing these rhythmically coordinated and patterned signals, and the evolved sensitivities of newborns to recognize and reciprocate them (at a stage of development when they have few other psychological capabilities), argues for their primal importance in infancy. Even older children and young adults with profound mental handicaps (for example, restricted mobility, limited ability to use language) can participate in and enjoy such interactions with sensitive caregivers, strongly indicating "a biologically robust system of basic emotional communication" (Burford 1988).

That these kinds of behaviors influence neurophysiological, endocrinological, and immunological systems and are required for adult physical and emotional health indicates their evolved importance in human well-being—not only in infancy but throughout life. As humans, we evolved to be the kind of creature who *needs* the signs of mutuality— praise, recognition, encouragement, comfort, affectionate touching, and fond smiles—just as we evolved to need food, water, and light. Otherwise, we are incomplete and can even perish. Lacking mutuality, we lack humanity.

THE MOTHER–INFANT PAIR AS THE "CRUCIAL LINK" IN REPRODUCTIVE SUCCESS

All readers of these pages are testaments to their ancestors' reproductive success. If our parents and theirs in turn, back through time, had not met and mated precisely when they did, we would not be here to read books, ponder our origins, and mate and reproduce in our turn. Of course, successful reproduction requires more than mating strategies. Not only finding the right mate but also all the things people do that affect their lives—perceiving, thinking, and acting in all the various circumstances in which they by chance or design find themselves—contribute to survival and reproduction, as does the care that is taken of offspring.

Yet it is interesting to see the emphasis in current biosocial research on issues related to actual mating. In the fifty articles from two volumes (twelve issues) of *Ethology and Sociobiology*, the official journal of the Human Behavior and Evolution Society, in 1995–96,[12] twenty-three (or 46 percent) concerned mating strategies or sex differences that affect mating strategies. Ten (20 percent) reported on various attitudes or social practices within families that indirectly affect fertility—for example, incest avoidance, birth spacing, or economic and property inheritance patterns. The remaining seventeen studies treated a variety of topics that are difficult to categorize: for example, attitudes toward homosexuality, cultural practices such as body scarification or holding a child on the right or left side of the body, the association between mood and landscape preference, evolved cognitive preferences that affect the choice to assist others, and effects of wording on moral decision making. Only two articles of fifty (4 percent) directly addressed maternal care of children and its contribution to reproductive success.

Obviously, sex in our species is more appealing to researchers, male and female, than are maternal-infant interactions. One should not be surprised. But it must nevertheless be pointed out and emphasized that between the Result of a Successful Mating Strategy (that is, a fertile conception with a live, healthy outcome) and the Completed Offspring Who Is Capable of Being Favored by Kin with Strategic Choices (for example, with longer birth intervals or a big inheritance) and Who Then Embarks on Successful Mating Strategies of Its Own is an overlooked crucial missing link: the literally linked mother-infant pair. Without their jointly evolved capacities for mutual interest and involvement, all human mating strategies would be so much seed cast into the wind, and all kin-investment attitudes would be unnecessary. Everyone *knows* this, but interest within the field of evolutionary psychology has overwhelmingly centered on getting the gametes together or on differential investment (whether deliberate or inadvertent) in the resultant offspring.

Yet let us just look at some of the multitudinous inborn capacities that contribute to mother-infant mutuality—evidence of its crucial contribution to reproductive success. Newborns, even premature newborns, are receptive to human voices and will quieten to listen to them in preference to any other sound. They can recognize their mother's voice, which

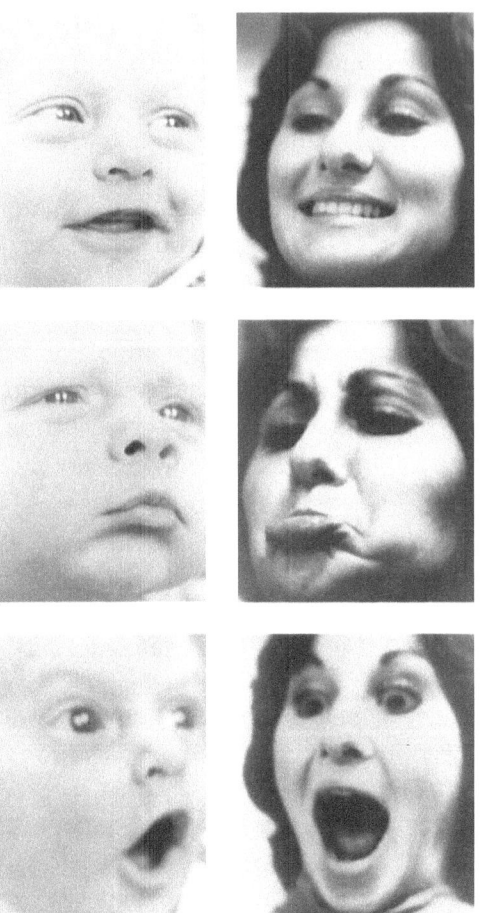

Newborn infants (average age 36 hours) respond to happy, sad, and surprised facial expressions of an adult. Photographs: Tiffany M. Field.

they have become accustomed to from within the womb, and prefer it to the voice of another woman (DeCasper and Fifer 1980). They are also sensitive from birth to configurations of human faces, especially to eyes— looking at them ten times longer than at the mouth at seven to eleven weeks of age (Haith, Bergman, and Moore 1977). Contrary to some psychological theories of the 1940s and 1950s, which claimed that newborns could not see, hear, or feel, newborns have even been observed to imitate facial expressions (such as eye-closing, eyebrow movements, protruding the lips or tongue, or opening the mouth), vocalizations, and hand opening and closing (Kugiumutzakis 1993; Meltzoff and Moore 1977).[13]

Far from being passive recipients, responding only reflexively to stimuli—as was once thought—babies come into the world actively ready to communicate their needs, feelings, and motives to other persons, as well as ready for sympathetic engagement of vocal, facial, and gestural expressions. Even a fetus has areas of cerebral cortex that are specially formed to engage in cultural life and to acquire traditional skills (Trevarthen 1987, 107; 1997). From analyses of filmed baby-talk routines we have learned that babies themselves elicit from adults the sorts of sounds, movements, and actions that are necessary for normal growth of their minds (Greenspan 1997). After all, adults act and speak with babies as they do because that is what babies so demonstrably *like*. Mothers spontaneously recognize or learn (because they are rewarded with smiles, coos, and even more subtle signs of attunement) that their babies require this extreme behavior, which, produced for anyone else, would seem embarrassing or silly.

Baby talk is an excellent example of a behavior that evolved, over time, between two people who had to pay close attention to and respond to each other. The signals each gave had to be rewarding to the other: "I will look into your eyes and smile and you will smile back and make those wonderful faces and entrancing sounds (that, though neither of us realizes it, help my brain develop)." Then: "I will speak and act in this silly way, and you will smile and chortle and join in the rhythm, and we'll both be flooded with delight."

No one teaches infants to smile: they spontaneously produce this universally recognized social signal of receptivity and friendly intention without any knowledge that it will be used on thousands of future occasions. Similarly, they automatically make vocal sounds that many months later will develop into spoken language. The usual view of language is that it evolved to help us label the world and became additionally useful in enabling us to think and convey information to each other. This assumption is reasonable, but it is important to be aware that what we communicate to each other is rarely, if ever, simply factual, verbalized information.

Baby talk, as just described, has nothing to do with the exchange of verbal information about the world and everything to do with participating in an impromptu expression of accord and a narrative of feelings, ideas, and impulses to act. It is this wish to share emotional experience that motivates early vocalization (or "talk before speech") and sets a child on "the path to spoken language," as the neurobiologist of language John L. Locke (1993) nicely described it—not the instrumental need to request or name things, which comes later.[14] In this view, language emerges from and first expresses emotional needs of mutuality and belonging, although

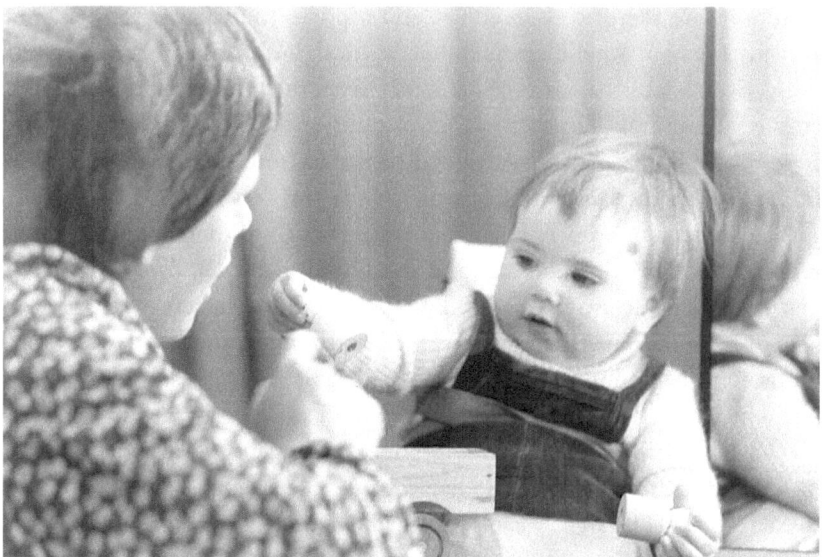

As mother points to the truck, her year-old infant holds out a toy for her to place in it.
Photograph: Colwyn Trevarthen.

it will eventually become also an instrument of symbolic reasoning and intellectual analysis.

These preverbal origins of language and communication are generally disregarded (if not dismissed [e.g., Pinker 1994, 40]), as is the fact that in adult speech emotion continues to be expressed in features such as intonation (speech melody), rhythm, stress, tempo, amplitude, pauses, and voice quality. Contemporary psycholinguists, philosophers, and literary theorists frequently discuss language as if it had to do only with signifiers and symbols—words—and their grammatical and syntactical organization. Considering how language originates and develops in the prelinguistic infant provides a wider view and suggests that, like music, it is built upon a primal emotional communicative ability inherent in every infant.

The innate drive to mutuality seen in the earliest protoconversations is evident in other untaught behaviors of small children. One-year-olds and toddlers spontaneously hand things to others and expect them to be handed back. This early penchant for reciprocity—for showing and sharing—arises from our ancestral hominid nature. Bipedality left the arms and hands free for carrying and handing things to others. Unlike our primate relatives, who procure their own food and—not being able to transport it except by mouth—eat it on the spot, all hunter-gatherers carry food home to share with others (Lancaster 1978).[15]

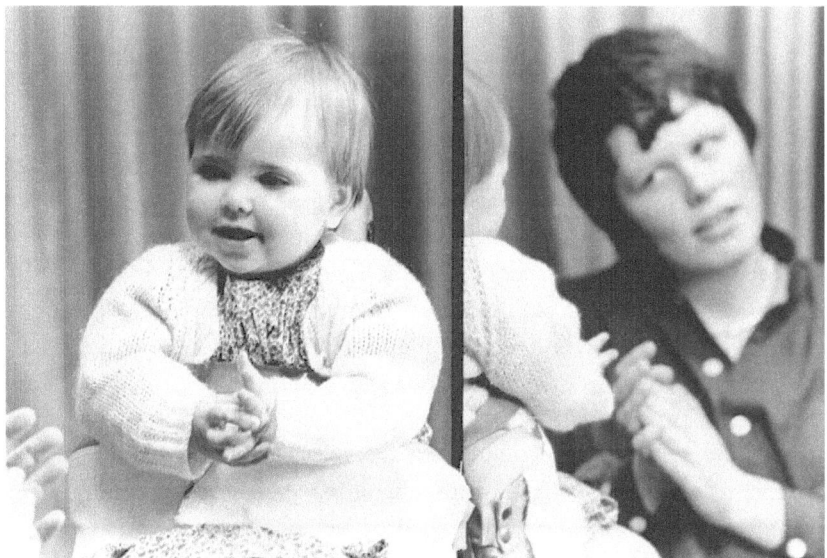

A one-year-old infant imitates her mother clapping. Photograph: Colwyn Trevarthen.

Infants (even newborns), babies, and small children also naturally imitate others, changing over time in what they choose to imitate. They want not only to be pleased by but also to please others. Imitation remains an unconscious way to please: even in adults, matching or mirroring behavior unconsciously induces positive feeling in a conversational partner, literally communicating accord. Adults talking to one another are temporally synchronized—a kind of imitation—like mothers and babies in engagement, who also unconsciously respond to split-second changes in unconscious signals from their partners in an ever changing improvisation of emotional and motivational messages that will later underlie spoken conversational exchanges of information.

As children grow older, they spontaneously imitate the activities of their elders—pretend cooking, shopping, driving. We call this kind of imitation "play" or "make-believe." Like the spontaneous playful smiling, sharing, and synchronizing in mother-infant mutuality, later deliberate play further instills culture by giving practice in doing what is natural and necessary for a particular way of life, as play hunting teaches kittens how to hunt. Children's play may be viewed, like animal play, as "competitive," testing one's mettle against that of others. Yet play also teaches children how to fit into a group; it provides opportunities to please others and to receive positive attention and approbation. It helps them to feel valued and validated and, of course, to use their imaginations.

That children are innately prepared to play (as they were earlier innately ready to smile, imitate, synchronize, and reciprocate) indicates how important sympathy and cooperation have been to our species—too important to leave to chance. Thus the traits that grow out of mutuality are as fundamental to human nature as self-interest. Indeed, we can think of traits of selfishness, ruthlessness, anger, and greed not only or even primarily as *needs* but as *tactics* to get what we need, or rather what we think we need because our material or psychological needs were or are insufficiently met. Long-term studies have shown that children who turn out to be leaders are those who were friendly in play groups—showing signals of appeasement and conciliation, not aggression, during incipient conflicts (Morgan 1995, 148–49).

As humans developed divergent ways of life, there was the possibility for more variation in customs, including child-care traditions, that were given symbolic value and passed on verbally, by precept, as well as by example. Each cultural group has developed traditions and conventions about raising its young (as about every other important matter).

Yet the variety of child-rearing practices seems to be built upon the common readiness in infants (and preparedness in mothers) for developing and sustaining mutuality—the rhythmic-multimodal sensitivities and competencies that enable matching, turn-taking, synchrony, and other indications of sharing an emotional state. Thus I believe we can look upon the inborn tendencies in all infants to imitate, smile, and synchronize as behavioral adaptations from ancestral times, as are the corresponding tendencies in caretakers, especially mothers, to respond to them with tenderness and reciprocity. Even in a society such as the Gusii of Kenya, mentioned earlier, which avoids eye contact and talking to babies, the babies were nevertheless ready for such interaction. When Western investigators urged Gusii mothers to play with and talk to their babies, the babies obviously enjoyed it, responding with cooing vocalizations, big kicks, and large smiles (Dixon et al. 1981).

It is not too much to say that infants are born "expecting" a caring other to be there—a Virtual Mother. Their readiness from birth to find the human face and voice of riveting interest, to imitate facial movements (before even knowing that they possess a face), and to adjust their bodily movements to the rhythms of human voices seems convincing evidence that they are innately ready for relationship. Adults' preparedness to provide the cues that infants need (the most attention-getting kinds of facial expressions and bodily movements, and the vocalizations with the most appealing intonation, volume, undulations, and rhythm), along with their preparedness to adjust and change these features to match babies' changing requirements, indicates that they are inherently able to help their young grow up in mutuality.

LEGACIES OF MUTUALITY

Affiliations with others (including the varieties of love mentioned at the beginning of this chapter) are prefigured in the mother-infant relationship. There, each of us first encounters the bodily mechanisms of mutuality and learns about elaborating them. The dictionary definitions of "mutual"—directed by each toward the other; having the same feelings one for the other; shared in common; joint; characterized by intimacy—describe very well the interactions that psychologists have observed in mothers with their babies. They also describe the most satisfying moments between close friends, even among a group of friends, and between lovers, the memories of which may be carried for a lifetime. The profound unions that we feel in what Freud called "oceanic experiences"—sexual fulfillment, the complete understanding between intimate friends or lovers—are foretold in the union of mutuality. All are positive, "flowing," boundless experiences, the most significant that we know. At the end of chapter 5, I suggest that even the feelings of transcendental oneness that can arise while making or experiencing the arts or in religious and other noetic or spiritual transfigurations are at least in part based on these innate propensities for mutuality.

Although humans are predisposed for rhythmic-modal expressions of mutuality with caretakers and other close familiars, and although such interchanges are even necessary to infant survival, they eventually take their place as means to other ends. Expressions of mother-infant mutuality occur in brief bouts that may last only a few seconds, and in hunter-gatherer and other similar societies (to be described in chapter 2), they can take place with several or even many other people. They are not exclusively with one person and soon are replaced by similarly structured and longer-lasting group events that unite numbers of people.

In succeeding chapters I show how in small-scale (and probably ancestral) societies these expressions are transformed into feelings of belonging to a group and sharing its ideals. In heterogeneous modern societies, where we have relationships of various kinds (not necessarily even face-to-face) with a variety of people who know us only in certain roles or at certain times of our lives and who often do not know one another, mutuality and belonging are less inclusive and well defined. Perhaps this disruption to our evolved nature accounts at least in part for the obsession with sexual or romantic love in modern society's popular songs and pastimes.

I wonder whether the excessive amount of time and effort some of us spend in seeking, finding, and then recovering from love affair after love affair, and our frequent bitter disappointments in love of this sort, is not driven at least partly by the desperate attempt to fill a void that in ancestral times did not exist. I daresay that no other society is as preoccupied as is contemporary America with romantic love as the primary meaning of life.

It strikes me that the word or concept "bonding" became part of popular culture at about the same time that the traditional bonds between married partners and between parents and their children were found to be no longer immutable.[16] Perhaps our own insecurities required an acknowledged psychological process or entity, as if that would make it somehow more reliable than "attachment," the term that had been used by ethologists for human and monkey mothers and infants in the 1960s. If one can attach, presumably one can detach—but bonding, like epoxy glue, sounds indestructible.

The growing trend for working parents to deposit their infants in day-care for thirty-five to forty hours per week from as early as six weeks of age (or government imperatives that single mothers leave welfare—and their young children—in order to work) does not appear promising for building the sorts of mother-infant relationships that have evolved to characterize humans over tens (if not hundreds) of thousands of years.

Cross-cultural studies indicate that infants may not require an exclusive relationship with one caretaker, as some Western attachment theorists (e.g., Schore 1994) have claimed. In Aka pygmy societies, for example, infants between one and four months are held by their mothers less than 40 percent of the time and are transferred among adults and older children more than seven times per hour (Hewlett 1991). Efe pygmy infants spend 39 percent of their time in physical contact with persons other than their mothers at three weeks and 60 percent at eighteen weeks. These interactions are described as "positive and playful" (Tronick, Morelli, and Winn 1987). One can hope that American day-care center personnel, like the Aka, interact with and stimulate infants throughout the day, "talking to, playing with, and showing affection" to them (Hewlett 1991, 32).

2

Belonging

HUMANS ARE NOT biologically or psychologically prepared for being
unloved and unwanted. Unlike bull elephants or orangutans and leopards
of both sexes, which prefer to live entirely alone except for brief periods
during which they mate (or, in the case of female orangutans and leopards,
have young), hominids have always required intimate coexistence with
others of their kind. Mutuality with other individuals and belonging to a
group are as necessary to human life as food and warmth. They are emotional food and warmth.

As described in the previous chapter, we humans evolved to be lovable and to attune ourselves to others from the moment we are born. From
these tenacious roots of mother-infant mutuality grow our need and readiness to belong to a group. As it feels good to love and be loved in mutuality by another, it feels good to feel valued by and validated in a group.
Just as important, not having these things feels bad, or worse than bad:
incomplete.

It is interesting that among social animals who care for their young—
whether mammals, birds, or even insects—affective interchange usually
occurs between adults as well (Eibl-Eibesfeldt 1989, 144), often in ritualized behaviors (like feeding one another, "billing and cooing," or making
infantile sounds and movements) that are derived from infant care. In contrast, iguanas (which, like most other reptiles, simply lay eggs and give no

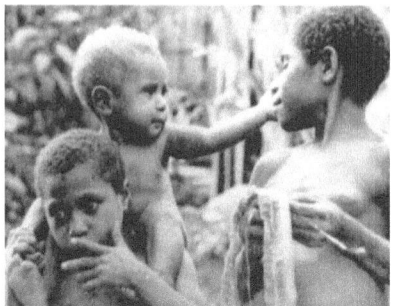

a

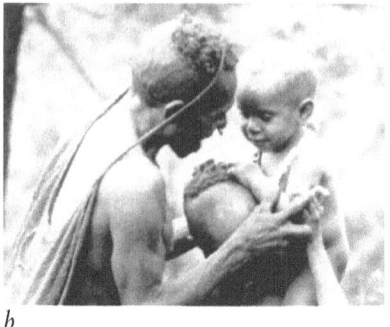

b

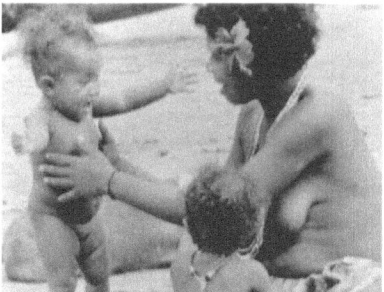

c

In small-scale societies the world over, children easily engage in a larger social world of kin and other familiars. Photographs: I. Eibl-Eibesfeldt.

a. Infant boy on older girl's shoulders solicits contact with a young woman, who responds. Eipo, Irian Jaya.
b. Male greets infant riding on another adult's shoulders. Eipo, Irian Jaya.
c. Year-old infant solicits contact from adult female while a younger infant looks on. Trobriand Islands, Papua New Guinea.

further thought to their offspring) are gregarious but not really sociable. All their communication is restricted to display of mood or intention, without give-and-take interaction.

In humans, the rhythms and modes that characterize mother-infant interaction also seem to have provided raw materials that have been used for building relationships outside the parental association, which in their turn—as I show in this chapter—help individuals to identify with the social group. This sense of belonging then makes it possible for the group member to acquire a sense of meaning and competence for his or her life (see chapters 3 and 4). We see the seamless and early progression from primary infant mutuality with the mother to mutuality with others in the group in the lives of small children in present-day hunter-gatherer societies (such as the Khoisan of southern Africa, Aborigines of Australia, and Congo pygmies), as well as in numerous other small-scale foraging and horticultual societies, which suggests that this was the ancestral human pattern.

For example, among the Kalahari Khoisan (Konner 1977), the mother-infant bond is "of long duration" and very close and indulgent.

The baby rides on the mother's hip, with constant skin-to-skin contact, in a special sling that allows maximum movement of arms and legs and continual access to mother's breasts and to the ornaments around her neck. At the same time, there is the possibility for eye-to-eye contact at child-level with other children, who show much interest in coming close and interacting.

Although in other Bushman groups, such as the !Kung and Hadza, there are some minor differences in parental indulgence and age at weaning, these infants also spend most of their first year riding on their mother's side or back (Blurton-Jones 1993). In all Bushman societies, the close mother-infant relationship exists within a dense social context where the pair is in constant contact (including face-to-face interaction) with relatives and friends of all ages. The child moves from (almost literal) physical as well as emotional attachment to the mother to gradual social embeddedness in a group of other children of different ages, who then grow up together, sharing the same experiences and knowing the same people.

In other hunter-gatherer groups, too, mutuality may be established between the infant and its mother and, almost at the same time, between the infant and other close kin. In these sociable enclaves where people are well known to one another, all welcome the new arrival and remain eager to pick babies up, hold and handle them, and carry them around. As Annette Hamilton (1981, 29) has described for Aboriginal infants in north-central Arnhem Land:

> [An infant] has a very sociable time. It is passed around the group and people constantly look at it, placing their faces close and making sounds to it, or saying "you are my [kin]." If it is fretful it is fed, and if still fretful, rocked and joggled up and down. . . . In the main the infant lies on its back in the cradle, over its mother's knees, surrounded by the movements and sounds of the camp.

Soon after birth, infants of Efe pygmies in the Congo Republic (formerly Zaire) are passed around among the women, some of whom may suckle the babies whether or not they are lactating. By three weeks of age Efe infants spend 39 percent of their time in physical contact with people other than their mothers, and by four months, 60 percent (Tronick, Morelli, and Winn 1987). At three weeks they are passed to someone else nearly four times per hour on average; at seven weeks, five to six times per hour; and at eighteen weeks, over eight times an hour. Every baby is immediately attended to, being cared for by an average of fourteen people. Observers of these positive and playful interactions conclude that the Efe pattern of multiple caretaking maximizes a baby's interactive skills, allowing it to learn gregariousness, cooperation, and mutual support—values that are integral to Efe society (Tronick, Morelli, and Winn 1987).

A similar pattern exists in Aka pygmies from the Central African Republic and People's Republic of the Congo (Hewlett 1991). Babies are carried in a sling on the adult's side, where they have much face-to-face interaction with their caregivers or passersby. Although the mother is the primary caregiver and attachment figure, the Aka father also participates readily, as do numerous others. Between one and four months of age, while in camp, an infant is held by its mother less than 40 percent of the time and during a typical hour may be transferred to seven different people. Outside camp, however, the mother holds the baby 90 percent of the time, and it is transferred only two times or so per hour.

Despite small differences, the general pattern of infant and child care in these hunter-gatherer societies is remarkably similar: even when there is multiple caretaking, the mother and infant sustain a close relationship that easily and naturally branches out into lively social interaction between babies and others. The mother-infant duo exists within a supportive group of kin and other familiars, and the child is absorbed gradually and smoothly into this larger unity.

Humans and their societies are nothing if not variable, and in groups with different types of subsistence we see other permutations and styles of mother-infant interaction. Yet the propensity for encouraging early social interaction with others is strong in virtually all small-scale societies.

For example, in a number of groups—including Kaluli in the Southern Highlands of Papua New Guinea (Schieffelin 1990), Fais in Micronesia (Sostek 1981), Marquesas (Martini and Kirkpatrick 1981), Kanela in Brazil (Sorenson et al., cited in Sostek 1981), and Ganda in Uganda (Ainsworth 1967)—small babies are held facing outward as if to maximize their association with others.

A Marquesan mother spends much time playing with her infant, holding it supine on her lap in a face-to-face position for about 60 percent of the time when the baby is six to fourteen weeks of age. Once the baby can sit more comfortably, she facilitates face-to-face play with other children by turning it to look outward from her lap. From about four to nine months babies are routinely held sitting or standing face outward, and caretakers (who may assume much of the baby's care by the time it is five to six months old) deliberately set up interactions of three or more people with the baby as the focus. Thus the brief interactive routines of the mother and baby are rather quickly generalized to interactive routines with others (Martini and Kirkpatrick 1981).

From birth the attention of Kwaia'ae infants in the Solomon Islands is directed away from their own feelings and toward the social group around them. Caregivers stimulate, talk to, and include infants in social conversation, speaking for them and translating their baby sounds into Kwaia'ae. They use special "calling out" routines to encourage six-month-olds to repeat the contour of the sound, thus helping them learn to vocalize correctly (Watson-Gegeo and Gegeo 1986).

Kaluli children greet and address infants, and in response a mother will turn her baby outward and speak "for" it in a special high-pitched nasalized register, moving the baby as she speaks. For example, here is a mother speaking in this altered voice for her three-month-old infant to a three-year-old child:

> *"My brother! My brother! My* ko! *[affectionate name] My* ko! *My brother!"*
> *Brother smiles at baby: "Yes!"*
> *Mother again speaks as above: "My brother, carry me a little."*
> *After her own interchange with the older child, the mother speaks again as her baby: "Abi [older brother's name], I'm going to drink the breast." (excerpt from Schieffelin 1990, 71)*

Although Schieffelin expressly says that mothers rarely talk directly to infants (except during the first months of life, when they "greet [them] by name and use expressive vocalizations"), this sort of "speaking for," in a special register, nevertheless utilizes short repetitive phrases and physical movements that are reminiscent of the "typical baby talk" described in the previous chapter.

In some societies in Africa and Papua New Guinea, direct eye-to-eye contact or vocal play is avoided, yet observers report that mothers are absorbed by, preoccupied with, and attuned to their infants (e.g., Ainsworth 1967; Dixon et al. 1981). In these, as in the small-scale societies just described, babies are patted, stroked, and bounced up and down, and it is rare for a caregiver and infant to be alone together. Thus we can surmise that despite variations in styles and components of play and in details of carrying (seated on adults' shoulders, encased in a baby sash on mother's

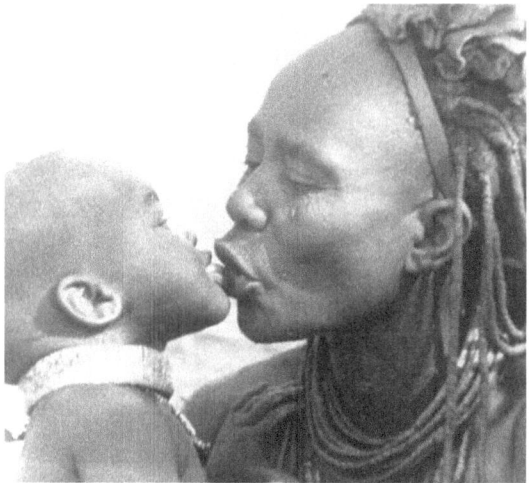

Grandmother-infant kiss feeding. Himba, Kaokoland, southern Africa. Photograph: I. Eibl-Eibesfeldt.

back as she works or even dances, or slung atop her hip), there is ample opportunity for babies to interact physically and facially in the rhythms and modes of mutuality with others.

I suggest that the broad similarities one finds in hunter-gatherer child-care styles be viewed as closest to the "ancestral norm" from which both the dramatic and vocal engagements of modern Western mothers and the more restrained interactions of other societies have diverged and differentiated.

In any small-scale society, babies are born into and grow up within a community, acquiring wide experience with many different others, all of whom know each other. They are ever aware of ongoing life surrounding them—people working, talking, laughing, quarreling, haranguing, complaining, grieving, playing, singing, telling stories. Babies sleep with their mothers in the same rest area if not on the same mat, often with a group of siblings and cousins. They are fed on demand with breast milk until the age of two or three or even longer; other food may be premasticated by the mother or pushed into the baby's mouth with her fingers or, in some societies such as the Eipo, from her own lips.

It is evident that in such small-scale societies, infants and children have socially and physically stimulating lives amid a homogeneous group of other people, many of them family and kin. Although in some of these societies small children may be teased mildly or even vigorously, and like children everywhere they do not always get everything they demand, their lives appear to be far more "secure" in the sense of being part of a group—of belonging—than do the lives of children in a modern society. As anthropologist James Chisholm (1983, 38) reminds us, only in industrial Europe and North America does the small, isolated nuclear family predominate. In the rest of the world, and from the remotest beginnings of hominid evolution, the social environment of infancy ordinarily includes a large number and wide variety of siblings, aunts, uncles, grandparents, cousins, and familiar neighbors.

In such societies, except for death, long separations are hardly known and certainly not feared or expected. "Commitment" to others, or another, is rarely if ever a choice, but part of the way things are. Such societies are far more cohesive and communal than ours—difficult to imagine for people like ourselves, whose boundaries from others have been encouraged from the earliest months by sleeping alone in a crib, perhaps in a separate room, riding in a stroller or car seat rather than on someone's body, and being consulted about our individual preferences in food, clothes, and activities. Being born into a diverse and stratified society of strangers from whom one is kept separated is something quite new in the human repertoire.

CREATING AND SUSTAINING AFFILIATION

Although human infants are innately programmed to "attach" to a caretaker, emotional "detachment" has not been built into human psychology because it was not a biologically viable possibility. Unattached infants would have died and failed to pass on their genes for self-sufficiency. Rather, the rhythms and modes of mutuality and attachment with a single protective figure seem to have gradually overflowed into attachment to close others and eventually to the group itself.[1]

Ancestrally, the hunter-gatherer way of life evolved to suit mobile cooperative bands of around twenty-five individuals, many or most (but not necessarily all) of them blood relations. Seasonally, several bands known to each other probably came together, allowing for meetings that could lead to intermarriage and other alliances and providing the sorts of get-togethers that, despite a very different way of life, people still enjoy today.

Getting together is one thing. Getting along and staying together is another—whether as pairs, small groups such as families, or larger extended-family groups of twenty-five. Being social may be imperative,

but it is (and was) not always easy. Consequently, the human need for belonging has demanded incentives and reinforcements to maintain that
state. All animals possess what ethologists call "behavioral mechanisms"
that help them get along together, usually by preventing bad moods, dis-
agreements, or conflicting interests from escalating to actual physical
fights.

There are visual and behavioral signs of *appeasement*, when you realize that someone bigger or otherwise more dominant than yourself might
have misinterpreted something you have said or done. Appeasement signals usually are ways of making oneself look smaller, more inconspicuous,
and therefore less threatening: lowering or bowing the head, reducing
movement and sound, averting the gaze, and saying submissive things like
"I'm sorry" and "excuse me."

Like the appeasement signals of other animals, ours may also recall
infancy (when one is indeed small and unthreatening). Dogs roll on their
backs or squeal like puppies. Macaques bare their teeth in a silent grin.
Humans smile, speak (if at all) in softer, higher-pitched voices, make our
eyes larger, or perhaps even weep to garner pity or sympathy rather than
fury. In Awlad 'Ali (Egyptian Bedouin) society, where the highest values
include personal honor, self-mastery, and propriety, people may punctu-
ate an ordinary conversational exchange with an improvised poem called
ghinnawa (little song) that expresses sentiments of vulnerability that would
otherwise be socially unacceptable. Chanted or sung in an altered voice,
these poems make use of metaphorical terms that evoke childhood, re-
vealing feelings of longing, sadness, and even self-pity. By being expressed
in a childish way, the poems attract sympathy and help for the speaker
rather than moral criticism (Abu-Lughod 1986).

Appeasement is a reaction to perceived threat or disapproval. Animals also have evolved positive or constructive means to create affiliation
and accord between individuals. Chimpanzees, our closest ape relatives,
smack their lips and smile to indicate reassurance or as a friendly greeting.
They use gentle touching, grooming, and even embracing and kissing—
as we do—as signs of reconciliation. These expressions of affiliation reduce tension and promote accord (de Waal 1989).

The rhythms and modes that build mutuality between caretakers and
infants, like the unthreatening behaviors and appearance of infants themselves, have become a sort of reservoir for human appeasement and affiliation signals—that is, effective ways to reassure others and to create or
strengthen social and even sexual bonds. Courtship, for example, in our

own species and in others, sometimes makes use of infantile or parental cues that act to dispel unconscious reluctance or self-protection. Thus male sparrows shake their wings toward an intended mate like a juvenile asking for food (Eibl-Eibesfeldt 1989, 146), and male ravens make a silent coughing motion of the head that resembles parental feeding (Morton and Page 1992, 96). A courting male hamster utters contact calls like those of baby hamsters (Eibl-Eibesfeldt 1989, 146). Bonobos (a close chimpanzee relative of humans) copulate face-to-face, with prolonged gazing into each other's eyes—the only other creature besides humans to do this.

In humans, love songs and courtship speech frequently use childish words and refer to childish things to create and display intimacy: "Cuddle up a little closer, lovey mine," or "Baby I want you." We say our sweet nothings in a soft, undulant voice. It seems likely that the fondling and nuzzling of the female breast in human mating is derived from (or evolved alongside) an adaptation that first made the nipple and areola pleasurably sensitive to the suckling of infants.

In occurring far in excess of what is required for procreation, human sexual behavior is different from that of other animals (except bonobos). Indeed, human females have evolved to be sexually receptive outside the estrus (or fertile) period, even during pregnancy, as if sexual engagement is important in itself, apart from reproduction.

In bonobos, sex seems to be a sort of tension-reducing device, as frequent and casual as stopping for a quick break for coffee or a cigarette. In humans, sex is usually more discriminating and more elaborated, as if its purpose is less to reduce tension than to reinforce a mutual bond.

Both sexual and mother-infant interactions make use of similar rhythms and modes: unfolding dynamic temporal sequences, "matching" and "turn-taking" of voice, gesture, and movement, and building to an anticipated but not precisely predictable climax—thereby achieving emotional union and communion. In these features, both kinds of engagement also resemble the ritualized affiliative "dances" or "performances" that, much more than the brief, indiscriminate copulations of bonobos, engage the interest of and synchronize some courting animals such as cranes. Although it may at first sound strange, it is not really far-fetched to suggest that human mating, though not so "hard wired" as that of cranes, echoes and elaborates upon the mother-infant mutuality. Foreplay "works" in human sexual bonding because its rhythmic and modal elements evolved to create attunement in the equally important relationship between mother and infant. Although it is not strictly necessary for the

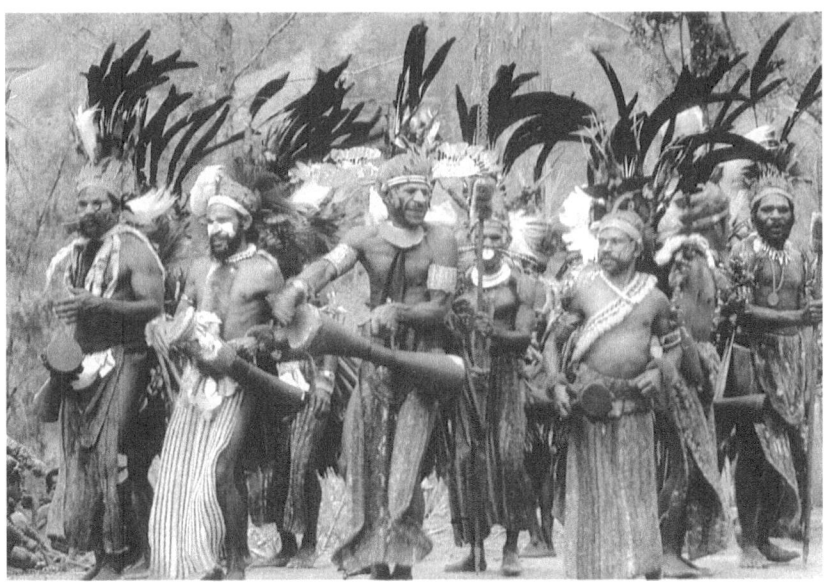

*Sharing the preparations and experiences of a ceremony unifies a group of individuals.
Kairuku nut festival, Gogime village, Chimbu Province, Papua New Guinea. Photograph:
Maureen MacKenzie.*

attainment of copulation, it is essential to *lovemaking*, where affiliative
emotions and sensations are periodically reinforced and sustained.

Rhythmic and modal elements such as synchronizing, turn-taking,
imitating or matching, and sequentially patterning movements and vocalizations are also the stuff of ceremonial ritual—a universal and age-old
practice that will be discussed in more detail in chapter 5. Occasions and
expressed reasons for ceremonies include resolving interpersonal conflict
and reducing tension, displaying resources, providing formalized avenues
for competition, expressing thanksgiving, assuring prosperity or success in
ventures, averting defeat or other misfortune, "transforming" individuals
from one life stage or state to another, curing illness, and requesting ab-
solution or other beneficence.

A particular ceremony may or may not ultimately achieve its intended
purpose, but it nearly always makes people feel as if they have addressed
their problems. What is more, it literally brings individuals together, unifying and coordinating them—at least for the duration of the ritual—in
common purpose. Using structural and performative elements drawn from
the rhythms and modes of mutuality, social groups achieve similar ends of

sustaining emotional bonds (communal, rather than dual), reinforcing the individual's identity with the group, and instilling cultural norms. For example, some rituals are dyadic, using alternation and imitation as a way to create or express understanding and unity. Others may be concurrent, with all individuals performing actions together and thereby creating and confirming unity. Both styles may be used in the same ceremony, as they are used by mothers and infants in the same interaction.

Just as it was essential during human evolutionary history for mothers and infants to establish mutuality, so was it essential for members of groups to work together in confidence and harmony rather than to act individually, selfishly, or haphazardly, without reference to tradition and communal purpose. Presumably, if ceremonies had emphasized only unrestrained individualism, perpetual novelty, and loyalty only to immediate self-interest, the individuals and groups who practiced them would have dwindled and vanished.

Although ritual elaboration will be described in more detail in chapter 5, we can look now at four examples of ceremonial use of the rhythmic and modal elements that characterize mother-infant mutuality.

CEREMONIAL REINFORCEMENT OF BELONGING: FOUR EXAMPLES

Until recently in Karelia (once eastern Finland, now part of Russia), women performed *itkuvirsi*, a kind of improvised but ritualized lament (Tolbert 1990). With roots in ancestor worship of ancient folk religion, laments were traditionally performed in the context of funerals—or weddings, where they expressed sorrow at the bride's leaving home. They also might be called forth when old friends met after a long separation, to complain about the hardships of life. As in the Bedouin *ghinnawa*, a ritualized voice and context made it possible to express things that could not otherwise be said, and also to gain sympathy and solidarity rather than censure for frailty or ill humor.

A Karelian lamenter did not simply weep or cry aloud but used formalized descending sigh-motifs sung in crylike exhalations along with stylized sobbings. She cried "with words," not with tears. Rather than spontaneously expressing an individual's own sadness, a lament was symbolic or metaphoric of grief, meant to move all who heard it into a collective expression of sorrow. Lamenters felt certain that even the most hardhearted person would be moved to weep.

Laments were set off from everyday life and speech in numerous ways. Their words were uncommon and difficult to understand, being metaphoric, grammatically intricate, and sometimes even chosen for their sound rather than their meaning. Often terms denoting childhood or mothering (for example, "my dear little nursling") would be used. The repetition of initial sounds (alliteration) was deliberately utilized and prized. Although the utterances lacked regular meter, the rhythm was different from that of ordinary speech. The lamenter used a dialogic form, asking the deceased person rhetorical questions ("Why did you leave?" "What offense moved you to go?" "Do you need anything where you are?"). As the improvisation proceeded, vocal tension increased: that is, pitch rose, and there was increasing use of microtones and microrhythms. The lament ended with acceptance that the inevitable (death, leave-taking) had taken place, thus achieving both a formal and an emotional closure or reconciliation.

It does not seem inappropriate to point out that even apart from direct and indirect references to infancy, much of the Karelian women's lament was based on features that promote mutuality and attunement in mother-infant engagement—for example, words whose meaning is emotionally rather than semantically understood, expressive vocal contours, dialogic structure, frequent repetitions, development of intensity, and a final resolution—and achieved a similar end. The "appeasement" function of weeping, derived from childhood helplessness and need, was an additional infantile feature.

In the courtship "dance" of the Medlpa in the Southern Highlands of Papua New Guinea, beautifully adorned young couples sit side by side and initially sway their bodies toward and away from each other while moving their heads in parallel, to a background of adults' singing. Then, placing their foreheads together, they turn or roll their heads (which must always be touching) from back to front, and when their cheeks are together, make a bow. After these movements have been repeated several times, there is a "cutoff" activity, such as looking down or turning away, before a new bout resumes. Each couple creates its own common synchronous rhythm, not necessarily that of the vocal background. They adjust to one another—the young man initiating and controlling the form of the movement and the young woman the fine variation in speed (Pitcairn and Schleidt 1976).

Here, kinesis, or movement, is the main medium that allows physical and rhythmic communion between a performing pair, and as in mother-infant mutuality, the engagements stop and start, occurring in "bouts" that are broken off by one or the other. The achievement of mutuality is a joint endeavor, and—appropriately for a courtship ritual that is meant to explore whether or not a couple is "suited"—prefigures the coordination that takes place in actual sexual intercourse as well as other forms of physical and emotional attunement and communication.

Among a number of musical rituals of the Kalapalo of central Brazil (Basso 1985) is one that is dyadic, called *akina*. A narrator tells a sung story with the participation of a listener-responder (called a "what-sayer") who rhythmically punctuates the narrative flow with remarks like "yes," "I told you so," "wow," and *"kitsi"* (disgust), or by repeating the focal phrase or clause. The responder can direct the narrator's flow of speech into side channels of greater explication or elaboration and help the narrator to recall details that might otherwise be omitted. How the what-sayer responds to the storyteller is crucial to a successful performance.

Narrators manipulate their vocal pitch and other prosodic features to take on the voices of other characters, and they use a a variety of structuring and conventional devices that organize their story into segments and additionally help to create, maintain, and develop the audience's anticipation and awareness of such narrative features as connection, perpetuation, progression, and conclusion. These devices include intonational contours, parallelism, and vowel lengthening (for surprise effects).

Like members of other premodern groups, Kalapalo cannot sing without moving the body and are thereby unified by moving in synchrony. Music is explicitly considered to be a way to control and channel aggression and to merge individuals together into a larger whole in which people feel a unification of space and time and a collective solidarity.

The multimedia nature of Kalapalo performance, the use of a dyadic form in which two people are necessary for developing the narrative structure and story, the use of vocal and narrative variety, and the buildup of anticipation all recall the rhythmic and modal means for building mother-infant mutuality.

Relying on prosodic and poetic devices as well as the subject matter of infancy, the Kaluli, a rain-forest people of the Great Papuan Plateau in the Southern Highlands of Papua New Guinea, reinforce group cooperative values (Feld 1982). Their major ceremony, called *gisalo*, recounts the legend of a boy whose elder sister refused his requests for food, after which he turned into a *muni*, a type of fruit dove that utters a plaintive call. In this ceremony the Kaluli interweave a complex associative web of bird sound, human weeping, melodic song, and poetic language to express and reinforce major cultural themes that promote reciprocity and obligation—such as food giving and sharing, comradeship, assistance, and caretaking—and at the same time express fear of isolation, abandonment, and loss.

The *gisalo* song voice has a conventionalized evocative vocal register and uses descending intonation that, because of its association with a child whining for food, makes listeners feel sorrow or pity. The song voice also uses devices of delaying expectation and plays on the audience's deepest childish fears of abandonment and isolation until the desired responses, weeping and anger, occur in a sort of dramatic catharsis.

MUTUALITY, BELONGING, AND IDENTITY

In chapter 1, I described how inherent mutuality between mother and infant evolved because it was essential for the survival of the baby and the reproductive success of the mother. I explained that the feelings of loving and being loved that were nourished by mutuality's vehicles—among them imitation or matching, reciprocity or turn-taking, and emotional communion—also set the infant on a pathway that led to belonging to a larger social group.

The adaptive value to individuals of living in unified social groups, like the adaptive value of bonded infants and caretakers, seems clear. Cohesive societies would have prospered more than fragmented and uncooperative ones, and the individuals within them would have had better chances for survival. Individuals who felt intrinsically part of their group would want to contribute to it and defend it.

It is not surprising that societies all over the world have developed these nodes of culture that we call ceremonies or rituals, which do for their members what mothers naturally do for babies: engage their interest, involve them in a shared rhythmic pulse, and thereby instill feelings of closeness and communion. The inborn propensities for imitation, reciprocity, and emotional communion in infancy have become further elaborated and used in ritualized and ceremonial forms that themselves build and reinforce feelings of unity among adults, all of which ultimately serve to hold the group together.

From mutuality and belonging emerges what we call today a *sense of identity*, which can be thought of as a set of circles of varying sizes with degrees of overlap with other circles—or, let us say, drops of watercolor paints of different colors that enclose or encroach upon one another. In the inmost center is our own selfhood, prepared as in every creature for self-preservation. As humans, our sense of selfhood may vary according to the way in which our social group conceives of selves—as dependent, interdependent, or independent; as proud and isolate or inextricable from the selves of others; as unified and balanced or composed of separate elements such as faculties of reason and emotion, private or public spheres, or upper and lower souls. And there are many variations or even unresolved combinations of such ideas.

No matter how the person conceptualizes this self, and even if it is not clearly conceptualized, this "central core" includes what can be called the "biological self," which is motivated to do what it perceives as necessary to stay alive: to eat, drink, sleep, avoid danger or harm, seek approval, and so forth. In circumstances of ultimate, unquestionable danger—on a sinking ship or in a burning theater—it will struggle to save itself. Perhaps it will try to save others, too—but not always, or not reliably.

In the evolutionary view I present here, the core human self is both "individually biological" and "biologically social." It requires mutuality and involvement with other selves and has an identity in terms of others— an immediate caretaker or caretakers—which then extends to others with whom mutuality is shared: family and close kin. This social self, one might say, becomes a "Hatfield" or a "McCoy." In ancestral times and for most individuals even today, in most parts of the world, this circle of kin usually completely encloses the core self.

Other circles also expand out from or overlap the core self and family circles with other, sometimes simultaneous, sources of identity: for example, community (perhaps totem, clan, moiety, tribe, neighborhood, village), age set, occupation, religion, social class, city, state, nation, race, gender—affected too by how our familiars regard these various things. Depending on circumstances, we feel various degrees of closeness to others who are in these same identities, so that in a foreign country we may form a friendship with another person simply because we are both of the same national origin. We might feel more compatible with a stranger who, like us, is a teacher or a "thirty-something" than with a bank teller or a person in her fifties. That is, we share an identity (we "belong"), even though in other circumstances we might not notice this particular identity because of being more involved in another, more immediately embracing one.

Identities in small societies are fewer and less ambiguous or conflicting than those in large, pluralistic, anonymous societies, where the water-colors may create incompatible and confusing boundaries.[2] Thus, in ancestral times identity was easier and more certain. In small, homogeneous hunter-gatherer communities, individuals each have an acknowledged place, and although their choices might to us seem limited, in those limits is a security that we were evolved to accept and even require.[3] In such societies, accepting and following traditional ways does not feel like "coercion" or loss of freedom, since everyone else of the same age or sex or identity behaves and is expected to behave similarly.

Increasingly over the past century, however, instead of automatically entering into a prescribed role in a familiar, supportive group, people in modern mercantile societies are expected to fashion an identity—find a niche or means of livelihood. That is not all, for we must then—at least in the United States—learn to "sell" that identity and niche to strangers who themselves have no special reason to value a stranger and are, moreover, similarly preoccupied with their own identity and self-worth. "Expressing one's individuality" and "being original" have replaced fitting into a community and conforming to its age-old, tried and true maxims. Rather than sharing, people now "go after what they want." Individual "freedom" replaces obligation; we are largely taught to value rights of individuals over responsibilities to the group.

Yet once within our modern fluid and self-conscious "in-groups," we behave remarkably like our Paleolithic ancestors. Today, as then, people feel closest to those with whom they do things—eat, work, or worship—together. Positive social sentiments are strongest with respect to those with whom daily life is shared, because mutuality and belonging are continually reinforced. Our conversations are built upon a nonverbal scaffolding of synchrony and turn-taking; we agree in rhythm and mode. We come together with our closest associates to do things that are jointly perceived to be important and valuable.

As members of the human species, we all enter the world prepared for mutuality and belonging. Infants require love, attention, and validation, or else their hearts atrophy. Their brains are ready (that is, they feel the need and motivation) to respond to signals of affiliation and love and to return them. If things go according to plan—if there are effective, reliable responders to these needs—a youngster is adequately set on the human pathway as it evolved to be in ancestral environments. If there are no such responders, he or she will be diminished, deficient, less well adapted, and less adept than human ancestry prepared the child to be.[4]

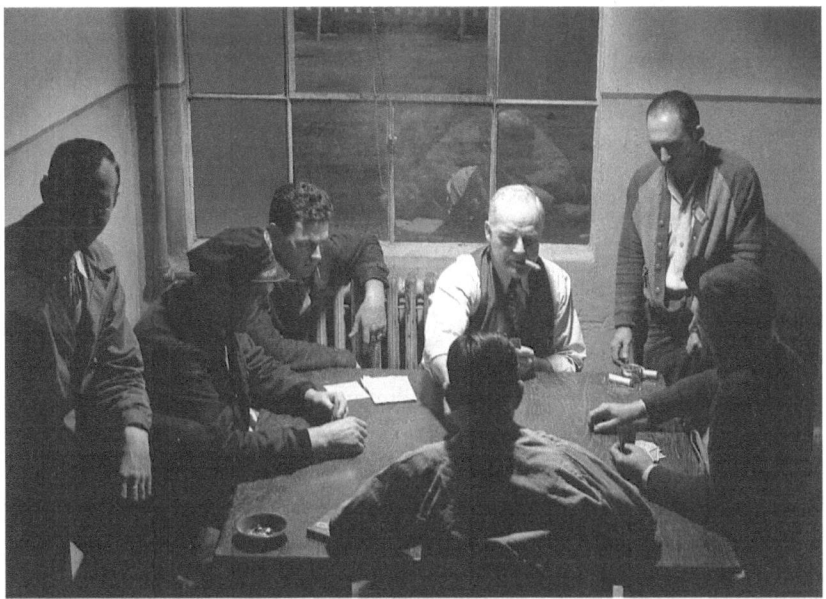

Truck drivers at a rest stop relax together and play pinochle. Photograph: Sol Libsohn (Photographic Archives, Ekstrom Library, University of Louisville).

If it is in our human nature to require mutuality and belonging, it is also in human nature to respond to other circumstances of life based on whether or not these needs were satisfied or denied. Persons deprived of mutuality or belonging, whose inborn tendencies toward affiliation and sympathy have not been answered and activated, easily become selfish, insecure, unable to make or sustain close relationships, perhaps violent and self-destructive, even sociopathic;[5] they lack a sense of identity and self-esteem and are defective in the "social emotions" (Mealey 1995) of love, shame, guilt, remorse, and sympathy with others. Conversely, persons whose mutuality and belonging needs *are* met will be more easily generous, sociable, sympathetic, and secure. It sounds simplistic but it makes sense, since we evolved to be one way and not the other.

It is well to remember, however, that these kindly traits fostered by mutuality and belonging are expressed most strongly within the group with whom one maintains those ties and rituals, those familiar modes and rhythms. The ties that bind easily become the nets of nepotism, and they can serve as stiff barriers to the acceptance of others. That also is the way humans evolved to be.

If belonging makes possible the security of group unity and identity, it also predisposes us to think of other groups, not our own, as wrong or worse than wrong—as deserving of ridicule, avoidance, or even eradication. In many small-scale societies, the group calls itself by its word for "human" or "people" and seldom uses the same word to refer to people of other groups.

Thus racism, too, grows from the need to belong, for belonging means that others belong elsewhere. Particularly when resources are scarce or unpredictable, others can be blamed or viewed as competitors. In prejudice and racism we demonize and cast aspersions on others, thereby bolstering our sense of belonging to a superior group, whether the unity is that of a common race, religion, class, political party, or other ideological group.

It seems clear that in hunter-gatherer societies there must have been strong selective pressures for young males to have the propensity to bond and work harmoniously and loyally in groups that performed dangerous, skilled, and exciting physical activities together—such as hunting large game, with its attendant risks and cooperative skills of locating, tracking, killing, and bringing it home. In other environments, this predisposition can take other forms such as raiding nearby villages for women and other booty, participating in team sports (or, in an age of specialization, watching others participate and sympathetically—usually according to "hometown"—identifying with them), enlisting in the armed forces and fighting in wars, and joining militias, SWAT teams, the Guardian Angels, or neighborhood gangs.[6]

Men go to war for their country (or they used to) to defend their flag, their loved ones, their freedom. But in the terrifying tumult and confusion of actual battle, these abstractions may not sustain them. Commanders instill loyalty within the group so that men will fight and even die *for their buddies*, as parents will die for their children. The camaraderie of battle may seem the farthest thing imaginable from a mother and baby at play, but it draws on the capability for sympathetic mutuality and the loss of self or emotional joining-of-selves that was so essential in ancestral mothers and infants and in small interdependent bands.[7] Military drill itself accomplishes, through shared rhythmic movement, "muscular bonding" (McNeill 1995).

The unspeakable horrors perpetrated in civil and tribal wars are testament to the power of the emotional bond of belonging. The more the other group hurts you, the more united your group becomes in order to maintain—by vengeance—its honor, which comprises land, goods, people, and other resources. Leaders and warriors all over the world employ bards (or lackeys) who regularly recount and embroider past glories in order to inspire future exploits and victories.

Few insults incite anger and violence more than the loss to another of something loved, or the threat of such loss. Aggression, violence, and greed rush in when one's comrades, way of life, or reputation and identity (as self or group) are threatened or perceived as being under threat. Crimes of passion are crimes to avenge or punish disrupted belonging or intolerable loss.

Group loyalties can shift when circumstances require. In Somalia, every person is born into a clan, a descent group originating from a single male ancestor. Such clans are at the heart of Somali culture, so that pledging allegiance to, honoring, and defending individual clans are what lives are about. To separate from one's clan is to separate from one's history and identity. Since independence from Britain and Italy in 1960, power struggles among clans and subclans have sundered the country, creating thousands of refugees.

Yet in their new countries, Somalis' clan differences tend to dissolve. "We can't afford to be divided here," said one refugee who now lives in Seattle. "We need each other—all tribes, all clans. We have forgotten our differences, our problems. There's no talk of clans. We meet together for prayer, for weddings. . . . We eat together and help each other; we talk and laugh, and we forget what is going on in Somalia" (Tizon 1995).

LEGACIES OF BELONGING

Mutuality is a kind of taproot formed in the elemental loam of the mother-infant relationship. From it arise shoots that can grow into the radiant and sublime blossoms of friendship, love, and affiliation and also proliferate into hateful clumps of violence and slaughter.

Evolutionary psychologists emphasize the importance of self-interest in human evolution. They say that humans are, at bottom, egoists who routinely use manipulative deceit to get their way with others. There are valid arguments that underlie this position, and viewing "nature" films makes us graphically aware of the imperative in nature to eat or be eaten and of the relentless winnowing of billions of seeds, larvae, insects, fish, birds, and other animals, all of which are "competing" to live and to reproduce.

Ruthless competition is all too evident in human social life as well—globally, locally, even in families where husbands and wives or siblings try to gain advantages over the others for their own gain. Cheaters in business, at school, on the job, in diplomacy? "That's human nature," we say.

Even the mother–infant interaction can be interpreted as primarily concerned with the individual's genetic advantage. The baby has evolved manipulative ruses of looking cute and gaining attention in order to serve its survival interests; the mother has evolved loving responses that fool her into willingly forgoing her personal comfort in order to serve her larger genetic interests of reproductive success.

I would like to point out, however, that to consider "unreal" or "deceitful" the messages of communion that the two exchange and the overflowing emotions they feel is rather like saying that the furnishings in our houses *really* consist only of empty spaces between molecules. These ways of putting matters may be justified at the level of abstract theory, but for all practical purposes the existence of mutuality and belonging and the feelings that undergird them are as real and sustaining as the comfortable beds and armchairs that reliably embrace us. Amid and despite the challenging clashes of egos in the outside world and even at home, the mother–infant duet is the archetypal origin of authentic affiliative, sympathetic, and moral capacities that make (and have made) human culture—and human existence—possible. Despite their "selfish" origins, continuing to cultivate and expand these capacities has been and even today is our only hope for continued survival. If we do not strive to care for and please others as well as ourselves, we are as emotionally deformed and incapable of survival as an unlovable baby or an unresponsive mother would have been in ancestral times.

Although humans are certainly born with the potential to be xenophobic and racist, we are not thereby destined to be unregenerately selfish or even fundamentally self-centered. The challenge to us in our high-tech, fast-changing environments, so different from those in which we were evolved to thrive, is to find ways to enlarge our in-groups, as well as to be aware that people whose emotional needs for mutuality and belonging are inadequately met or whose material and social needs are threatened will act in *more* selfish, "tribal," inhumane ways. In chapter 6, contributions of the arts to this challenge are discussed at some length.

The propensity for individuals to gather together in communality and oneness is part of human nature, whether for reasons and ends that seem good or bad. We are not fated by our biological heritage to be either paragons or villains. Most of us in most societies are not asked to develop either our best or our worst, and even fewer are urged from within to the extremes of being either saints or monsters. But none of us escapes being influenced—blessed and cursed—by these earliest emotional predispositions for mutuality and its natural extension, belonging. Our susceptibility to their emotional effects ensures that we will be receptive to the values and ways of our intimates.

3

Finding and Making Meaning

TO DISCUSS "MEANING" in an age hipped on hype and stupefied by oversimplification is not a welcome prospect for either reader or writer. The word is almost meaning*less*—vague and even faintly embarrassing. "The politics of meaning," a slogan of the early Clinton White House, was perhaps intended sincerely (itself an embarrassing word), but, like most things people yearn for, was indistinguishable from all the other transiently marketable catchphrases of a commercial society and therefore easily trivialized, ridiculed, and discarded.

While philosophers and makers of dictionaries define "meaning" and "meaningful" disinterestedly, most people use these words informally to express personal feelings about the seriousness or importance something holds for them. "The movie had layers of meaning" suggests there was more than an obvious interpretation to the story: it provided something of significance to think about. "Our conversation was really meaningful" indicates that for the speaker it had "value"—a deeply felt conviction of significance, even truth. But because in a heterogeneous society one person's "meaning" is often another's platitude or illusion, the terms have additionally lost precision and hence general usefulness.

In the infancy of the individual, as in the infancy of the species, "meaning" is equivalent to biological importance—that is, importance to survival. The baby cannot articulate or even conceive that smiles, undulating vocalizations, or mother's nipples are "meaningful" (significant or valuable), but it responds positively to them because they indicate the sorts of features that will give it life. An infant does not create meaning so much as recognize what is meaningful—security, warmth, physical and emotional nourishment.

Similarly, in the infancy of the human species, as in the lives of other animals, what was meaningful was what "felt right"—a full stomach, a safe environment, nearness of familiar others, or ways to acquire these. Again, these meanings were not created so much as biologically endowed—naturally recognized and sought.

As human infants grow, they want—like other young animals—to explore and "make sense" of their surroundings. Instincts guide them to use their mouths, hands, limbs, voices. But for humans, instincts are not enough. Or rather, instincts guide young humans to look to their elders in their search for what is meaningful.

Over the millennia of human evolution, the mind increasingly became a "making-sense organ": interrelated powers of memory, foresight, and imagination gradually developed and allowed humans to stabilize and confine the stream of life by making connections between past, present, and future, or among experiences or observations. Rather than taking the world on its own terms of significance and value (the basic survival needs, sought and recognized by instinct), people came more and more to systematize or order it and act upon it. Eventually, this powerful and deep-rooted desire to make sense of the world became part of what it meant to be human—to *impose* sense or order and thereby give the world additional (what we now call "cultural") meaning.

What cultures systematize and value derives from the basic biological requirements for survival and well-being—such essentials as finding, preparing, and assuring the continuance of food; rearing children; and maintaining social relationships, social practices, health, safety, prosperity, and competence. Biological meaning—significance or value—implies that we have emotional investment in these fundamental things: that is, we have evolved to care about them. Cultures have in turn evolved to assure that we care by appropriately emphasizing what we need to care about most. Cultural knowledge and practices direct our attention to particular biologically significant things and help us know what to think and do about them.

There are limits to cultural invention, of course. It is conceivable that a culture might introduce practices that are counterproductive—say, standing on one's head before taking a mouthful of food, or elaborately carving every log for the fire, even if eating and staying warm are highly important and worth caring about. Expending effort on really trivial matters, too, such as applying butterfly wings to the soles of one's feet, would fail to contribute to the evolutionary success of individuals or cultures that advocated it. Thus the biological significance of any cultural practice tends to keep it viable, even though many cultural practices may seem fantastic and strange (just as the peculiar structural features and instinctive behaviors of many evolved creatures seem bizarre until we understand how they contribute to overall successful survival). Additionally, many cultural practices (for example, whether water is drunk during or after meals) have little if any vital advantage or disadvantage; they merely "ride along" with a general biological requirement—in this case, assuring in one way or another that water is imbibed.

In chapters 1 and 2 we saw that as children move from mother-infant mutuality to belonging to a group of others, they are innately or automatically predisposed to acquire the worldview and ways (that is, the cultural meanings, significances, and values) of this group. What to do and how to live are not instinctive. These lessons must be learned, but the predispositions of mutuality and belonging, and the rhythms and modes that instill them—the motives for affiliation and relationship, the emotional bonds, the states of interest and pleasure, the desire and ability to match, mirror, and imitate, the intention to please—are also the predispositions for acquiring the cultural meanings of those among whom we grow up and who share our lives.

In this chapter we look at evolved human needs for finding and making "meaning"—needs for system and story—which are addressed and satisfied by cultures in myriad marvelous and singular ways. Chapter 5 considers more specifically how these systems and stories are manifested, instilled, and reinforced by rhythmic-modal elaborations in ceremonial ritual arts.

SYSTEM AND STORY

Each vanished aboriginal society is like an extinct animal species whose unique body plan (with, say, its striped neck ruff or broadly curved crimson claws), voice (with its ponderous bass tones or liquid trill), and distinctive habits (such as brachiating in the branches of mahogany trees, dipping chinaberries in dew before feeding them to mates, laying three perfectly round pale pink eggs) will remain forever unknown and even unimaginable.

Anthropologists today routinely pillory their predecessors for misrepresenting the now-assimilated or eradicated cultural groups they lived with and described fifty or seventy-five years ago. Yet to read these early ethnographic accounts, even with their inevitable assumptions, biases, and misinterpretations, is to become aware of how intricately and aesthetically the different parts of a people's worldview and ways can fit together. It is almost as if someone all at once—not a group of nonliterate people over centuries—made it all up to be a beautiful, unexpected yet inevitable whole, a work of art like a Shakespeare drama or a Vermeer painting, everything in its place and bearing upon every other thing. Laura Thompson, writing in 1945, referred to the "logico-aesthetic integration" of the Hopi Way, with its harmonization of the personal, social, and cosmic in an annual cycle of ceremonies.

To read about the rich and profuse traditions of these lost and dwindling societies is also to become aware of how fragmented and tawdry our modern replacements are—how flawed, *un*aesthetic, and unintegrated. While some modern philosophical, scientific, and mathematical systems may have beauty, inevitability, and unity, they do not permeate everyone's consciousness and are not what anyone, not even their adherents, *live by*.

Human minds were adapted to be born, grow up, live, and die within these vanished and vanishing, communally shared, and significant wholes. Our displacement from such ways of life is no doubt why they continue to intrigue and tantalize modern imaginations like some lost Golden Age or Garden of Eden.[1]

To illustrate one society's "logico-aesthetic integration," I have chosen the Yekuana, Carib-speaking subsistence horticulturalists and huntergatherers in Venezuela and the upper Orinoco of Brazil. Here, and again in subsequent chapters, I try to convey something of their worldview and lives. As I am summarizing at second hand a detailed and sensitively interpreted and written book of nearly three hundred pages (Guss 1989), the limitations of my account are obvious. Still, I believe that it effectively introduces my more general remarks about the human need for system and story.

System and Story in the South American Rain Forest

At the time David M. Guss and his wife lived with the Yekuana—in 1976–78 and again in 1982–84—they were a small indigenous population, just over three thousand people. In their dense rain-forest habitat, Yekuana men hunted small game, using poison-dipped darts. Their main sustenance, however, was *tapa* (or cassava, also called manioc), a food plant

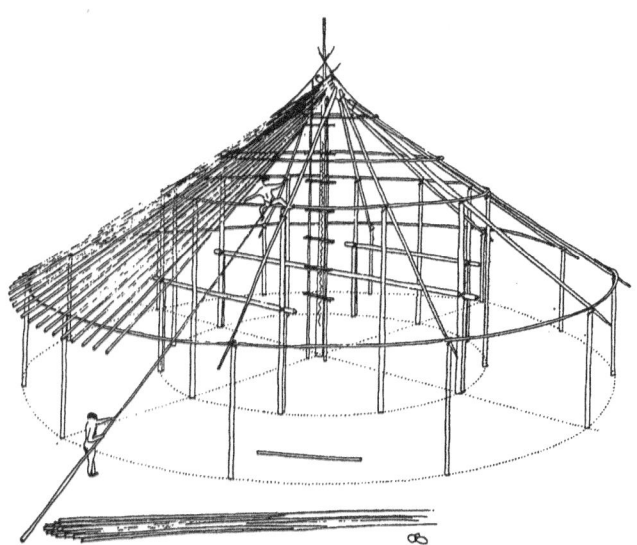

A Yekuana communal house, in which an entire Yekuana village lives.
Courtesy Antropológica.

grown and prepared by women. Highly toxic in their natural state, *tapa* tubers had to be painstakingly treated to remove their oxalic acid before they were cooked and eaten. In addition to meat and manioc, both sexes obtained fish by using a poisonous plant preparation called *barbasco* that temporarily removes oxygen from the small bodies of water in which the fishes live.

Yekuana believe (or at least did at the time of the Gusses' fieldwork) that every material object—animal, vegetable, or mineral—has an invisible double, a spirit being, that is both sacred and eternal. Such spirits live in a "parallel world," although they may sometimes appear to humans disguised as fish or game. Although spirit beings are potentially uncontrollable and disruptive, the art of dealing with them can be learned.

The Yekuana's metaphysical dualism, and its associated notion that danger can be humanly controlled, seems to arise logically from the inherent toxicity of their major food source, *tapa*, which requires cultural transformation in order to become safe and usable. The further use of poisons for obtaining other food such as game and fish reinforces an awareness of dangerous otherness. But as principles, dualism and danger have been generalized to inform the Yekuana view of the world; they are manifested in all their artifacts, activities, concepts, and stories.

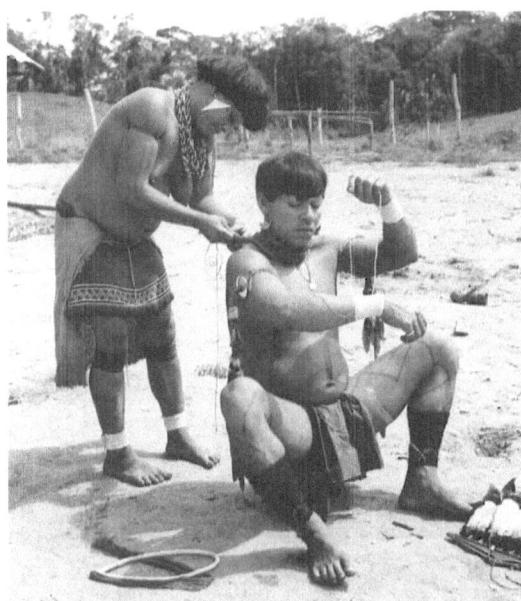

Preparing for a festival, a Yekuana man puts on wrist bands while his wife adjusts his necklace. Note the tight upper arm and leg bands (the latter made of human hair). Photograph: Barbara Brändli.

For example, the communal house (in which resides the entire village of several extended families, some forty to a hundred people) is formed of two concentric circles. The outer one, considered to be profane and ephemeral, is divided into living compartments for ordinary life, and the inner one, considered to be sacred and eternal, is used by males for craftwork, for discussing dreams and other important matters, and for shamanic curing. Conceived of as a self-contained universe whose external walls are a barrier to foreign spirits and persons, the communal house is constructed as a replica of the way Yekuana conceive of the cosmos.

Each individual adult person is also a microcosm of the dualistic universe, with demarcated areas of the body echoing the inner and outer zones of the cosmos-house. On the limbs—at the biceps of the arms and just below the knees—bands and strands of beads or human hair are wrapped so tightly that they leave marks when removed. Around the neck are various necklaces, and a loincloth is tied just below the stomach. These bands, beads, and other encirclements mark off the trunk of the body as an inner or sacred zone, differentiated from the outer limbs and head. A second, outer circle is demarcated by rings of white beads wrapped around the wrists and ankles. (There are other analogies between the body and the house that I do not have space to describe. For example, the cut of the hair and the thatch of the house roof each have perfectly finished edges.)

Gardens, too, have a central and an external area: the outer region is used for food production, and the inner, sacred one, for traditional female rituals, including the practice of herbal magic.

Guss describes *Watunna*, the Yekuana creation epic, as being "like an invisible sleeve holding the whole culture in place." One might expect that it would be told to the group as a narrative in special sessions, but that is not so. Instead, it is "everywhere," without a beginning or an end. One can approach or enter it at any point, since every activity, whether ritual or material, is determined by the pervasive and underlying configuration of symbols of duality and the related necessity in every aspect of Yekuana life for cultural transformation of wildness and dangerousness. All actions communicate the same essential messages and meanings: "To tell a story, therefore, was to weave a basket, just as it was to make a canoe, to prepare barbasco, to build a house, to clear a garden, to give birth, to die" (Guss 1989, 4).

The Gusses found that the Yekuana had no neatly framed storytelling events; rather, the whole "story" was constantly manifested in every activity. In a pluralistic or fragmented, secular society like our own, perhaps the nearest we might come to such an encompassing master life narrative is in times of war or crises such as the Great Depression, or in a rare individual's sense of life mission to which everything else is subordinated and through the lens of which everything else is viewed.

Ritual (which is, of course, rhythmic and multimodal, making use of sight, sound, and movement—chanting, singing, acting, and applying special substances) permeates every Yekuana activity, no matter how mundane or material it might appear. The Gusses came to understand that for Yekuana the distinction between sacred and profane was not a distinction between religious ceremonial practices and secular activities but between a ritually safe state and an uncontrolled, toxic one. The challenge for the Yekuana was, in all acts of life, to transform the contaminated and impure into the culturally infused and human. This—no more and no less—was the meaning of life. Examples of these transformations are given elsewhere in this and succeeding chapters.

Human Needs for System and Story

Nonhuman animals are born generally knowing what to do: they build nests, seek food, find mates, and bear and nourish young, largely without being taught. Humans, by contrast, have to learn the rules and schemes that make their world orderly—comprehensible and manageable. We are not born knowing such survival skills as how to make a shelter, find and prepare food, or care for infants. We must learn social skills, how to act and what to think, so that we will be regarded positively by those with whom we live, those we love. Compared with humans, other animals have a much more straightforward path to maturity. Yet the rhythms and modes of human infancy and childhood predispose us to acquire systematic and storied accounts of the world into which we are born.

Although ways and worldviews differ from one group to another, all cultures, like the Yekuana, have, or have had, frameworks or rules for living, along with stories about themselves and why things are as they are. The mythical, social, and practical orders are inextricably interwoven. Adherents of an individual culture's systems and stories consider them to be foreordained, unequivocally right and meaningful, logical and aesthetic. The Yekuana call themselves So'to, meaning "human" or "person," as distinguished from any other species, human or nonhuman. This word refers to their unique heritage of common culture and language, what was called in chapter 2 "identity." Guss tells us that the Yekuana, like other small-scale cultural groups, have utter confidence in the propriety of their way of life as opposed to any other.

No matter how isolated or technologically impoverished, every human culture has, like the Yekuana, an account of the cosmos, its creation and maintenance, and the origin of themselves and other beings. The cosmic order includes the natural order—life and nonlife, male and female, human and animal—along with the divine and the mundane. There are notions of an "other world," different in some way from this one, concepts of souls and spirits, things unseen as well as seen, and an eschatology of what happens at and after death.

From a modern standpoint, the cosmologies and supernatural beliefs of traditional peoples are "myths," meaning fabrications. Yet for their adherents, they satisfy the need to explain, within an accepted order and system, why and how things are as they are. Our more abstract metaphysical systems—whether theological, philosophical, or scientific—are similarly ways of ordering and explaining the world, of understanding ultimate reality.

Along with metaphysical systems come rules that regulate social, familial, and sexual relations. Every society recognizes duties and benefits that accompany different ages and stages of life, with acknowledged procedures—rites of passage—for entering or leaving these stages or roles: ceremonies for weaning, first menstruation, circumcision, marriage, graduation, or inauguration, to name a few. On the occasion of a Yekuana girl's first menstruation, a "new person" ceremony rehumanizes her from her toxic and wild state. In a practice reminiscent of clearing and creating a new garden, all the hair on her head is shorn and she is isolated for three months. Then, to the accompaniment of special chants, she is transformed—painted with special substances, given protective arm and leg bands, and restored to the community.

In such ways are social roles confirmed and their requisite behavior and privileges regulated—often in hierarchical structures with dominants and subordinates and with clear ideas of boundaries. People learn what to expect, depending on whether they are boys or girls, men or women, husbands or wives, parents, mother's brother or father's brother, elders, and so forth.

Inherent to small-scale communal societies are the encircling pools of identity described in chapter 2. A person's identity emerges at or soon after birth, is connected to the identities of others, and remains hardly conceivable apart from the group. Identities of sex, age, family, or moiety usually entail socially endorsed conventions of appropriate and acceptable behavior. Because there is little or no choice of identity, there is no requirement, as in modern societies, to choose or construct it, nor is it expected that one will almost automatically rebel against social convention as part of a life stage called "adolescence." Individual wishes are generally subsumed within the authority of the group. No one requires an explanation of the necessity for a "new person" or a weaning or naming ceremony; no one questions the custom of thanking a game animal after it has been killed or wonders why someone from a particular family is a leader.

Far from being born free or created equal, humans evolved to require the restraints of custom and authority which, within a small-scale, self-contained society, provided psychological security and satisfaction—a familiar and desired wrapping. These restraints may be felt as oppressive after exposure to different cultures with alternative ways, although Yekuana even yet consider the ways of European settlers to be inferior to theirs.

All human groups develop systems of social organization that include such things as principles for governing, settling disputes, dealing with deviants, dividing labor, and apportioning inheritance; residence rules and property rights; and methods for population control. Other regulations concern who mates with whom (for example, incest prohibitions and customs of polygyny and polyandry), kinship terms, practices of naming, and other ways to indicate individual and group identity. There are rules of etiquette—sometimes extremely complex—including norms of personal modesty, propriety, and self-discipline. While to an outsider such restraints and regulations may appear arbitrary and even irrational, they logically complement and aesthetically echo other of a group's customs. Yekuana values of personal restraint, obedience, self-control, and avoidance of contaminants reinforce their fundamental notion of duality and their conceptualization of each village as a separate world—while also facilitating social harmony. Suffused with notions of sacred origin or sanction, such concepts and values provide a necessary stable structure to human relationships.

Other systems within human social groups provide taxonomic classifications of plants, animals, and other important parts of the environment—types of snow, behavior of livestock and game, or ocean waves and currents. There are food taboos of varying duration and restrictiveness, and other "superstitions." In Sri Lankan villages, children learn not to whistle after dark and not to overtly praise another's prized possessions in case they inadvertently tempt misfortune; in the United States, we whistle a happy tune so we won't seem afraid, and we compliment others on their beautiful garden, new car, or new baby.

Along with rules and schemata, humans utilize lore, traditional knowledge of how to do what is necessary and appropriate to solve life's problems and thereby manage or affect the world—that is, to do things necessary for subsistence and well-being. In all small-scale societies there are right ways to make and preserve fire, fashion serviceable implements, cure and heal, attract game, bear a healthy child, avert danger, minimize conflict, propitiate supernatural beings, interpret dreams, predict the future, and have right relationship with the forces of nature. And as there are right ways, there are right times to do things—plant and reap, celebrate and mourn, fast and feast. Learning these things gives people a sense of competence or aptitude for their lives. Yekuana women learn to grow *tapa* and to prepare it for their families to eat safely. Yekuana men learn to hunt. Additionally, and of equal importance, over a lifetime they learn how to weave baskets of increasing complexity in pattern and meaning.

Knowledge and belief systems, whether aboriginal or modern, have grown out of inherent mental aptitudes that made it possible for ancestral humans accurately to perceive, peruse, and utilize their environment. We evolved to think in terms of resemblance or correspondence, continuity, contiguity, coherence, duality, and cause and effect. Over millennia, these ways of mentally acting upon the world have proved to work. To adapt a crisp epitome from Joseph Carroll (1995, 78): organisms that were consistently mistaken about their environment and how to think about and act upon it did not survive to perpetuate their genetically constrained disposition to error.

As humans are natural system-builders, they are also natural storytellers. To some degree we tell stories and hear those of others as part of everyday interaction—"The Visit with Susie's Teacher," "Car Trouble on the Way to Work," "The Dreaded Job Interview," "The Trip to Hawaii." Such stories may well be informative, but they are more than that. Using devices such as vivid detail or suspense that will engage the hearer, they call for and receive empathy and interaction.

We have evolved to respond to archetypal images and narrative structures that touch upon fundamental existential themes and interests: being and nonbeing, birth and death, the life course from infancy to old age, males and females, mothers and fathers, sons and daughters, wise elders, helpless children, heroes and villains, wild animals, and bodies and bodily functions such as eating, drinking, urinating, defecating, and copulating.

From fundamental human struggles and outcomes—failing or succeeding (escaping harm, overcoming, losing or gaining), giving, loving, being demeaned, admired, or rejected (Lazarus 1994, 307)—arise such common emotions as joy, grief, desire, anger, frustration, and anxiety; experiences of plenty and want, love and loss; and expressions of violence, duty, obligation, shame, and redemption. While such features are the stuff of popular entertainment and everyday conversation, they are also the substrate of age-old myths, epics, and scriptures.

Stories move people in ways unlike other uses of language. They provide a certain kind of knowledge: a person has done this or that, and this is what came of it (Burkert 1996, 56). Children at two and a half years of age recognize that to tell a story is different from other uses of language (Olson 1997).

Children notoriously like to hear the same story over and over again. So do adults, when the story is a "good" one. We wait expectantly for the punch line or the denouement, even when we already know it—and then laugh or feel the appropriate emotions of sadness, disbelief, outrage, amazement.

A good tale is easy to remember, even if heard only once. We do not remember or reproduce it as a sequence of sounds or words (like a melody or an address) but rather as a sequence of events and actions that, even with different words, *makes sense*. A story is, as Walter Burkert (1996, 58) described it, a structure of sense.

A Russian folklorist, Vladimir Propp (1968), identified thirty-one constant or recurring structural or narrative elements of plots in folktales. Although not every element occurs in any one story, and some elements may be in part repeated, every tale contains some combination of these elements. Burkert (1996, 58) has described Propp's scheme in an abbreviated version:

> The tale starts with some damage, lack, or desire (8); the hero is told to go somewhere (9) and agrees to do so (10); he leaves home (11); he meets some being that puts him to a test (12); reacting to it (13), he receives some gift or magical aid (14); he gets to the place required (15) and meets an adversary with whom he has to interact (16); he is harmed in some way (17) but is victorious in the end (18); thus the initial damage or lack is put right (19). The hero begins his homeward journey (20); he is pursued (21) but saved (22); he comes back without being recognized (23); there is a wicked imposter (24), a test (25), and final success (26); the hero is recognized (27); the imposter is punished (28); the hero marries and becomes king (31).

Stories that use these structural or thematic motifs are diverse and inexhausible: Burkert gives examples from Greek, Sumerian, and other early mythology. While other scholars have, like Propp, described universal themes and principles of narrative construction in world literature, they usually assign them to psychological predispositions without recognizing their evolutionary *adaptive* significance.[2]

Burkert, in contrast, points out that Propp's general scheme, which can be called "The Quest," follows the biological program of action for finding food or more generally summarizes the primary pragmatic function of solving a problem. (He also shows that some quest tales appear to have shamanic origins, and others describe the progressions familiar from ritual sequences where there is separation, ordeal, and reintegration.)

Joseph Carroll (1995, 1999) and Robert Storey (1996) have also recently treated literary motifs and themes as they reflect evolved psychological propensities that have biological salience. Carroll's application of evolutionary theory to literature shows how and why its subject matter is

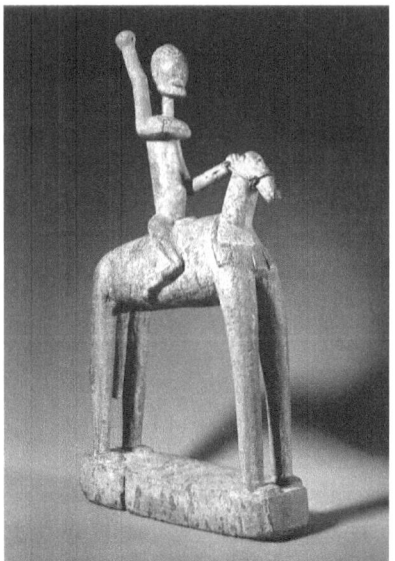 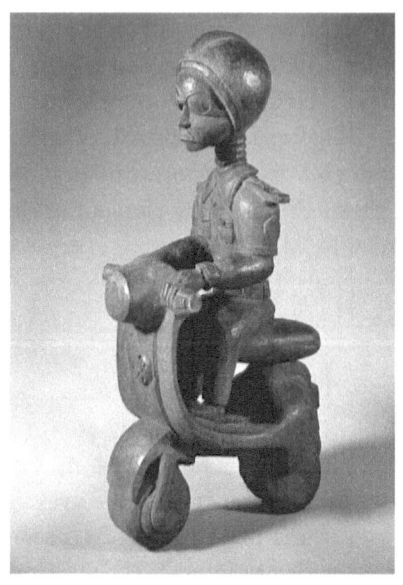

Dogon horse and rider. Courtesy of   *Yoruba on a Vespa. Courtesy of Elaine*
Helen Kuhn.   *and Bram Goldsmith.*

and always has been the subjective quality of human experience, since "life is the central source of imaginative power." By not taking into account the many specific features of human nature that have evolved and that enter into the production of literary works, orthodox academic analyses of literature overlook valuable corroborating support for their own schemes, which frequently are tacitly based on putatively universal psychological, linguistic, or social predispositions.

Evolutionary perspectives such as Burkert's, Carroll's, and Storey's do not challenge so much as embrace and incorporate earlier schemes that view the elements of stories as psychoanalytic complexes or mythographic archetypes. Herbert Cole (1989) has identified five major images in the visual arts of Africa, which are of course also the subject of story and song: the male-female couple (two as one), the woman and child (maternity and abundance), the forceful male (hunters, warriors, and heroes), the mounted leader (riders of power), and the stranger (ambiguous aliens). The brief synopses of television shows in each week's *TV Guide* suggest that these themes—sometimes adjusted for such novel permutations as surrogate mothers, custody battles, and invasions from other galaxies— are wider than the traditional arts of Africa. Indeed, for good biological reasons, such themes are universal.

Literature, whether from the ancient oral traditions of people without writing or from the latest bestseller, has always dealt with the vital interests and concerns of humans—such prosaic but elemental and inexhaustibly myriad matters as staying alive and well, being accepted and thought well of by associates, developing normally both physically and socially, learning the ways of one's fellows, engaging in activity that is materially, emotionally, and socially rewarding, finding a mate and mating, successfully producing and caring for offspring, helping one's offspring thrive, overcoming threats, and otherwise affecting the outcomes of things one cares about. Whether they appear in Homer or Lady Murasaki, Dostoyevski or Danielle Steele, grand opera or soap opera, news features or television commercials, we are attracted by these and other humanly relevant themes that derive from evolved needs and interests. They invariably capture our fascinated attention.

Such crystallizations of stories have become cultural property, passed on as truth and accepted without question because they "worked." In Belau, in the western Caroline Islands, for example, one frequently told story emphasizes such important necessities of living with others as reciprocity and loyalty, caring for the aged, and restraining personal greed. Hearers are reminded that successful social life is not to be taken for granted but is, rather, a fragile entity that has to be defended against dispositions and behaviors that can undermine it (Thomas 1995, 175).

Although far from simplistic, traditional knowledge and belief is humanly conceivable, with a place and reason for everything. Graspable, reasonable "laws" explain in a contained, self-sufficient way why and how things happen as they do; compelling narratives suffuse these explanations with sacred meaning. As mind is consonant with world, myth as system and story is consonant with mind.

LEGACIES OF THE NEED TO FIND AND MAKE MEANING

In ancestral societies, uncertainty and misfortune were usually addressed by ceremonies, charms, and imprecations composed largely of viscerally felt and emotionally satisfying rhythmic-modal elaborations (see chapter 5). A group's lore included these tried-and-true methods for coping with mysterious forces, both natural and supernatural, and, if they failed, explanations of what went wrong.

In the modern world, science (with its stern-countenanced partners, rational thinking, and technology) has become our institutionalized method for satisfying needs for order and system and for affecting the world. The systems and stories that provide meaning to modern people are less likely to be flavored with emotion-rich rhythms and modes than to be permeated with by-products of the scientific worldview. And just as we are often unsuspecting of the chemicals added to our food, we may be unaware of the traces and residues of science in our thinking or beliefs.

This may or may not be welcome news, since attitudes toward science as a human achievement and method of understanding have become polarized today as never before. At one extreme are those who believe there is a technological remedy for everything. At the other are those who wholly distrust science, finding its mechanistic and reductionist approach to the world not merely distasteful but inadequate and even dangerous.

Understanding the human need for system and story helps to explain, first, why science and technology have been so attractive to our species, and second, why they are not enough. The human need for order is quickly seduced and gratified by the discoveries of science—its laws, tables, taxonomies, axioms, theories, principles, and formulas that classify and systematize the seen and the unseen world. Today we can appreciate as never before the geological and archaeological past, the mysteries and wonders of living things (even long-vanished beings such as dinosaurs), the extent of the universe, the structure of matter, the intricate interdependence of the parts of our bodies and of whole environmental ecosystems.

Without science we would know none of these things. Yet as humans evolved, their need for meaning was (and still can be) satisfied with nonscientific explanations, with the complex logico-aesthetic integrations—cosmological, theological, social, and psychological—that have been devised by every human culture. Intricate, allusive, and compelling, they explain the world and satisfy the need for meaning—even without being completely understood. Sacred revelations may be mimicked without comprehension, as the recitation of scriptures by young boys in Hebrew, Sanskrit, and Arabic attests. Eventual scriptural understanding consists in continuing restatement or reinterpretation, not in verification or cumulative alteration and even replacement as with historical and scientific laws, facts, and theories.

In chapter 2, I briefly described four examples in which the rhythms and modes of infancy were adapted to make systems and stories compelling, and I devote chapter 5 largely to this human penchant for elaborating meaning. As surely as human minds are predisposed to categorize or make narratives, they are inherently receptive to certain structural and performative elements—concrete imagery, striking musical and poetic devices—that by their very nature compel emotional response.

Many of us today remain powerfully affected by dramatic, age-old traditional stories that give emotional significance to our lives. Like stories from every other society, these have been handed down from ancestors—in our Judeo-Christian case, from the Neolithic desert pastoralists and farmers of what is now the Near and Middle East. Yet these revealed scriptural stories sometimes mingle uneasily with an ideal of scientific objectivity and analysis that originated in the Classical world and now irreversibly coexists alongside our ancestral revelations.

Holding mutually contradictory beliefs is called "cognitive dissonance." But I think that with regard to the mental juxtaposition of myths and scientific theories it is not so much dissonance as a matter of using two different mental perspectives, much the way we look at an optical illusion and see first a duck and then a rabbit. We don't ask which picture is the "real" one. Both are. We can approach this duck-rabbit or myth-science conundrum by examining and better understanding the effects of recent cultural developments and living conditions upon minds that evolved over millennia to comprehend and act in ancestral environments and ways of life.

Just as the ability to use spoken language made it possible for our ancestors to think in ways quite unavailable to nonverbal species, one might say that the invention of writing made possible a kind and degree of detached, analytic thinking that is literally unthinkable to preliterate humans. Such mental operations, which led to the invention of modern science, of course are inherent in the evolved architecture of the human brain: today's scientists and analytic philosophers were themselves once preliterate children.

However, when a symbolic system (such as language) can be stored externally—on a clay tablet, papyrus, or parchment sheet, between the covers of a book, or in a computer file—new methods of organization and analysis can be employed that in their turn affect the very way the brain thinks. This is not to say that all readers or even all scientists invariably think analytically, or that scientific thinking has intrinsic superiority. It is to say, however, that the Neolithic agricultural revolution, with its eventual invention of writing (and the consequent practice of reading), enabled previously uncalled-for operations and circuits in our Paleolithic-adapted brains and set our ancestors on an unwitting path leading to a quantum leap in human thinking (see also Donald 1991, 18–19; Mithen 1996).

Literacy and Meaning

It is difficult for people who have learned to read and write fluently to imagine or remember being nonliterate. The magic wand of literacy does more than give access to stories and ideas from many sources, enriching as this may be. Rather, reading, *and only reading*, makes possible habits of mind that were unnecessary and irrelevant in Paleolithic lives, simply because no one had ever used his or her mind in such ways. We go to school—a difficult task for many people—in order to acquire new methods and strategies for treating things in the world and new expectations about their nature. Preliterate people, for example, do not tend to consider the world in terms of "information" or "data."

In a stimulating study, Merlin Donald (1991, 273–74) presents a partial list of products of analytic thought that are generally absent (or rudimentary) in what he calls "mythic" cultures: formal arguments, systematic taxonomies, deduction, verification, differentiation, quantification, idealization, and formal methods of measurement. A formal *theory* is a system of thought and argument that predicts and explains, says Donald; unlike preliterate systems, it is "verifiable" (and falsifiable) in ways very different from supernatural proofs of significance.

With their tables, charts, and graphs, readers and writers increasingly rely on the attainment of ever-refined conditions of exactness, efficiency, predictability, rational inquiry, repeatability, definition, and standardization, leading to the presumption that humans are able to impose systematic organization in almost every domain.

Unless one can *record* and *store* information (at first on a two-dimensional surface but today electromagnetically in many media) and later *retrieve* it, it is difficult to demand, say, precision of measurement (see also Crosby 1997). In Sri Lanka, to give a humble example, my use of recipe books (and even measuring cups and spoons) for cooking was considered peculiar by my unlettered housekeeper, who could make hundreds of different curries and delicious baked goods without any of the external contrivances for accuracy that I required. One might say that her reenactment of cooking a curry was subtly different from my reproducing its recipe. (And my "memory" for methods and correct quantities of ingredients was far inferior to hers—another effect of my being able to rely on an external source such as a cookbook.)

In a similar way, unvarying word-for-word accuracy in anything—say, the "text" of a story, the recounting of a past event, the recollection of what someone said—is not a preliterate consideration: repeatability is, of necessity, approximate. Despite sometimes amazing feats of memory, there are limits to what can be stored in an individual head: simply being able to write allows the compilation of lists, cross-references, and statistics that can be checked and cross-checked, added to and subtracted from. Without written numerals, one cannot perform more than the simplest arithmetical operations. For most preliterate people, counting is also approximate, and many societies have only a few number words (for example, "one," "two," "a few," and "many").

Perhaps the most salient bequest of literacy is a greater possibility for disinterestedness, or *objectivity*. Once something is written, it becomes a thing that is separate from what it refers to. To be sure, a spoken name or word for a person or object is different from the person or object itself, but this is not always immediately evident. Children think that they *are* Sally or Tracy or Jim; preliterate people think that the words they say, especially names and adjectives, are attributes of the objects referred to. Apart from a few pioneers such as Rousseau, it was less than a century ago that the nature of language became itself an object of study and a subject for philosophy.

It is no accident that it was the Greeks who produced an early protoscientific sort of thought. Their unique alphabetic writing allowed a kind of ease or "transparence" in reading denied to users of syllabic or pictographic systems. Plato's philosophy of Pure Forms abstracted an individual object (my armchair) from the category "all chairs" and the preexistent ideal or Idea of chair. But even Plato, or Democritus (who first identified "atoms" as the smallest constituent of matter), or a pre-Socratic philosopher such as Thales (who proposed that everything was fundamentally composed of water and was himself also a geometer and astronomer) was not "scientific" in the modern sense.

Individual components of science are evident in preliterate thought. Toddlers readily classify, as when they learn to recognize individual people, animals, vehicles, foods, and so forth as members of a specific class or category such as men, women, dogs, cats, cars, or cookies.[3] Preliterate people develop and use complicated, orally transmitted taxonomies of kin, plants, birds, clouds, and other important parts of their world. Inference—noting cause and effect—is a fundamental cognitive skill. Close observation is essential to important areas of preliterate life. Making associations and testing and judging among alternatives are also universal processes of human cognition.

Modern science became possible not only because of literacy or alphabetic writing; for its realization it also needed the invention of the printing press in the fifteenth century (Eisenstein 1993). When printed, people's observations, tests, and conclusions could be much more reliably preserved and widely distributed than when they had to be remembered from a single oral presentation or laboriously copied individually by hand. People could build upon and improve earlier knowledge—for example, details of maps and anatomical drawings of plants and animals could become increasingly accurate; lists of measurements or components and numerical information, once they were preserved in print, could be used and reused. Correlations would emerge, with looking and checking, that might not be evident from simply remembering what one had been told or had seen weeks before in the only extant copy of a treatise in manuscript at some faraway library.

The scientific method, whereby one forms a hypothesis and tests it by gathering factual evidence, making objective observations, and drawing conclusions—all of which can be repeated by someone else—has been much scrutinized. Such notions as "fact," "impartiality," and "evidence" have been challenged and in some cases modified (for example, falsifiability is now accepted as a better characteristic of a good hypothesis than verifiability). The very project of science itself is today viewed by many as "merely" a cultural construct, and its findings are averred to be as relative or biased as those of any other construct.

Without digressing into a discussion of the epistemological status of science, or appraising its ultimate social costs and benefits, it is nevertheless indisputable that science has had immense influence and practical application in human lives. Even its detractors are affected by its discoveries, so that we can barely imagine living without anesthetics, antibiotics, air travel, electricity, newspapers, telephones, the automobile. It is a truism—but, like most truisms, true—to say that these things have made our lives in innumerable ways quite unlike the lives of people who lived only a century ago.

But we may be less aware of the important respects in which such devices, and the mechanical and mental procedures used to create and modify them, have made our minds different from prescientific minds. Despite growing alarm at the runaway ills that have accompanied technological progress—environmental degradation and pollution, the proliferation of ever more destructive weaponry, pervasive consumerism and mechanization—we remain resolutely reliant on literate and scientific habits of thought.

In schools, "language" skills are overwhelmingly concerned with reading and writing, not, as in medieval Europe or ancient Greece and Rome, with oral rhetorical ability. We value and teach our children what is called problem solving and critical thinking—such skills and abilities as planning ahead, impartially examining and weighing alternatives, and organizing ideas efficiently and clearly in outline form with headings and subheadings. We pay lip service to "creativity," but this usually means creative solutions to analytically framed problems. We assume that there is a best truth that can be found or imposed—an accurate, objectively verifiable reason, diagnosis, verdict, result, answer, or solution—which in turn may be constantly improved upon as new knowledge is accumulated. Contrast these procedures with acceptance of the great mythopoetic creation epics of every major or minor religion from every region of the globe, an acceptance in which knowledge is not sought or imposed but is taken as *revealed*. Some decades ago there was a useful term—"poetic knowledge"—for the kind of knowledge one receives from ideas that lack exact reference but nevertheless have a compelling force of truth (Laski 1961). Simply because we lack empirical verification does not mean that such knowledge is without value and relevance.

Literacy and rational thought are fine, as far as they go. We live in a world largely made by science and have to learn to manipulate and understand this world on its terms. The most recent additions to the scientific enterprise, of course, are those electronic receptacles of analytic-literate operations—computers—which are heralded as further agents in revolutionizing human minds.

It is good to be reminded once again that ancestral humans did not need to read, write, or compute, or to analyze to a high degree. The importance of this fact is not that they lacked the *ability* to do these things (for with good schooling, most of us do learn to do them) but that humans were not evolved to find a high degree of involvement, ease, or satisfaction in doing them.[4] Although they lacked literate vocations and avocations, the lives of our ancestors were nevertheless humanly full and rewarding.

Ancestral environments encouraged biologically relevant abilities such as skillful tool making, tracking or navigating, using one's body for work, play, and locomotion, telling and responding to stories, dancing and making music, and conciliation and other socially useful skills. Practicality and efficiency would not have extended to the degrees we consider normal today—making every moment count, living one's days according to a "schedule" of precise times, remembering to take the shirts when leaving the house so they can be dropped at the laundry after work on the way to the gym, or buying a birthday card for Aunt Abigail so it can be mailed before the three-day-weekend postal holiday.

That people can do these and countless other similar planning and organizational tasks is testament to human adaptability—even though not everyone is particularly adept at doing them. But it is perhaps most important to remember that even though they are learnable, they may not satisfy the evolved need for meaning in the same way as the exercise of ancestral skills. Granted, some people are able to find fulfillment and significance in balanced checkbooks, completed reports, tidy desks, and early Christmas shopping. Others love their hyperanalytic work as scientists, engineers, programmers, and academics, or their hyperverbal work as editors and writers. Such people thrive in modern societies.

But many do not thrive. There are legions of young men who look to me as if they would be more productively and happily occupied spearing woolly mammoths or constructing a longhouse with their buddies than attending high school or sitting eight hours a day, five days a week, in an office. Apart from this enormous cohort of young males who cannot find a place in the contemporary world, many others, women and men, just hang on, feeling always rushed, stretched, overloaded, and behind, if not just plain incompetent or out of control. Such feelings scarcely seem adaptive.

It seems important to note that even those who can negotiate and enjoy the complexities of modern superliterate life usually look for meaning in the sorts of satisfactions (or their derivatives) that would have been selected for in ancestral lives. Benign pastimes include socializing, cooking or otherwise making things by hand, gardening, sports, vicariously participating in fictive lives, and other activities that will be described in succeeding chapters.

For millennia, humans lived in societies with firm understandings of the way the world works and of their place in it. It is not apparent that we can easily exchange one belief system for another, or cynically espouse nihilism, and still feel that there is order and meaning in our lives. Not surprisingly, one finds in our "secular" age a spectacular variety of marginal religious or quasi-religious pursuits and practitioners—astrologers, psychics, mystics, gurus, nature religions, "alternative" therapies, complex diets, and other forms of body control and maintenance. They offer systems and stories that give meaning to the world and provide techniques and paraphernalia for affecting it positively. If order and meaning are not provided by societies, individual minds look for and find them where they can.

Meaning Today

If literacy and the alphabet have changed the way humans think, events in western Europe and the Americas following the Renaissance and Industrial Revolution have changed the way we and the rest of the people in the world live. Minds and lives, both, have tasted of the fruits of the tree of possibility as well as of knowledge, trading meaning for meanings. The logico-aesthetic integration of our ancestors' lives and their certainty of knowing what is true and good have gradually dissolved, along with culturewide acceptance of divine providence or a destiny that shapes our ends.

Ironically, despite all the knowledge and sophisticated technological mastery that have arisen from contemporary science, its most advanced ideas reveal fundamental principles of uncertainty, relativity, and the infinite—whether of outer space or inner matter—that inescapably confront our wish to understand with what is humanly inconceivable. Although natural science separated itself from theology centuries ago, the entities with which it now concerns itself—superstrings, quantum gravity, and black holes, for example—seem as mystically alluring and beyond human understanding as intimations of the divine. Uncertainty and relativity have become articles of faith even in the humanities, as professors teach that we are incapable of knowing what is true or real, and doctors of philosophy maintain that all knowledge and reality, being mere interpretations of cultures and individuals, are unavoidably partial.

Although the larger implications of science may give rise to wonder and even mystical speculation, as a tool it addresses quite specific questions about nature, such as how things work and what they are made of. Although its findings have given us order and powerful ways to affect the world, it remains the case that human minds evolved to require from life more than discovery and problem solving. Analytic thinking requires an unnaturally high level of training and vigilance and can easily be overridden by wish, desire, anxiety, or strong authority. It does not address or answer questions of ultimate meaning, purpose, intent, and justification for the ways things are; instead, it narrows its focus to description, subsumption, and probability.

Yet judging from ancestral and traditional examples, the systems and stories that keep society orderly and individuals secure work best when they are vividly presented as part of a compelling belief system and irradiated with convictions of transcendent truth. What we call "religion" and "art" were for countless centuries intrinsic to the order of ordinary life and to the motivations of human minds. They were not optional practices to be indulged one morning each week or when there was nothing better to do, nor were they superfluous pastimes that could be rejected altogether. Pueblo Indian cosmology may seem quaint and dubious compared with Los Alamos physics, but it satisfies human needs and addresses nonscientific questions to which people want answers.[5]

Where do we come from? What are we? Where are we going? Why do the innocent suffer? What should we do to make things better? These are questions answered succinctly and without hesitation by religions and political ideologues, but not by the American Association for the Advancement of Science. The former are more popularly convincing about the truth of their convictions than scientists are about the probability of their hypotheses or the applicability of their conclusions.

For important reasons, scientific and other academic "-ologies" present their findings dispassionately, in abstract terms. Even when discussing the birth of stars, the beginning of life and the finale of death, or the rise and fall of empires, their accounts describe impersonal antecedents and consequents, unpicturable principles and processes. Although such analyses allow a useful, rationally expressed general understanding, they deliberately distance themselves from a humanly relevant world with its mysteries, wonders, and dramatic personal conflicts or satisfactions. Faced with a painful disease, people may be instructed about viruses or defective genes. But these "explanations" still don't answer the more urgent question, "Why me?" Sorcery or witchcraft provides a more tangible explanation, with a built-in course of action.

Human minds evolved, like those of other animals, to pursue and find meaning in their own interests (which include their own kin and close associates). Appeals to concern for the common good are typically less effective than demonstrations of how policies will affect your paycheck or the health of your family. It remains all too true that for most human minds it seems insufficient simply to find and make order, nor are our minds easily convinced of something unless it is presented with emotionally appealing personalized relevance.

Ten thousand years after the invention of writing, the kind of disembedded, critical thinking that writing makes possible remains difficult and even irrelevant for many, as is evident to anyone who observes general public discourse and its assessments of complex social issues. It is not difficult for "evidence" from one's feelings and senses to outweigh arguments addressed to one's reason. Juries find it difficult to separate the personal and dramatic from the evidential and legally admissible and may base their verdicts more on the former than on the latter.

The mythopoetic expressions that we evolved to respond to and require are concrete and vivid, embedded in the world they explain, and based on analogies with human actions and emotions: they catch us up in dramatic, descriptive narrative. There are heroes, villains, good and evil, transgression and retribution. No wonder stories about amazing adventures and celebrities' lives appeal far more to human minds than descriptions of the complex history of a political crisis or careful analyses of global problems and economic trends.

We view with alarm many traditional beliefs and their attendant practices—such as subjugation, scarification, or mutilation—and consider them to be ignorant or enslaving. Kenneth Maddock, in a sympathetic book about Australian Aborigines (Maddock 1973, 183), points out that what we regard as illusions and even oppression often are inherent in beliefs and practices whose *absence* removes meaning from life and renders it mediocre or even insupportable. Such meaning-rich practices frequently involve rhythmic-modal elaborations.

In the laudable post-Enlightenment endeavor of dispelling illusions and casting off oppression, it is easy to leave a desolate void that is all too ready to be filled by other emotion-laden explanatory schemes that satisfy the needs for belonging and meaning—say, conspiracy theories, obedience to mind-controlling cults, or fanatical adherence to fundamentalist doctrines both secular and divine.

The strongly felt belief that something is meaningful does not, of course, make it true or right. This shortcoming was of little importance in small-scale societies whose ways changed little over centuries and who in any case seldom met or came into conflict with other people whose ways were different. In today's overpopulated, complex, and interdependent world, our evolved readiness to accept the meanings of the groups to which we belong leads to many of the manifold horrors reported every day in newspapers and on television screens.

One thinks of suicide bombers (or the kamikaze pilots of World War II), whose feelings of bondedness and loyalty to their group and its worldview fulfilled the need for both belonging and meaning. In the recent wars of "liberation" in Africa and Asia (as elsewhere), boys as young as eight or ten have been recruited as soldiers by militia leaders. They are first given good food, bicycles, or other toys as indications of belonging, along with the privilege of helping to carry equipment. Eventually they are taught to use weapons. One Liberian boy told Jonathan Randal (1995) of the *Washington Post* that the first time he killed a man he felt "floating, unconscious." The dissociation from reality produced in a naive youth by taking a life was condoned, absolved, and transmuted when a practitioner of local medicine (the *juju* man) made four incisions on each of the child's arms near the shoulder and pronounced that henceforth killing would be easier. The boy then went on to kill at least twenty more enemies and recounted watching the "necklacing" of a fellow militiaman with a gasoline-doused tire for having killed five men of his own squad and a *juju* man. "I watched him burn to death, pleading for mercy," said young Alfonso, "but felt no regrets. It was only right that the man be killed in turn for killing his own men."

The experience of patterned, painful wounding by a charismatic figure of authority, accompanied by assurance of invincibility, gave both meaning and a sense of belonging to his present life and helped the young killer cross a line of no return. Another boy was also "terrified" the first time he killed, but the *juju* man also gave him courage so that he was able subsequently to kill without remorse anyone his commander told him to. While some might call this simple conditioning, one could ask why it is not just as easy to "condition" youngsters to *resist* the imprecations of authority figures and the expectations of one's group. To just say no.

It may not give much comfort to know that for millennia it has been adaptive for humans to be receptive and vulnerable to the appeal of group meanings, whether or not they are in today's terms rationally testable or verifiable.[6] Ancestrally, the times when such beliefs "didn't work" in an immediate context were apparently less detrimental to a person's survival than certainty about culturally relevant practices and purposes, congruent with a logically and aesthetically integrated worldview, was ultimately beneficial.

In any event, the meanings that were conveyed as true and good by individual traditional societies over centuries were obviously biologically true and good within their particular environmental contexts, or they— the beliefs and their believers—would not have endured. Over time, groups whose verities did not adapt to changing circumstances dwindled and perished. In circumstances of scarcity or other trouble, if one group's interests were challenged by those of another, their different customs and beliefs could become reasons for mutual disdain and even attack.

Today, as accelerated, externally imposed changes (rather than slower natural changes) have increased, ancient "true" and "good" principles of aboriginal societies all over the world have become maladaptive in the sorts of societies imposed by more technologically powerful and "rationally" motivated conquerors. The pluralistic, individualistic, secular, and rapidly changing culture of modern Western societies has largely eradicated the certainty of ancestral worldviews. It is no wonder that fundamentalists in every country are threatened by Western ways and demonize and try to resist us so vehemently.

Modern ideas of progress, efficiency, and having new experiences may be exciting and challenging to the young, but human individuals and societies have not evolved to prosper in an atmosphere of insistent and accelerating change. Not only have new technologies made age-old occupations obsolete, but also newer technologies have made those of a generation ago, or even less, irrelevant. Knowledge and procedures now metamorphose as quickly and relentlessly as the shapes of clouds in a fast-moving front, so that *in*experience and hence openness to the new have become the prized qualities for success.

In contrast, for millennia humans have found comfort and certainty in the repository of wisdom that their elders won through experience over the years. Today, when change is the norm, potential elders are redundant before they are fifty. They and the certainty they once embodied are instead replaced by "freshman" politicians and new business school graduates whose assurance comes not from mature minds but from limber brains.

Yet I question whether many of our species, even among the young, can be so comfortably confident about the promise of the ever new. Depending on their source and strength, threats to one's worldview result in emotions of confusion, anxiety, and anger. Prejudice and stereotyping easily emerge as "default options," in Frederick Turner's (1995, 147) memorable metaphor, when the cultural software program doesn't work. Suspicion of and disdain for authority lead to an erosion of standards, and their replacement with the trendy or expedient may not be so nourishing as more moderate and time-consuming fare. When endless choice becomes a self-justifying virtue, one outcome may be restless dissatisfaction.

Although we live in an age of technological "control," we feel increasingly unable to influence macro-forces that govern our lives—the economy, the political system, environmental pollution, overpopulation, crime and violence. Humans, like any other animal, have a fundamental need to reduce psychological uncertainty (Kalma 1986). Studies indicate that "healthy" and "hardy" people have a greater sense of control over events in their lives, tend to be committed to others and to themselves, and tend to possess a belief system that includes a sense of the meaningfulness of life (Kobasa 1979).

Indeed, studies have shown the important effects of hormones such as cortisol and testosterone on bodily functions of immunity, growth, reproduction, muscle action, and cognition (Flinn et al. 1996). Elevation of cortisol may be felt as negative (for example, anxiety and worry about an uncertain situation) or positive (for example, mild excitement when playing competitive sports). Testosterone levels are elevated in certain social situations in which men experience a sense of control, success, or pleasure—for example, winning in a competitive game, enjoying increased status, hunting, engaging in moderate exercise and in sexual or erotic stimulation. Such "stress responses" have been adaptive in motivating action to reduce uncertainty and in allocating energy to different bodily functions. We are familiar with the psychological deterioration of native peoples whose worldviews and competence were eradicated in a generation by an alien conqueror, although they had until then been able to cope with normal stress and had lived healthy and hardy lives for untold centuries.

Citizens of states all over the world have had to deal with rapid modernization, with revolution and counterrevolution, throwing into disarray what their parents and leaders had proclaimed as the way things were supposed to be. It is hardly surprising that the twentieth century has been marked by unprecedented anxiety and angry aggressiveness, which were once adaptive responses to the threat of losing, or the humiliating loss of, the meanings that one needs and holds dear.

4

"Hands-On" Competence

WHEN A NEWBORN baby is given to its mother for the first time, she nearly always takes or touches its tiny hand. Father, admiring relatives, and family friends also seem to find it natural to insert a finger into the small fist, pick it up, and gently move it back and forth in welcome and kinship as if to say, "You are one of us."

This gesture of taking or touching hands is reminiscent of Michelangelo's depiction of the creation of Adam, showing the instant just before God bestows life upon his creature, the first human, by reaching out to touch his limp—and thus as yet useless—hand. The beauty of hands, even in repose, is in their latent mobility. Dancers must be as aware of their arms and hands as of their legs and feet, since the hand is so expressive— the tool of the soul as much as of the will.

In choosing the adjective *habilis* ("handy" or "able") to designate the earliest fossil representative of the genus *Homo*, early paleoanthropologists acknowledged the importance of the hand and the crucial distinguishing capacity it bestowed—the ability to handle and make. Another name used sometimes to refer to our species was *Homo faber*—the making or tool-making human.

For millennia hands were the primary instruments for building and making the human way of life. Everything humanly relevant and recognizably human was made by human hands. To be human was to make.

Of the eight most common verbs in the English language—do, make, be, have, take, give, show, say—at least half imply hand use.[1]

Just as belonging to a group predisposes us to learn the meaningful systems and stories of our fellows, it also prepares us to want to follow the example of our associates and learn to make things for our lives. Human brains and minds evolved to enable the learning of manual skills from others and the devising of practical solutions for the requirements of ancestral environments—to cope, "hands on," with the demands of life. Simply by doing what we were born to do evokes a sense—subliminal or fully felt—of competence, of being at home in the world. Such a sense is often undeveloped in modern humans, because they inhabit a prefabricated and electronic environment and pay others to provide their food, clothing, shelter, utensils, and everything else.

If making things for our lives was necessary, then manual interaction with the natural world (the source for all those things from which ancestral lives were constructed) would also have to be inherently satisfying. Hating one's work, feeling demeaned by it, failing or being unable to do it would have put individuals at such a selective disadvantage that they would not have propagated these negative predispositions or ineptitudes.

Because the human hand is a specialized anatomical adaptation of physical precision and emotional expressivity, it seems reasonable that we should naturally find both pleasure and meaning in making. Additionally, because our bodies (skin and senses) are our primary means of knowing the world, we should find active, pragmatic intimacy with natural surroundings and materials to be emotionally, physically, and mentally gratifying and significant.

Manual involvement and material interaction with the world are multisensory—multimodal. With our hands we pat, stack, smear, wipe, press, gouge, dig, mark, scratch, pick, prod, stroke, caress, squeeze, brush, flick, flex, stretch, bend, turn, twist, and twirl. What we handle has resistance, pliability, elasticity, softness, hardness, moistness, dryness, warmth, coolness, shininess, slipperiness, stickiness, pulpiness, pastiness, gumminess. It sounds crackly, squishy, rustly, bubbly, ploppy, squeaky. Manual movements are dynamic, taking place with more or less intensity or force, and speed. They have rich associations with each other and with other parts of experience—some universal, others private. They are among our earliest experiences of our bodies and of the world, and they become part of the funded tacit knowledge with which we continue to experience it.

Infant development and inclination suggest that hand use and involvement with the material world are integral parts of our species program. *Not* to do these things contravenes our fundamental nature. All together, the psychological traits that emerge from mutuality—a sense of belonging and identity, a reliance on shared meaningful systems and stories that explain the world, and a hands-on relationship with the natural world—lead to a basic sense of competence, or aptitude for life.

THE PLEASURE AND MEANING OF MAKING

The hands of monkeys and apes are specialized for grasping and manipulating: they can be used to swing hand over hand from branches, to pick apart tasty morsels, and to peel fruit. As primates, early hominids inherited this dextrous and flexible instrument which, because they walked upright, became liberated and therefore available for even more complex things.

When hands are not used for locomotion, they are free to wave and signal. Persuasive theories have suggested that human language began with gestures, and certainly hands add eloquence and even precision to the things people say. Hands are able to carry, so that babies can be more helpless: they do not need to cling. Hands can touch other hands and bodies, subtly conveying intentions and feelings. Even chimpanzees touch hands or pat one another as a sign of reassurance and desire for reconciliation (de Waal 1989). Emancipated hands can more easily investigate— not only potential food or other useful material but also interesting rocks or beautiful shells can be picked up, examined, and brought home. Significantly, hands that are free can make tools and, unlike the hands of even the most inventive primate, use tools to make tools.

In any case, although chimpanzees make tools, the chimpanzee way of life does not *require* their manufacture and use. The lives of humans, in contrast, have been dependent for at least 1.8 million years on the tools they make. For most of that time, the only extant artifacts of our hominid ancestors have been stone and then bone tools, implements that helped them to obtain and prepare food and other of life's necessities. Handmade tools could scrape skins for shelter and clothing, fashion utensils and vessels, make weapons. Such a defining human characteristic as skillful and varied tool making would strongly favor a corresponding need (or predisposition) to manipulate—the word itself comes from the Latin word *manus*, or hand. And to be sure, like sociability, handling is precociously evident in infant development.

The Beginnings of Hand Use [2]

Pleasure in handling is "hard-wired" into human nature for very good reason: it predisposes us to be tool users and makers. The infant's drives to reach, grasp, and investigate with mouthing, looking, and dropping have critical biological importance. And as critically important biological drives they are things all babies everywhere *want* to do. You can't stop them.

Within the womb, the hands of human fetuses, like those of monkeys, already seem to begin to reach and grasp. From birth, rudimentary spontaneous hand movements of the human baby foretell its future career as a preeminent tool exploiter and peerless communicator. Although the earliest hand movements of infants are emotional and self-regulatory (Trevarthen 1986, 154), they soon start to make pre-reaching movements in the direction of objects that their eyes track.

It is interesting that natural selection seems to have co-opted the primate inclinations to use the hands not only for manipulating or making things but also for expressive communication. Even in early infancy this gestural use of hands is distinct from other uses. At around four weeks, when babies begin to respond to others' faces and sounds with social expressions and sounds of their own, their hand movements resemble conversational gestures. They impulsively move their hands up and away from the body, often with one or more fingers extended and the palm facing downward or forward, and they coordinate these gestures with their own lip and tongue movements and vocalizations. (Similar gestures are also made by newborns, but with less well-defined orientation to the expressions of their "conversational partner.")

At this early stage of intense *emotional* communication with caretakers, pre-reaching toward a "target" temporarily declines. By two months of age, infants' hand movements have characteristics that will be used in eventual speech. These gestures are "conversational," synchronized with the rhythms of others' gestures and voices, directed toward others, and emotionally dynamic—that is, depending on the baby's level of excitement, they display more or less force and speed.

But as babies' hands become more refined instruments of interpersonal communication, they must also begin to deal with—or literally *handle*, with increasing control, coordination, and goal-orientation—the material world. In the human brain there are different paths for perception (that is, for organizing information coming in through the senses) and for acting on the world. Coordinating the pathways of eye and hand

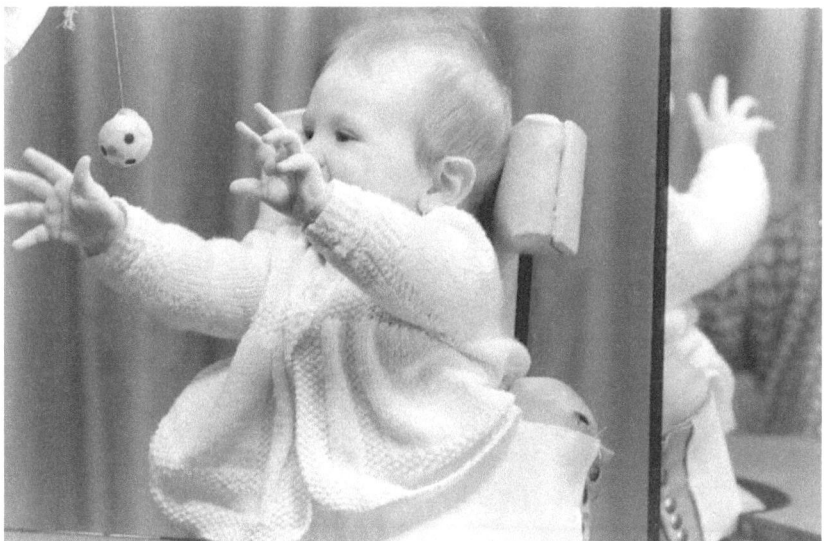

An infant of twenty-eight weeks efficiently reaches for a toy with both hands. Photograph: Colwyn Trevarthen.

begins when babies practice bringing their hands together and eventually "playing with" them; then they reach out more successfully and precisely to things in the outside world and ultimately truly grasp them.

Once babies can reliably reach for, aim at, and grasp objects, they bring them to their faces and investigate them orally—with tongue and lips. These are the first action or motor areas to develop in the cerebral cortex, no doubt because of their importance to feeding, and in infancy there are twice as many nerve endings in the mouth area as in the fingertips. In any case, the face and mouth areas of the primary motor cortex lie close to the areas that govern arm and hand movements. Mouths and fingers seem to retain a primitive psychobiological connection, as when we bite fingernails, idly or nervously manipulate our mouths with our fingers, or make small movements with lips or tongue when concentrating on a precise motor activity such as writing or threading a needle. Mouths, too, are rich sources of modal sensations and associations.

As every parent soon discovers, babies endlessly repeat the activities of reaching, grasping, and investigating with eyes, hands, and mouth. This allows them to learn not only about how things in the world look, taste, smell, sound, and feel but also that their actions can have an effect

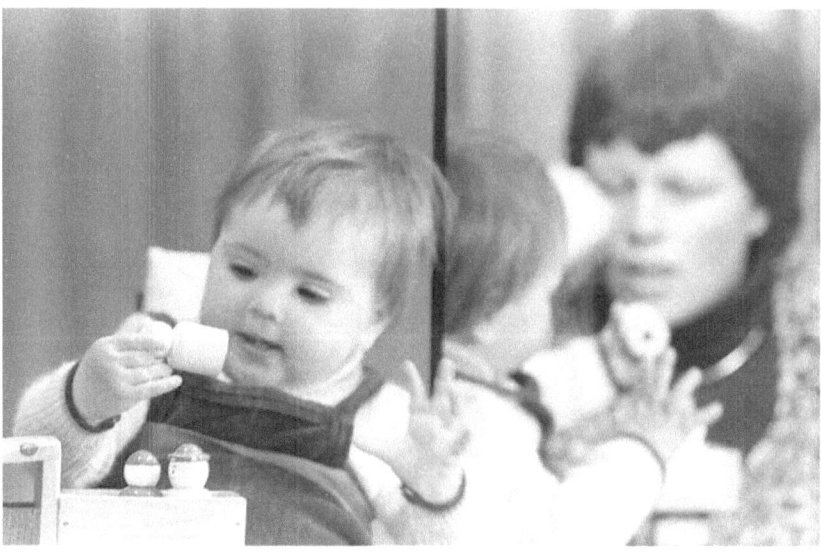

A year-old infant looks intently at the doll she is holding. Photograph: Colwyn Trevarthen.

on many of those things, including the most amazingly reactive of all—people.

Thus, from the very beginning, sense perceptions and motor skills have beneficial effects on cognition. For example, at first a baby can release its grip only by accident, but when the coordination to let go deliberately is finally achieved, dropping objects becomes as enjoyable as grasping them was earlier. Not only is there an immediate, observable effect on the world, but *planning* to drop something and *predicting* that someone will pick it up and hand it back have the ultimate result of developing these cognitive pathways in the brain, even though to the baby—if not its weary care-taker—such practice is simply having fun. Subsequent developmental stages of motor activity include integrating the uniquely human precision grip of opposable thumb and fingers with the improved coordination of eye and hand.

Manipulative skill is also developed in the social context of person-person-object games, in which babies and their partners hand objects back and forth and do things with them. At six months of age a baby's rhythmic banging is synchronized with syllable babbling, indicating the pleasure inherent in coordinating modalities and in moving to a regular beat. At this age, as with hand expressivity at one to two months of age, handling and using are normally inextricably connected with interaction and communication—reaching out to and affecting others as well as the inanimate world.

The most elementary motor activities of every normal baby—beginning with simply picking things up and setting them down ("placing")—can be used as the basis for developing "learning tools" for children who for various reasons lack this normal motivation or ability to investigate and play and hence are developmentally delayed. Katrin Stroh and Thelma Robinson, developmental therapists in London, have noted the features of continuity, effort, pleasure, and endless repetition that characterize the body activity of children under two years, and the child's total lack of fear of failure at this age. In normal development, such characteristics lead naturally through play and exploration to increasing competence.

In working with children older than two years who have language problems, learning and understanding problems, emotional and social difficulties, limited attention spans, and little interest in or ability to play, Stroh and Robinson (1993) provide opportunities for parents and caretakers systematically to facilitate the early motor activities—picking up and placing, banging, pairing, matching, sorting, building with bricks, sequencing, and drawing. These are the ways in which children in every culture begin to learn, understand, and solve problems. Such hands-on activity lays the foundation for future learning, understanding, and communication.

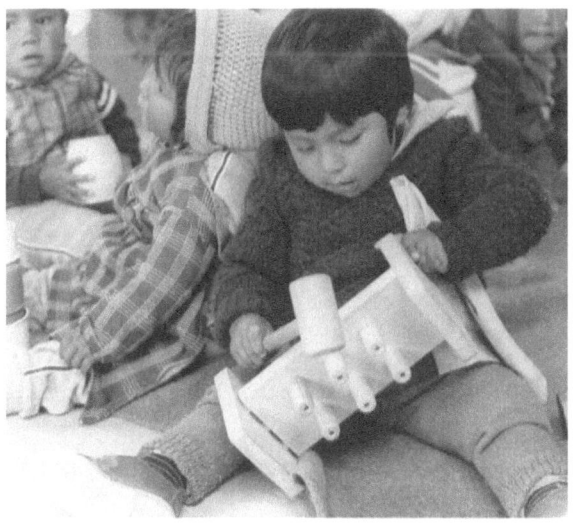

Bolivian boy with hammer and pegs. Photograph: Ray Witlin, UNICEF.

Making

The anatomical specializations of our bodies and brains for manual activity, including their psychobiological and social components, are sure confirmation of the importance of hands to the human adaptation. Quite simply, using our hands is something we were born to do. If adults make and use tools, children will too. If adults do not, then children will not either, and their natural drive to move seamlessly from handling to making will atrophy just as surely as the predisposition to smile or share will wither if not encouraged or mirrored by positive example.

In ancestral environments, the infant and child need for (and pleasure in) handling objects would have developed naturally into using and *making* them—implements, dwellings, regalia. In the biologically important behavior of play, children imitate the activities of adults and thereby learn the ways of their society. Western children simulate adult activities in their imaginations, with toys, or vicariously on television, but in many parts of the world girls and boys actually begin very early to contribute with their hands to family subsistence. In villages in the Sepik River area of Papua New Guinea, *naven* ceremonies mark the "firsts" in a child's life—the first fish caught, first yam planted, even first carving made. On these occasions, as the group sings, dances, eats roast pork, and watches an amusing, grotesque, ash-colored dancer, a youngster is made to realize that his or her new ability is an occasion worth noting.

Our early ancestors made everything needed for their lives from natural materials such as fiber, grass, leaves, mud, stone, cane, bark, and wood. What they made had human scale and relevance. People saw and used the results of their actions: they lived in the houses and wore the clothing they had made. It was of vital importance that handmade tools and implements worked properly—would the roof leak, the spear work, the basket fray?

The Yekuana, whose worldview was described at some length in chapter 3, use a word, *tidi'uma*, to refer collectively to the handmade artifacts that are necessary to their lives. Derived from the verb *tidi* ("to make"), *tidi'uma* translates to "things made" and includes the implication that these are all the things that one must learn to make in order to be considered a Yekuana. (In contrast, objects that are acquired through trade or chance are *mesoma*—"stuff," a general term for undifferentiated, alien objects.) *Tidi'uma* are rather like all the badges required to be an Eagle Scout, or the things an apprentice must know how to do in order to become a master craftsman. Although it may take years to become a fully competent Yekuana, the requirements are clearly knowable and attainable to those who apply themselves to accomplishing them.

In modern societies, I should add as an aside, all cultural signals point to the accumulation of money, possessions, prestige, and an indefinable but recognizable attitude of "coolness" as indicating that one has "made it." What is lacking are instructions as to the precise steps for obtaining these desiderata. Moreover, "coolness" is a kind of competence that is dissociated from any worthwhile task—its very message of "no big deal" discloses its nonutility.

Interestingly, Yekuana "making" includes not only manual but spiritual attainment. In learning how to make the various objects necessary for life in a Yekuana world, a person simultaneously learns about the society's underlying meanings, since ritual actions accompany all material ones and the incorporation of meaningful symbols is part of the manufacture of all *tidi'uma*. All functional design participates in a greater cosmic design. "To become a mature Yekuana," writes Guss (1989, 70), "is to develop not only physical skills demanded of one's gender but also the spiritual awareness that the preparation of these goods imparts." By making an artifact, one tacitly repeats or restates the message encoded in the story of its origin.

The importance of baskets and basketry among Yekuana *tidi'uma* gives the lie to facile jokes in American popular culture about "basket weaving" being the nadir of intellectual challenge (as opposed to rocket science or brain surgery at the other end of the scale). Baskets are particularly important because of their use in almost all Yekuana material activities—for transport, storage, hunting, fishing, and the many tasks required for transforming *tapa* into edible cassava. The technology of basket making includes finding and preparing the fibers as well as their actual plaiting.

Most Yekuana baskets are in bichrome black and white (like the basket illustrated in the appendix), thus fluently conforming to the dualistic worldview described in chapter 3. All incorporate stylized designs of potentially poisonous creatures such as coral snakes, toads, bats, and dangerous spirits. Weaving such a symbol is analogous to using human agency to convert natural poison to human use, as when making curare from toad venom (and thus bringing life to humans when curare-dipped arrows are used to kill animals for meat) or when transforming *tapa* to cassava. Once again, it is reiterated that poison, which is deadly when natural, can become life supporting when *made*, that is, transformed by human weaving into a stylized cultural symbol.

Basket making then becomes a natural yardstick with which to measure the maturity and character of a developing Yekuana boy, who is not considered to be fully adult or ready for marriage until he is able to make every kind of basket. And as Yekuana become older, they devote more and more of their time to weaving—that is, to the perfection of combined practical and ritual skills. In their baskets, older people demonstrate the most skillful integration and complexity of forms and show the most ritual knowledge. Thus Yekuana making—weaving baskets—exemplifies ritual or spiritual meaning as well as providing the satisfaction of practical, manual activity.

ENGAGING WITH THE NATURAL WORLD

With their senses of sight, smell, and hearing, humans—like other animals—have awareness and experience of the external world at a distance; with their skin and tongues they touch and taste it directly. These senses and organs evolved precisely for the purpose of engaging with the natural world in its immediate materiality, and it is only natural that such engagement should be a source of satisfaction.

As I have just described it, humans evolved to live a literally "hands-on" type of life, handling and making what they needed. Although handling and making of almost anything are in themselves satisfying, I would particularly like to extend the meaning of the term "hands on" in this chapter to indicate also the pleasure and satisfaction inherent in having direct physical involvement with nature. For our ancestors, the natural world was the source both of practical and material requirements and of significant systems and stories.

To begin with, humans were intimately aware of and necessarily dependent upon natural cycles and their life meanings. The year, with its recurring seasons, brought warmth and cold; rainfall and dry weather; directional changes of winds, tides, and currents; varied plants with their successive blooms and fruits; birds and animals with their seasonal sounds and habits; the changes and regularities encoded on the face of the wheeling night sky. The daily round, with its periodicity of light and darkness, dictated times for going forth and returning, for coming together, for work and rest.

Ancestral humans were a part of nature and therefore must have behaved and thought more than we can now imagine like their fellow animals. Sights, sounds, smells were all profoundly attended to, because of their literally vital meanings. Such people used their own agency and energy to make things happen—not only their hands or fingers but also their breath and muscles. What contemporary people call "exercise" is how earlier people led their lives; the association of active energetic movement with an increase of endorphins, the brain chemicals that create a feeling of euphoria, is no accident. It is an adaptive reward for doing what life originally required and what humans were designed to do. Certainly in ancestral environments an evolved tendency to like to do the stuff of everyday life would better assure that it got done and that the fruits of one's labors were duly reaped. Even in today's subsistence societies, people distinguish far less than we do between "work" and "nonwork," or between what they "have to" and "want to" do.

It is rare today, at least for urban Americans, to do physical work or even to see others do such work, so we may not realize what animal grace and economy of movement there can be in human bodies engaged in natural activities. The anthropologist Stanley Diamond (1974, 61–62) described his reaction to the Anaguta in Nigeria with whom he lived during his fieldwork in the 1960s. For the first time, he said, he appreciated the

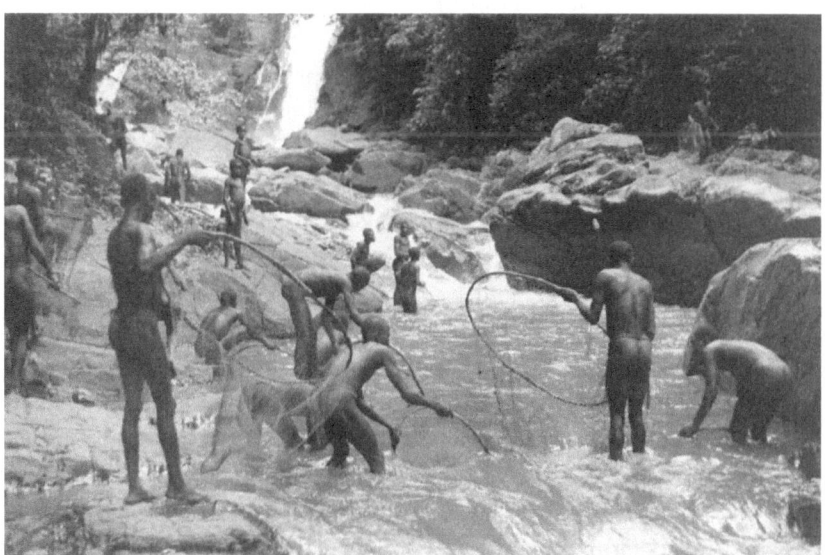

The annual fish drive in the Donga Valley, Cameroon. Photograph: Paul Gebauer.

beauty of a moving human body doing the work that it was made to do. This beauty had nothing to do with our conventional ideas of "beautiful bodies" from the fitness center, all invariably young and of starlet or stud proportions. Those are beautiful too, but the working, instrumental body of any age has a beauty that we have lost the opportunity and perhaps the eye to appreciate.

In Sri Lanka, on seaside holidays, we always stopped to watch fishermen on the beach pulling in their long, strong, handmade nets that twice daily were laid several hundred yards out to sea. In two widely spaced rows of perhaps twenty persons each, boys and men would spend an hour or more chanting and rhythmically pulling while moving backward in heavily accented steps, the rows gradually coming together, leaving loops of rope behind them on the sand. Periodically, the person at the end of a row would go to the front, and everyone else would move back to accommodate him. As the net was drawn nearer the shore and the two rows came closer together, the chanting increased in speed and amplitude along with the men's movements, growing to a climax as the catch—a tight bag of glittering living fish that seemed to pulse like a heart—was dragged onto the sand. Other rhythms characterized men scooting up coconut trees, or people bathing at a well who repeatedly lifted and poured buckets of water over their heads. Much of communal work—such as pulling a net, pounding grain, or transplanting rice seedlings—was accompanied by chants or songs, in part to coordinate the labor, in part to make it more enjoyable.

From their awareness of being dependent on nature arises the sense of duties and obligations toward nature that hunter-gatherer peoples then demonstrate in special observances and actions. A few examples are the Mbuti pygmies' *molima*, which sings the forest into being (Turnbull 1961); the Bladder Festival of the Kuskokwim Eskimos, in which the soul-containing bladder of every seal killed during the year is returned to the sea (after being "fed" and honored at an eight-day celebration) to unite with its bones in order to become a living animal once more (Himmelheber 1993 [1938], 15–16); and the *mbari* ceremony of the Owerri Igbo (see chapter 5), which forestalls adversity and maintains the natural order. Such attitudes are quite unlike the postindustrial assumption that nature is there for humans' continued, unlimited use. Connectedness with the natural world remains part of our heritage, however, in the sacred texts of religions and in the emotions that we all are still able to feel toward nature—curiosity, wonder, fear, and gratitude.

Certainly, selection would have favored a positive attachment to the natural world—the ability to find gratification from it and an aptitude for making practical use of its bounties.[3] Individuals would have better survived who could pay close attention to and remember flora and fauna and who could turn to account the details and peculiarities that conveyed important information about ripeness, edibility, or toxicity of vegetation or the condition and likely intention of animals. Tracking, homing, navigating, and finding water require ready ability to notice the possibilities and vagaries of terrain, wind, waves, and weather.

An individual's likelihood of survival would thus have been enhanced if certain kinds of signals and activities were innately fascinating, so that attention to them required no effort. Children everywhere take a rapt and precocious interest in living creatures of any kind, from ants to elephants—even as pictures in books. They learn the words for dog, cat, horse, and other animals earlier (and presumably more easily) than for common but inanimate objects such as a chair or door, or even for noisy and conspicuous mechanical contrivances such as telephones and lawn mowers. Even in an electronic age, older children love to climb trees, play in tree houses, make forts, go exploring, and sleep outdoors in tents. (I was grimly amused, however, to hear about a group of adolescents on a camping trip who watched a video—brought along by the adult supervisors?—of *Wilderness Vacation*, starring Dan Aykroyd and John Candy, in the lodge.) While many adults today may look upon camping as inconvenient and uncomfortable, millions of others continue to enjoy hiking, trekking, climbing, and a vast range of other outdoor sports. Most adults, like their children, find the animate world fascinating. We keep pets, look at them or at wild animals in zoos, and feel a vital connection. Their antics amuse us, and we are moved by their suffering.

Certainly gardening is a well-known source of personal pleasure and even therapy. In Seattle, a special facility provides "horticultural therapy" for patients with severe and chronic psychiatric illnesses and at the same time helps support itself financially by growing specialized crops and herbs—arugula, golden beet greens, thumbelina carrots, tarragon—for regional restaurants. Patients receive benefits from working side by side, as well as from the physical exercise and multisensory stimulation. "The very nature of working with plants, doing work that is predictable, routine and often repetitive, the very fact that they are working with a living material—it all helps," said a spokesperson (*Seattle Post-Intelligencer*, October 18, 1996, C8). Beautifying city parks in the aftermath of civil war in Bosnia gave people something "hands on" to do in order to regain a sense of humanity and dignity, as a means of "community healing."

Even our current preferences for homes and surroundings may have archaic roots. At least some Western psychologists have found that their subjects show a strong predilection for landscapes that are like that of the African savannah—that is, open grassland dotted liberally with trees (Kaplan 1992; Orians and Heerwagen, 1992). More specifically, the English geographer Jay Appleton (1975, 1990) finds that people optimally prefer environments that offer possibilities for *prospect*—being able to look out over a considerable distance—and *refuge*—feeling secure, protected from the climate and from intrusion. In combination, these reinforce one another, permitting us to see without being seen. Appleton claims that such preferences are genetically influenced, because of their evolutionary value.

Using Appleton's work, Grant Hildebrand (1991) has made a convincing case that the features of prospect and refuge are strong factors in the attraction to their homes felt by owners of houses designed by Frank Lloyd Wright, who apparently used those features unconsciously. For example, Wright consistently placed fireplaces in circumscribed interior areas and located living areas well above street level so that residents could remain hidden by terrace walls while looking out at people on the road below. Access to the living quarters was not straightforward: Wright's design required visitors to make a number of twists and turns in order to reach the entrance, which was inconspicuous and occasionally even concealed.

In chapter 3 I described how narratives and stories everywhere use archetypal images and themes—subjects, objects, and actions that engage ancestral predilections. Among these are important cues from the natural world that would have affected, positively or negatively, our survival: "the great outdoors," fires, caves, weather; things that are large, loud, fast-moving, pretty, shiny, unusual; and other people, including those who are especially attractive and babies and children. We are drawn with fascination to blood, physical danger, violent and adroit action. People who considered all these things uninteresting and preferred to look at blank walls or their big toes would not have lasted long enough to reproduce themselves.

Humans everywhere have been intrigued or excited by natural phenomena and natural forces, incorporating them into their creations, both actual and imaginative. The most impressive natural forms have become the abodes of the gods, or the gods themselves—the cosmic ocean; sacred mountains and mountaintops; the gods of thunder, wind, sun, and moon; the World Oak, Yggdrasil; animal spirits such as Raven or Coyote.

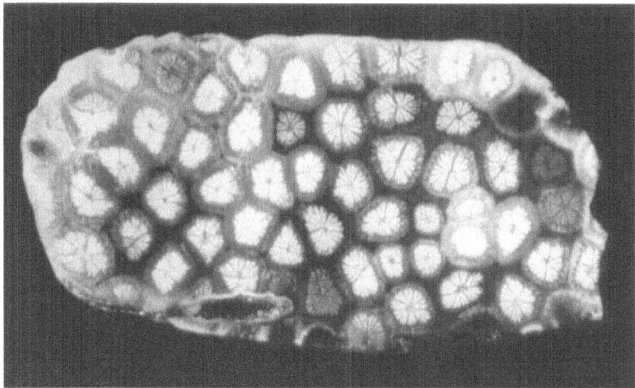

One of two pieces of fossil coral ("starrystone") found in Swanscombe, England, with conchoidal fractures indicating that they had been struck from the parent chert, one hundred twenty miles distant in Wiltshire, by human hands (Oakley 1981). Photograph: British Museum (Natural History).

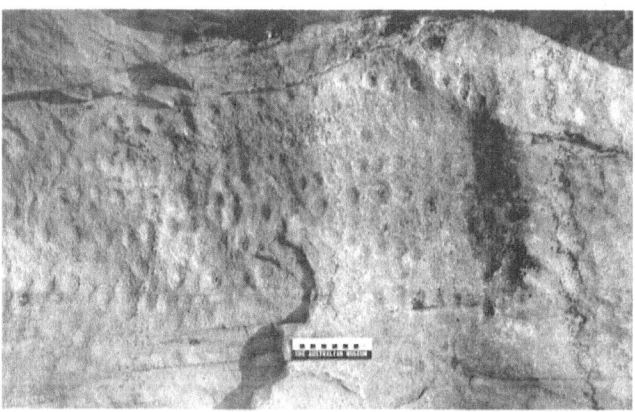

"Cupules" carved on rock-shelter walls, Jinmium, Australia. Photograph: Paul Taçon, Australian Museum.

Rocks and stones of every size seem always to have attracted attention, not only because they were durable and hence of practical use but also because of their beauty or sense of presence and power (Taçon 1991). Nearly a quarter of a million years ago, an archaic human picked up a piece of patterned fossil coral and carried it home from what is now Wiltshire, England, to Swanscombe, one hundred twenty miles distant (Oakley 1981). There is no other explanation for how it could have been transported. The apparent reason is that it looked unusual or beautiful, for it would not have been suitable for flaking. Did its discoverer want to keep it, or show it to another?

In widely dispersed parts of the world we find enormous stones, dressed and undressed, moved from great distances or left in place—stelae, dolmens, menhirs, cromlechs, and other megalithic monuments. Myths and scriptures tell of unhewn stones used for altars. In present-day Australia, at Jinmium (near the town of Kununurra), thousands of nearly identical circular markings, or "cupules," roughly 1.2 inches in diameter, were carved in neat rows on the walls of rock shelters (Fullagar, Price, and Head 1996)—some dated to many tens of thousands of years ago.[4] Like many European Paleolithic images of animals and humans, the cupules at Jinmium and nearby sites appear to have been placed so as to conform to the natural features of the rock wall (Taçon et al. 1997).[5] Their placement alongside or accentuating natural curves, cracks, joints, and boundaries suggests marking and movement through space.

It is important to note that humans do not always simply appropriate the natural world as it is but have everywhere recognized their difference from it as well as their dependence on and interdependence with it. That is, like the Yekuana, they make "cultural" transformations of nature.

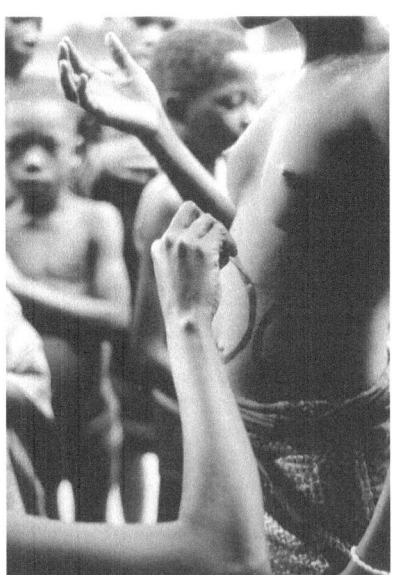 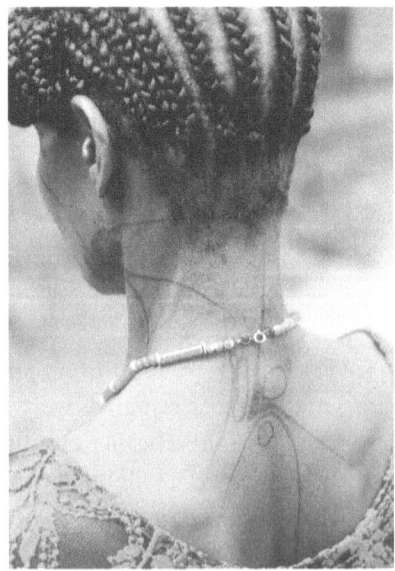

Uli *body painting of young Igbo women, Nigeria, serves to enhance their best features. Photographs: Herbert Cole.*

For example, they do not remain in their birthday suits, as other animals do, but adorn their bodies, sometimes with tattoos, piercings, or scarifications and with paint, beads, fiber bands, and other ornaments. They do not leave their hair unkempt, like animal fur, but restrain it by braiding, tying, or cutting it and adding leaves or bright feathers. They do not make just a rude nest or den but build regularized environments. They do not eat untreated food but cook and otherwise process it.

Early humans not only refashioned the skins, bones, and horns of other animals to serve as implements and tools but often decorated them, too. Regularized, repetitive geometric ornamentation seems to deliberately counteract the random or untidy look of natural forms. Careful decoration, as with the Jinmium rock shelter cupules just mentioned, can be interpreted as an imposition of system or order, perhaps as vicarious regulation and control. By departing from nature, an abstract human or animal figure would automatically appear otherworldly and extraordinary, an assertion of the ideational or spiritual.

Showing their difference from other animals by augmenting ordinary behavior and objects—shaping and elaborating them beyond the requirements of nature—is as defining a characteristic of humans as their manual dexterity, and it is accomplished with their hands. This important human predilection for elaborating and valuing extraordinary experience is treated separately in chapter 5. It grows out of evolved "hands-on" needs for handling, making, doing, and engaging with nature, as much as from the needs for meaning, belonging, and mutuality that were described in earlier chapters.

LEGACIES OF COMPETENCE

The chasm between contemporary life and a "hands-on" life is wider today than it has ever been. Only when a power failure temporarily disrupts the electricity supply do we need to be aware of the weather outside our door. We normally experience the natural world at several removes: dwellings are warm in winter, cool in summer, protected year-round from storm and wind. Water, even hot water, comes from a tap. With a simple switch we vanquish the night. What happens on television or computer screens is what is "real," and soothing recorded natural sounds of ocean waves or rain-forest murmurs artificially help us to "relax."

Compared with our parents and grandparents, most of us do next to nothing with our own hands. Kitchen gadgets, dishwashers, sewing machines, and clothes dryers have replaced hand stirring and chopping, soapsuds and dish towel, needle and thread, and clotheslines. But many people don't even bother with these machines and the raw materials they require. Instead, prepared food, disposable tableware, ready-made clothing, and commercial laundries are almost as cheap and are easily available. We even buy or consume entertainment in movies and on television rather than sing around a piano, play charades, and tell or read stories aloud, as our grandparents did. Such things are considered boring or weird. They take time we don't have.

Handwork and agency—making and doing—are rarities. We rarely need to walk but are transported instead in mechanical conveyances. We don't spin, weave, knit, and sew but buy clothes from the rack in one of dozens of shops at the mall. We don't even have to cook, much less grow or spear our own food, but can open a box and push a button or telephone the nearest Chinese takeout or pizza delivery service.

Deposited by some natural calamity in the wild and left to our own devices, most of us would not know where to begin. We would justifiably feel incompetent and terrified, and we would hate it—the reverse of the way the New Jersey writer Louis Sarno (1993) came to feel in central Africa after living closely with Ba-Benjellé pygmies. Eventually, like them, he found their periodic retreats to the forest to be at once more purposeful and more pleasurable than life in the village near shops and roads.

It is easy enough from a comfortable armchair to romanticize a hands-on life and chastise others for their indolence. The fact remains, however, that our bodies and minds are adapted to lead a life of physical engagement, and when born into it people find it agreeable, even richly rewarding. What is more, there are well-established negative consequences of physical inactivity and alienation from the natural world. One cost of boundless comfort and convenience, of course, is to become fat, flabby, and physically debilitated. Another is the debilitation of our environment. As we have mechanically subjugated the natural sources of our subsistence, we have also befouled them, damaging air, earth, water, and the other creatures whose lives in nature we once shared.[6]

These physical consequences are certainly cause for alarm and deserve to be emphasized at every opportunity. But they are well known, if not well heeded. Here I wish to emphasize another consequence of the repudiation of hands-on living that is less often described. I argue that we also insidiously promote *psychological* unhealthiness and damage by something that may seem paradoxical in an age of pushbutton convenience, namely, decreasing our ability to feel competent in our lives. I refer to that sense of helpless frustration we feel in a traffic jam or in a voice-mail loop. If only one could get out and walk, or speak to a real person—really reach out and touch someone.

For even as we greedily consume the products of science and technology, and as our minds are challenged and filled more than those of any previous humans with information and knowledge about the world, many of us in fast-paced, fast-changing, impersonal, pluralistic societies feel less and less that we personally affect our world. The more technological "control" we have, the less direct hands-on control, and it is the latter—what I earlier called an *aptitude for life*—that we evolved to acquire, like the Yekuana, over a lifetime. Humans need to believe and feel that their efforts are appropriate and likely to succeed. We want to know not only what to do but also that we are competent or able enough to do it.

No other animal has to acquire an aptitude for life. The very notion sounds ridiculous: aptitude for life is what they are born with. Although there is surely a continuum from so-called lower to higher animals in the degree of learning or fine-tuning required for taking up normal adult activities, and although no infant animal matures without external influence, nonhuman animals come into the world well prepared to lead the life of their kind. For young humans, by contrast, life is a succession of increasingly complex skills to be learned and problems to be solved, and youngsters are remarkably keen to assimilate the methods, rules, and explanations that their cultures provide as the "right" way, "the way things are done." In preindustrial societies, areas of competence require practice, but they are generally straightforward, presented as normal, necessary, and within the ability of nearly everyone. Life itself is composed of such activities. The effect of each one is immediately evident, and it seems therefore worthwhile.

By contrast, although the institutions of modern life demand many accomplishments if one is to be granted full membership—grades and examinations passed, certificates, licenses, and possessions acquired—we do not have a set of *tidi'uma*, things that all adults have made with their hands to demonstrate their participation in material and moral culture. Instead we, Americans in particular, acquire a sense of worth through competitive accomplishment and achievement.

It begins very early, as parents—at least those in what used to be called the middle class—note with interest when their baby first holds its head up, rolls over, sits alone, stands alone, takes a first step, says a first word. These abilities are not celebrated with a *haven* party, as in Papua New Guinea, which instills in a child a sense of being part of a social group. Rather, these individual milestones, and especially their precocity, prove that one child is smarter or better coordinated than another—and after this one step up the ladder of success an infinite number still remain. I do not remember preschool-age children in the non-Western countries where I have lived shouting insistently "Look at me!" as they successfully negotiate the sliding board at the playground or hang by their knees from the jungle gym. I think that already such claims for attention indicate the excessive need to be acknowledged for one's achievements that is fostered in contemporary individualistic societies. Even as adults we have to keep meticulous track of our own accomplishments on resumés, and we automatically report those of our families (along with their maturational milestones of birthdays and weddings) at the end of every year in one-size-fits-all holiday letters. So common is this that no one even thinks it odd.

To be sure, people everywhere want to be able to do what their cultures esteem as proper. If women's role is to have children, then barren women feel incomplete. If men are hunters or warriors or owners of many pigs, those who fail at these things feel inadequate. But the requirements of traditional societies generally fall within the range of average human abilities.

In modern societies, where success is measured by things purchased or things consumed rather than things made, adequacy (or competence) entails an unprecedented sort of exclusiveness. We have to *earn*, not make, a living, and so we choose (or fall into) one specialized field instead of addressing an array of tasks. People want not just any job but a *good* job—one that provides a lot of money to enable the purchase of possessions. The deck has been stacked, however, so that good jobs are not just a matter of "ability" but of one specialized ability: the manipulation of written symbols and information.[7]

Most people have never thought about the fact that of all the ancestral life activities that were performed over the tens of thousands of generations of human evolution, none required this most essential skill of contemporary life. The faculties and talents that sustained our species in ancestral environments for hundreds of thousands of years were evolved for activities such as making fire, tracking, finding raw materials and properly preparing them, fashioning implements and using them correctly, swimming, climbing trees, navigating, assessing distances, predicting weather, assisting childbirths and treating wounds or illnesses, dancing,

singing, playing games, telling stories. Even analytic skills such as naviga-
tion or assessing distances could be accomplished without numbers. Our
ancestors learned largely by watching and doing, not by reading or even
by verbal instruction.

Children, premodern and prehistoric people, and the rest of us
commonly and naturally use ancestral abilities that are visuo-spatial, mechanical, musical, oral-verbal, social, and bodily (or kinesthetic)—that is,
*non*literate. We vary, one from the other, in the degree to which we can
develop these abilities, but we evolved to have adequate competence in
all and skill in one or two.

In modern society, which exalts literate skill and analytic problem
solving, persons whose natural abilities are greater in these other kinds of
accomplishment are disadvantaged. And even these people, if they are less
than Olympic-caliber athletes or Juilliard or Cordon Bleu graduates, may
feel inadequate and discouraged because their skills are not good enough.
Yet in earlier societies, even at the beginning of this century, these skills
would have found a valued place, and their possessors would have felt aptitude for life. When nonverbal competencies atrophy, we remain unaware of their age-old satisfactions.

As the British poet Phoebe Hesketh (1994) observed, whirling spin-
dles have been replaced today by flickering screens.[8] Our marvelous,
long-evolved, specialized hands, which can weave baskets, fashion arrows,
or mold vessels, are now used chiefly for pressing buttons on appliances
and computer keyboards. Although the electronic world of computers is
praised for being so engaging to children and for allowing them to feel
more quickly competent (compared with the difficulties of learning to
read and write), there are significant differences from the kind of hands-
on dealing with the natural world for which young people are inherently
equipped. Even though computer literacy may be essential for life in the
twenty-first century, ultimately I believe that it still leaves important
needs for life aptitude or competence unsatisfied and even unacknowl-
edged (see also Bowers n.d.).

Yet the entertainments proffered by videotape players and computers obviously appeal to natural predilections, since so many children seem
irresistibly drawn to cartoons and electronic games, just as their elders are
addicted to television watching and the Internet. In her long career as an
art therapist, Edith Kramer has worked with many hospitalized children.
Until recently, she says, the opportunity to use art materials with a real
person outcompeted television every time (in Williams et al. 1997). But

with the availability of video games, children's preference for art making no longer holds. Why do mechanical contrivances now seem to satisfy their undeniable needs for attention, companionship, and physical activity? She proposes an intriguing answer.

Kramer likens video games to what animal behaviorists call a "supernormal stimulus." Many animals are innately receptive to certain clear signals that automatically cause them to respond adaptively, as when a female duck is stimulated to roll large, white, oval objects into her nest, or bird parents to stuff insects into a gaping, red-throated beak. In normal environments, a white oval object is a duck's own egg, which has become unlodged, and the open beak is that of one of the bird's offspring begging to be fed. But an experimenter can place an unnaturally ("supernormally") large white oval object next to the nest, and the duck will repeatedly attempt to roll it, even neglecting her own eggs. The parent birds will preferentially feed a baby cuckoo's larger, redder open beak rather than the smaller, paler gapes of their own young. Birds whose recognition preference is for stout sticks to build a nest, perfectly adaptive in the wild, may in cities choose pieces of wire instead.

Kramer suggests that by using evolved capacities to respond to easily recognizable, clear signals of lifelike figures in active movement, video games and other television programs "supernormally" engage children's normal appetites for action, excitement, competition, and mastery and their propensity for boundless fantasy—adventure, violence, magical thinking. Even chimpanzees in research laboratories find the constant colorful movement in television cartoons and advertisements engrossing.

Yet while children, like chimpanzees, are being distracted, amused, or mesmerized, other things are happening (or not happening). Compared with the superstars they see—comic superheroes or real-life sports and entertainment figures—children's own actions and inventions seem paltry. While stories for young people have always emphasized adventure and impossibility, the action, violence, and practical jokes of video games and television—their magical tricks and supernatural powers—are capricious and exaggerated: they promote faulty or false assumptions about what is real or possible. What is more, they do not lend themselves to deeper reflection or encourage development in a child's own imagination. If anything, they foster delusion. A good question to ponder in a quiet moment is, which is more "real," the virtual or the imaginary?

Although video games may satisfy a need for hands-on competence, they do so without the benefits of the lessons of *real* hands-on play, action, and adventure in an actual social and natural environment. Pressing keys or clicking a mouse is not like building or making real things. Real materials may resist as well as obey; they make clear their own sometimes unforgiving physical laws. Handling them generates a kind of exchange between body and mind that is absent in computer art. Nor does electronic play give the same kind of practice as material play in sustaining physical effort or learning to *use*, not escape, boredom. Kramer notes the "false fatigue" and desire to quit that can be met and overcome in a sort of psychological "second wind" that children can learn with persistence, often by encouragement from another.

Seductively "interactive" as it may be, or become, electronic communication remains cognitive and disembodied, the reverse of mutuality. It does not matter with whom we communicate, what kind of persons they are, or where they are (Alonso 1995). The emphasis is on the willingness of participants to continue to exchange information, not to share experience. (I find it noteworthy that the need for face-to-face communication is apparently so engrained in human nature that Internet intimates usually feel a strong desire to meet.)

Because they cannot learn the skills of reading others' facial expressions, forming friendships, building alliances, or making compromises, which require actual others in proximity, youngsters whose play is primarily with computers also do not develop physical agility, courage, or strength. Like laboratory or domestic animals, they may not know "what to do" outdoors. Attached to electronic devices, how can they learn the real possibilities of their surroundings?

No matter how essential electronic media become or how virtual the realities they provide for us, we are still living creatures who require interaction with the natural world. The young Wordsworth, roaming the hills of his native Cumberland, felt nature as "all in all," "the joy / Of elevated thoughts; a sense sublime / Of something far more deeply interfused . . . / A motion and a spirit, that impels / All thinking things, all objects of all thought, / And rolls through all things." In a world full of change and uncertainty, the natural world provides acquaintance with abiding and inspiring continuities and structure. It is where we came from, what we are a part of, and where we will go. If we do not know this, of what use or good is the rest of our knowledge?

Today's Wordsworths can hardly commune with nature on their rambles, since they are wearing radio headsets or talking on cellular telephones. And even when we stay at home (or do anything—ride in cars or airplanes, sit in airports, go shopping) we lead our lives to background commentary or music. The ever-present radio and audiocassette or CD player have made possible a world in which being quietly alone and idle is not so much a luxury as something unwelcome, something to avoid. People are more familiar with the voices of distant strangers in their ears than with the thoughts inside their own heads, which require silence—the growth medium of one's inner life—in order to take shape and rise to the surface to surprise or engage us.

At least video games are "interactive": they call for participation. How does the passivity of television watching, our involuntary absorption of its messages, affect our sense of competence for life? Between ages three and eighteen, says Neil Postman (1993), the average young person watches half a million television commercials. The primary values that are imparted are the opposite of the sorts of values transmitted by ceremonies of the traditional societies in which we were evolved to find identity, meaning, and a sense of competence.

First among these modern values is that self-fulfillment is the natural pursuit and meaning of life and that it is in large part accomplished by achieving an ever-heightened good time and freedom from constraint. Although the young in traditional societies are bound by custom and authority, this social swaddling serves as a security blanket. Severance from the apron strings of family and societal expectations, by contrast, can be exhilarating—but it can also make a young person feel like a solitary balloon released into emptiness. When the purpose of life is only to have fun, the good times can easily roll, pitch, and plunge headlong into a slough of despond.

A related modern value is intolerance for tradition, a hostility to rules (of courtesy, decorum, manners). Active priority is given to overthrowing authority, hierarchy, and structure—to "making it new." Fashion and obsolescence are built into every imaginable human pursuit. Different is good, as is constant, unceasing choice. In complex, fast-moving, technological societies, people must thrive on chaos, be flexible and willing to change. Thus change for its own sake becomes a virtue. Nothing is carved in stone; everything is written in sand—or in cyberspace, which makes it even more transitory.

In today's world, for the first time in human history, the fleeting and transient, the throwaway and ever novel, and the virtual or mediated predominate over what is lasting, substantial, traditional, and "real" or "true." Yet our evolved propensities for belonging and meaning suggest that humans require shared, believable systems and stories. Perhaps contemporary values of individual fulfillment, ceaseless fun, continual change, and limitless choice should themselves be regarded as supernormal stimuli that appeal to humans' adaptive attraction to independent movement, pleasure, and novelty, which once signaled or reinforced real things that needed to be paid attention to. Like similar attractions to sugar and fat, which could not be overindulged in ancestral environments because of inadequate opportunity, our appetite for these once-adaptive but high-calorie psychological states leads to pathology.

Social reactions to media oversaturation range from wholehearted acceptance to withdrawal or ostrichlike denial. Some of us "go with it"—either bravely or swept along in the tide—trying to keep up with new advances. Others find refuge in the past, advocating simple old-fashioned solutions such as returning to traditional ways: back to basics.

And indeed, keeping company (if not pace) with the relentless march to an everchanging future is a return to tradition and to nature. Cynics may place nostalgia and the great outdoors among other marketable fashionable pursuits—and they are often presented as such. But I think they are also, and perhaps even more, expressions of the fitful atavistic urges of a suffering, expiring creature to take in mortal sustenance.

Although machines have today released humans from wearisome labor, and although manual work is often considered boring or even contemptible, there is evidence that the "continuity, effort, pleasure, and endless repetition" of our first motor activities continue to be satisfying. People cook "for relaxation" and take cooking classes for recreation. A 1994 survey by the Knitting Guild of America found twenty-five million knitters in the United States. Attendance at their national conferences and conventions had grown by 25 percent in the preceding three years (Falick 1996).

Numerous craftspeople claim to enjoy the mundane, repetitive actions of scraping, sanding, planing, weaving, stitching, knitting, hatching, beating, throwing, turning, and polishing that are traditionally part of careful making. A young ceramicist, Tré Arenz (1995, 70–71), even deliberately commemorates labor, both in the time and physical care she expends on the objects she makes and in her state of mind as she works. Rather than "go through the motions" automatically, with an empty or wandering mind, Arenz chooses to work *mind*fully—as in careful striping, which is certainly repetitive but requires attention. Arenz paraphrases Walker Percy: "The most dangerous thing most of us will have to

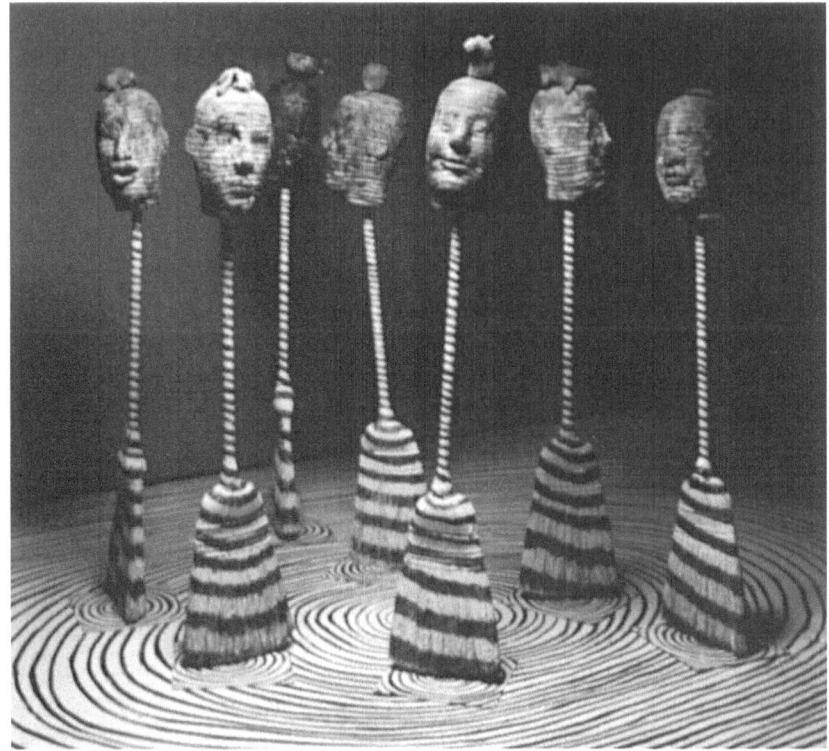

Tré Arenz, "Distractions," 1995–96, ceramic, fiberglass, broom, paint, steel. Arenz's work "involves a celebration of making through the use of multiple objects and repetition in relation to ordinary domestic routine or ritual. . . . But repetition can be mindful" (Arenz 1995). Photograph: C. Zaleski.

face is a lifetime of ordinary days." Yet by acknowledging the "malady of the quotidian" (to quote a line from Wallace Stevens),[9] she recognizes and celebrates it rather than acquiescing to the predictable and tedious, which all too easily deadens people into accepting things as they are.

Repetitive work can also engender a kind of contemplative state with access to remote parts of the mind seldom available to those who dash continually after novel experiences (except perhaps, to a degree, while driving long distances alone on superhighways, or on trivial assembly-line work). I have not done a controlled survey, but my subjective impression is that potters or ceramicists, more than people of other occupations, seem to be "down to earth," "grounded," and "centered." By this I mean that they lack pretension, are not adherents of insubstantial philosophies, and have

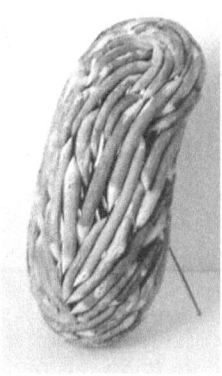 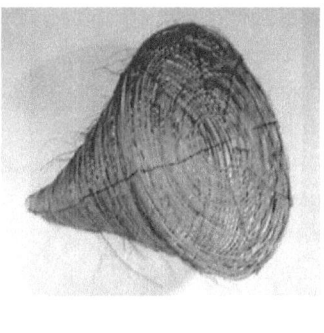

Sculptures from natural materials by Gina Telcocci, Santa Fe, New Mexico. "My preference is for simple, direct ways of working. There is something that happens when you work with a particular material by hand over time. You become intimate with it and with the process so that a kind of energy and spirit come through the object that make it special" (artist's statement, 1997).

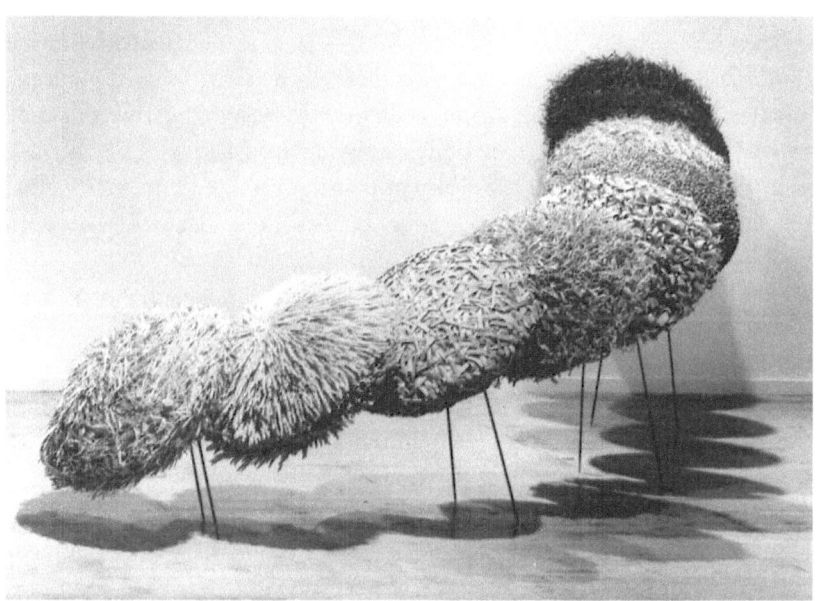

"Spinners," mixed media installation, 1997, by Lyndal Osborne, Edmonton, Alberta, Canada. Sage, day lilies, rhubarb seeds, dogwood, lime grass, yellow willow, cattail leaves, reeds, wire, spear-grass, gaillardia seeds, and palm leaves. The artist subjects her found materials to cutting, clipping, binding, weaving, dyeing, papering, painting, and casting. Repetition of both form and activity in her work is essential "to suggesting the flow of time which is a significant component of each object's full nature" (catalog essay, 1997).

considered ideas about their work and their place in the world. Although few hold doctorates, their reflections and ruminations (as expressed in, say, issues of *Studio Potter* or *American Craft*) often show a depth and clarity of insight that academic theorists might well envy. Perhaps clayworkers' handling of a humble yet elemental material like mud, their participation in the ongoing circular motion of the wheel, and their ultimate acceptance of the inevitability yet possible fecundity of accident in the firing of their work facilitate insights into the human condition and contribute to their integrity as persons.

Certainly hand use, like other activities of the body, can be a "way of knowing." The composer Stravinsky described, in hindsight, his own fascination with his creation of *Petrouchka*: "The different rhythmic episodes were dictated by the fingers themselves. . . . Fingers are not to be despised; they are great inspirers and in contact with a musical instrument often give birth to unconscious ideas which might otherwise never come to life" (cited in Gardner 1993a, 220). The connection between hand and brain is commonly noted by makers of visual objects and rarely expressed by composers, although surely *improvised* music (which, before there were written scores, all music surely was), such as jazz, also emanates from the rhythms and modes of hand and body. Indeed, artists, musicians, dancers, athletes, lovers—performers in all media—will attest to the independence and wisdom of the hand's or body's knowledge. Making then allows a kind of engagement with the real world and access to a kind of spiritual self-enlargement that, except for a few handworkers like artists, modern people have largely forfeited.

There is a subtle distinction to be made between the attributes "repetitious" (as boring) and "repetitive" (as recurring). If we find everyday work monotonous, let us not forget that nature itself is cyclical or repetitive, and human work in the world, concerned with the daily round and the cycles of the seasons, has a rhythm and recurrence that for millennia have given satisfaction to people because they evolved to be part of it.

Traditional life recognizes no sharp separation between work and leisure, a notion that has grown out of industrialization, where "useless toil" in factories replaced "useful work" for one's own life needs. In premodern life, there are tasks that need to be done, some more arduous than others, but little if any notion that these might be demeaning. Work is not simply a way to make a living but a framework for the rhythms and regularities of daily activity. As in the Yekuana house or garden, structure and system are inherent in the whole of life, and it is this whole, evident in all things, that provides meaning.

Ralph Waldo Emerson distinguished between what he called "job work" and the "main design" of life. He considered job work to be "the crime which bankrupts men and states" since it required people "to serve a turn here or there," thus deflecting them from their main design. This sentiment sounds odd today, when getting, keeping, and advancing in a job in order to make money has become the main design of most people's lives.

By "main design," Emerson meant, I believe, having a greater purpose to which earning a living is viewed as a means. "Nothing is beneath you," he said, "if it is in the direction of your life: nothing is great or desirable, if it is off from that." The notion is reminiscent of the master narrative discussed in chapter 3, the sense of life mission or divine plan to which everything is subordinated. Raising a child and building a marriage can be seen as other main designs in whose broader flow the tedious details become more easily sustained.

For our remote ancestors, as for the Yekuana, the direction or main design of their lives was inherent in its very living as their cultures presented it to them; their daily tasks, large and small, were all part of that main design. Since we, their descendants, are here many generations later, they obviously found the tasks of everyday life acceptable. Ancestral humans who found ordinary work despicable would certainly have perished and thereby removed from the gene pool their tendency to shun useful labor.

Modern cultures present most of us with job work as the means to purchasing the goods and necessities of life that we no longer make for ourselves. Job work is different from a person's "main design." Using Emerson's distinctions, I have observed that people who conceive of a main design to their lives beyond getting and spending are able to think of the menial routines of every day, including their "jobs," as contributing to this and making it possible, and thus are able to find "great and desirable" meaning rather than monotonous toil or bankruptcy in their lives. For most people today, however, it is the main design that has been lost sight of. (There is also the workaholic, whose job may seem to be a calling but is actually an addiction.) Job work bankrupts and is beneath us when it becomes the only pattern we can discern.

Between 1890 and 1910, in both the United States and Great Britain, hundreds of craft communities and workshops were formed in response to industrialism and its "morally destructive cycle of boredom and monotony at work followed by the pursuit of leisure completely unconnected with the work or workplace" (Ruskin, cited in MacCarthy 1994, 70; on the founding of communities, see MacCarthy, 602–3). John Ruskin, who with William Morris was a pioneer figure in the British Arts and Crafts Movement, thought that in the disconnection between work and leisure lay "social neurosis." He also challenged the distinction between manual labor and intellect: "The workman ought often to be thinking, and the thinker often to be working" (Ruskin 1851). The hero of George Eliot's 1866 novel *Felix Holt, The Radical* was an educated man who chose the life of an artisan.

A century later, in a now global economy, Morris's vision of communities of handworkers seems even more utopian than it must have seemed in Victorian Britain. Here and there, however, even today, such communities—guilds and schools of crafts—still exist. The fact that such places and the attitudes they embody are impractical does not mean they are misguided.

5

Elaborating

THE PREVIOUS FOUR chapters have introduced and described four psychobiological needs or capacities inherent in humans everywhere. They emerge during infancy and persist throughout life. To summarize, we are born with an unlearned readiness to seek and respond to mutuality, to belong to a group, to find and make (and share) meaning, and to handle and make things with our hands from the natural world, thereby acquiring a sense of competence for life.

These distinctive features of human nature were essential to the survival of our early ancestors and are still integral to the human way of life. They are called forth, expressed, and developed by means of special sensitivities to what I have called rhythms and modes that are experienced in emotional engagements with familiar others. They are infused with associations from interactions with the materiality of the physical world.

In this chapter I suggest that these same sensitivities to the rhythms and modes of love and natural being-in-the-world have further predisposed us to make and respond to the arts, and that it has been through the arts that humans have additionally called forth, expressed, and developed their penchants for belonging, meaning, and "hands-on" competence. In other words, contrary to contemporary understanding, I intend to show that the arts have been intrinsic to human life, inextricably entangled with the most fundamental endowments of human psychobiology.

Let us look again at the features of rhythms and modes that evolved to engender and sustain affiliative emotion and accord between infants and their loving caretakers. Those features are sounds, facial expressions, and movements (vocal, visual, and kinesic signals) that are temporally and spatially patterned, dynamically varied, multimodally presented, and multimodally received. These properties of rhythms and modes characterize not only the intimate play of mothers and infants but also ritual ceremonies—the songs, dances, and other means by which people have perennially become part of a group and have articulated (and felt) its meaningful systems and stories. Such rhythmic-modal properties further apply to the rudiments of creating and experiencing the temporal arts and suggest at least some of the motivations for and satisfactions of handling and participating with the forms and substances of natural materials in the living world.

What these rhythms and modes of mutuality, ceremony, and art have in common—making them different from ordinary communication and behavior—is what I call *elaboration*. I want further to claim that the degree and kind of elaboration is an outgrowth, manifestation, and indication to others of strong feeling or care. But how did this come to be? And why in our species alone should elaboration (ceremony and art) have grown from the attentions and exchanges of love (mutuality)? The answers (and their ramifications) are interesting and complex and will occupy the remainder of this chapter and indeed the rest of the book.

Although many other animals, like humans, have a social life with others and certainly have strong feelings about satisfying their needs, humans differ from other animals in the degree to which we can (and must) learn life-sustaining skills from our fellows and to which we are emotionally influenced by their actions and regard. We also differ in the cajolements of our highly imaginative and innovative minds.

The human abundance of sociality and wits has enabled interesting lives but also seems to have ensured that we are the most insecure of creatures. Unlike humans, other animals have no need to wear lucky charms or say prayers to help them find, or escape becoming, food. They do not waste time or energy worrying about the near or distant future or regretting and mulling over their past mistakes.[1]

Humans, however, do remember good and bad things and can imagine them happening again. Possessing foresight, we predict and plan and are aware of the desired possibilities and inevitable uncertainties of life. We *do* worry. Rather than rely on instinctive programs—chase, run away, don't move, lunge for his throat, erect fur and hiss, assume lordosis, sing like mad—we want to influence our lives, not only covering the bases but also stacking the cards in favor of our vital interests. We use our inventive brains to contrive myriad ways to influence the outcomes of these significant and valuable ventures: we create additional, extraneous meaning.

This peculiarly human response to the necessities and uncertainties of existence is usually called "religion," a property of human life that seems surely related to the arts and that (like art) is notoriously difficult to define or to discuss with universal applicability.

Like art, but unlike writing or gunpowder or democracy, religion cannot be pinned to a specific time or place of invention, although most prehistorians assign the earliest indications of both "religion" and "art" to between forty thousand and sixty thousand years ago. Both are found in every known society and have been remarkably persistent—for example, despite decades of well-organized atheistic education and propaganda, neither the Soviets nor the Chinese communists succeeded in eradicating either religion or the elaborations of song, picturing, and formal language that embody it. Although far more attention has been paid to religion as a human requirement than to the arts, in fact the two seem to be inseparable. This is because the meaningful systems and stories by which religions explain the world and join their adherents in common cause are everywhere garbed in—given potency through—rhythmic-modal presentations.

In a recent book, Walter Burkert, perhaps the most learned scholar today of early religion and its biological or evolutionary antecedents, describes three common characteristics of religion (Burkert 1996, 4–8).[2] First, religion deals with the nonobvious, "that which cannot be verified empirically." It thus commonly invokes special forms of experience (for example, paranormal or altered states such as meditation, vision, and ecstasy) that are accepted and interpreted by a majority of normal people as ways to get beyond the barrier of unclearness. Second, religion manifests itself through interaction and communication with nonobvious entities or partners such as spirits, demons, gods, and ancestors. And third, religion is profoundly serious—in the words of theologian Paul Tillich, a matter of "ultimate concern."

I would add a fourth characteristic to Burkert's formulations, or would derive an additional implication from them: religion's serious concerns, its acquaintance with special or nonobvious forms of experience, and its interactions with nonobvious entities or partners require and result in special kinds of elaborative behaviors, usually called rituals or ceremonies but in essence and in fact composed of rhythmic-modal behaviors, or *arts*.

THE RAW, THE COOKED, AND THE GOURMET

One of my most unforgettable moments was being handed a stone tool made by an archaic *Homo sapiens* and told by the distinguished paleontologist Kenneth Oakley that it was probably around two hundred fifty thousand years old. (Other tools made by hominid ancestors go back even further—over two million years, in fact.) I held it in my palm with what surely resembled the feeling of a religious devotee who has been allowed to touch a holy relic—a sense of privilege, humility, and wonder.

The tool was what is called a hand ax, almost exactly the shape and size of the inside of my open hand, made from a piece of flint of an army-jeep brownish green sort of color. Twenty-five times earlier than the invention of agriculture, someone not so different from myself had taken up a large cobble, assessed it, and fashioned this very tool. Of course he (or she?) could not have imagined the living room or city or time in which someone like me would one day come to hold it and wonder about the life and being of the person who made and used it. That asymmetry was one of countless others between us. And yet holding the hand ax like a talisman, I felt a connection to its maker that I still can retrieve (even if, just as with the person who touches a relic, whether of saint or famous athlete, the feeling has as much to do with me as with the material object or its owner).

In any event, I was interested much later to read an account the naturalist Loren Eiseley (1979, 270–71) wrote of his thoughts and emotions while he, too, held a flint tool shaped by human hands "hundreds of thousands of years ago." Admiring its purposefulness, he noticed something that he found to be even more remarkable:

> As I clasped and unclasped the stone, running my fingers down its edges, I began to perceive the ghostly emanations from a long-vanished mind, the kind of mind which, once having shaped an object of any sort, leaves an individual trace behind it which speaks to others across the barriers of time and language. It was not the practical experimental aspect of this mind that startled me, but rather that the fellow had wasted time.
>
> In an incalculably brutish and dangerous world he had both shaped an instrument of practical application and then, with a virtuoso's elegance, proceeded to embellish his product. He had not been content to produce a plain, utilitarian implement. . . . This archaic creature had lingered over his handiwork.

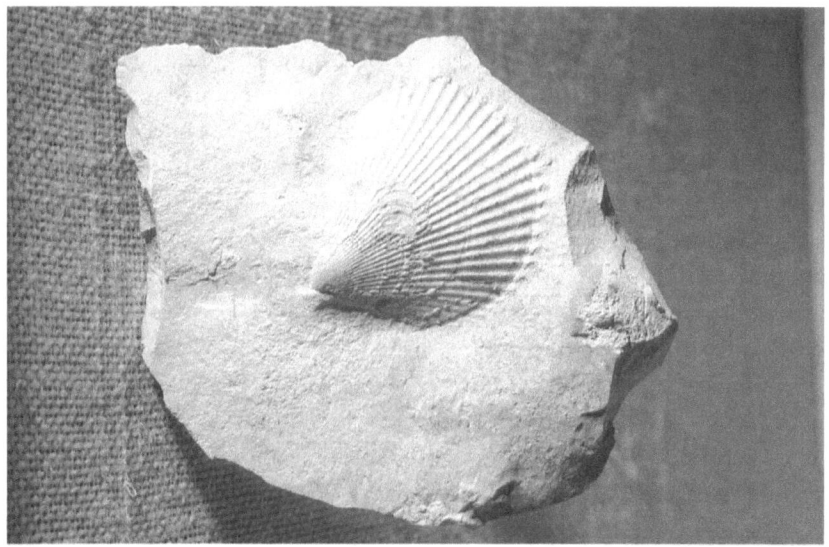

Paleolithic scraper, flaked with regard for its embedded fossil shell. Museum, Pech-Merle, Lot-en-Quercy, France. Photograph by Alain Turk; courtesy of Musée National de Préhistoire, Les Eyzies.

I had not noticed embellishment on the hand ax I had held. It had been enough simply to recognize human fabrication.

Eiseley was understandably impressed to see this early evidence of elaboration, that is, the taking of additional time and care. Indeed, Dr. Oakley had also that day showed me photographs of two different hand axes (again from two hundred fifty thousand years ago) that had been deliberately fashioned so that a marine fossil (a mollusc and an echinoid, each already embedded in the larger piece of rock) was in a central, focal position—almost like an insignia (see photographs in Dissanayake 1988, 54). Decades later I saw yet another example—a scraper rather than a hand ax—in the museum at Pech Merle in France.

French anthropologist Claude Lévi-Strauss (1969) titled a famous essay "The Raw and the Cooked" in order to describe the universal human imperative to transform "nature" into humanly usable "culture." Such transformations characterize humans everywhere, as when present-day Yekuana convert raw, poisonous *tapa* into processed and cooked edible cassava, when the earliest toolmakers worked flints into usable implements, and when modern technocracies turn silicon into microchips.

Herbert Cole, an American anthropologist, has given Lévi-Strauss's now axiomatic phrase additional explanatory bite by referring, he tells me, to the raw, the cooked, and the *gourmet*. Cole thereby calls attention to the curious fact that for humans, transforming nature into culture may not always be in itself enough, as it was not for the tool maker whose embellishment so impressed Eiseley. In his studies of the Yekuana, David Guss makes it also clear that for them it is insufficient simply to plant or reap, to set out in a canoe, to treat a wound or illness, to begin to menstruate, to kill an animal, to marry, or to die. As in other traditional societies, these are all occasions for elaborated accompanying actions and words, even though to a modern "bottom-line" orientation such elaborations may appear quite unnecessary.

Unlike other animals, humans characteristically do more than is necessary—they "waste time," "linger over their handiwork," gild the lily, go to extremes. They mentally transform the stuff of nature into "meaningful," culturally usable systems and stories, and then they make these even more elaborate and extravagant by vivid description, repetition, and other rhythmic and modal devices of emphasis, added figuration, or intensification.[3]

ELABORATING AS ADAPTIVE

The characteristic of human nature that I am calling here "elaborating" (elsewhere [Dissanayake 1988, 1992, 1995] I called it "making special") is, like art and religion, often overlooked by evolutionary biologists—it is assumed to be simply a cultural overlay, as if that were an explanation. To the unsentimental gaze of an evolutionary biologist looking for "selective value," elaborating is truly perplexing. What ends could it possibly accomplish? The other human capacities described here—mutuality, belonging, making meaning, and developing manual-mental competency—all clearly contribute to survival. But elaborating would appear to interfere with fitness, certainly not enhance it.

It is an axiom of evolutionary theory that successful creatures expend their resources on survival-related ends—finding food, protecting themselves from harm, putting aside for a rainy day, seeking mates and mating, caring for offspring, and, after all these are attended to, *conserving* their energy. Yet there we are, in every society: people adorning themselves, their artifacts, and their surroundings, making music, dancing, dramatizing, poeticizing, often expending vast quantities of time, energy, and material resources in this pursuit of specialness, of excess, of elaboration. Is this not dangerously impractical and frivolous—ultimate cost ex-

ceeding temporary benefit? The fact of elaboration, at least as a biological predisposition, might seem to embed a big fat thorn into the corpus
of evolutionary orthodoxy.

The usual evolutionary explanations for extravagant behaviors like
these have been that their individual male perpetrators are gaining reproductive success by outcompeting other males in displaying their mental
powers of creativity and protean expressiveness (Miller 1998) or their physical skill, strength, and stamina. By singing, dancing, or speaking well, or
by skillful building, males draw attention to the superior qualities that set
them apart from less talented or tireless males. They are then preferentially
chosen by the ladies, of whom they can take their pick. In the animal world,
there are visual, architectural, musical, and terpsichorean analogues to our
own species' male theatrics: the peacock's splendiferous tail, the bower-
bird's *chambre d'amour*, the songbird's territorial warbles, and the Indian
bustard's acrobatic dances all either repel rivals, seduce females, or both.[4]

Yet while we all know about the proverbial allure of the human artist-
stud—the sweet talker, the sexy dancer, the master builder—or of the
king whose power is evident in the palaces and monuments he is able to
command, sheer male competition seems to be only part of the explanation for human elaborations. Although male competition is an undisputed
fact of human evolution, as it has been in the evolution of many other animals, I do not think that it alone can adequately account for such products of human elaboration as, for example, Paleolithic cave paintings in
France, Spain, and elsewhere, the megaliths of prehistoric Europe, the un-
derground tombs of the Pharaohs, monumental sculpture, the temple of
Kailash at Ellora, the Gothic cathedrals of Europe built over centuries by
whole communities, Asmat *bisj* poles, Abelam and Arapesh *haus tambaran*,
feather capes in Hawaii (each requiring from eighty thousand to ninety
thousand birds), the whole-body tattoos of the Marquesans or the deep,
chiseled, full-face tattoos of Maori males, body designs in aboriginal Australia painted with a man's own blood, the months- or years-long preparations for visual displays in *mbari* or Gèlèdé or Carnaval, or the hours of
uninterrupted dancing, drumming, singing, and chanting in countless societies, near and far, past and present.

Although some of these activities are the province only of males or
are made possible only by a sufficiently powerful force that can coordinate the labor of many men, and although the talents and stamina of individual men may be given prominence, other evidence indicates that
male competition is only one, and not the most important, driving force

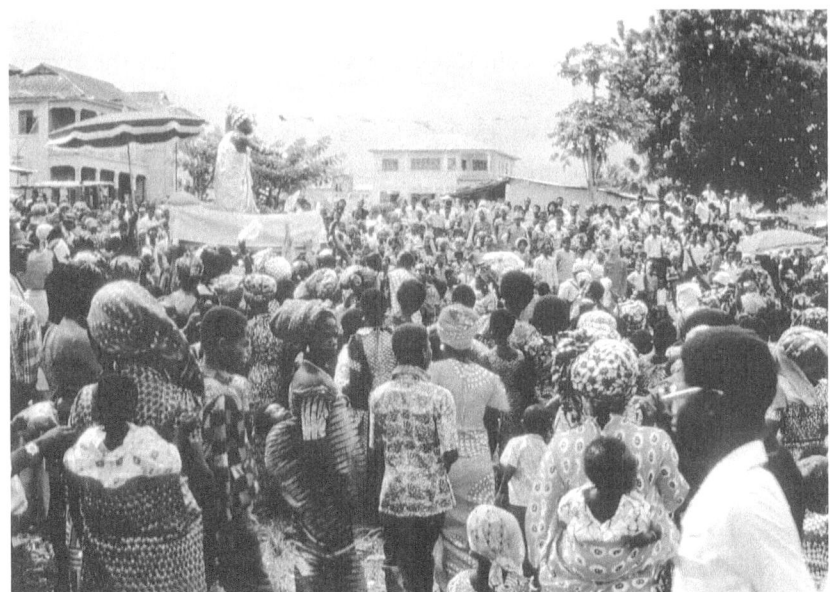

While artful rhetoric draws attention to the speaker, it also brings people together in common purpose. Akan festival, Ghana. Photograph: Herbert Cole.

for human elaborations. Male competition cannot account for the arts of females (which may be less spectacular and arduous than those of males but are as evident throughout human history), for the arts of men and women older than prime reproductive age (who may be the master elaborators in a society), or for the obvious fact that the arts, even when they also serve competitive interests, are often co-created and performed by more than one person. The last is especially the case in premodern societies, where the arts transmit valued systems and stories ("meanings") and unite individuals in social groups.

Nor does the male competition explanation account for the fact that in many instances even apparently mundane objects and activities may be elaborated. For example, in parts of India, the horns of the bullock that pulls a cart are painted—one red, one blue—and garlanded with a string of brass bells and large beads. The modest wooden cart may also be painted with little designs. At harvest, the threshing floor is painted with magical symbols. Drivers of buses, lorries, and cycle rickshaws outline the inside of their windshields with intricately cut frames of colored paper or chains of flowers, adding tinted pictures of gods. Before setting out on a trip,

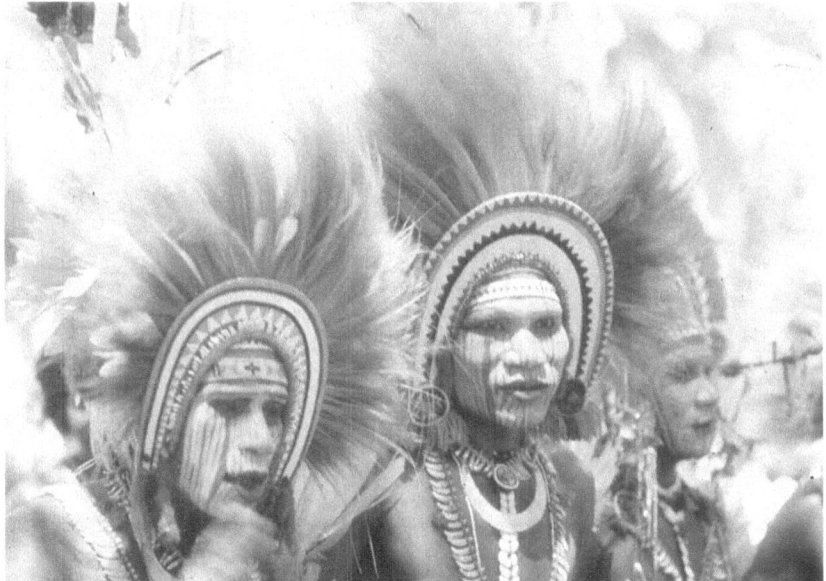

Mekeo males of Papua New Guinea look splendid with their yellow painted faces, headdresses of costly bird-of-paradise plumes, and valuable shell ornaments. In such attire they advertise group identity and solidarity as much as each man's individual difference. Photograph: Pamela Rosi.

some drivers light a stick of incense in a container on the dashboard. The fragrant smoke pervades the journey and sets it apart from the routine world outside.

The sorts of things that attract special attention and elaboration (for example, bullocks, carts, threshing floors, windshields, journeys—and, among the Yekuana, gardens, canoes, medical treatments, monthly bleeding, game animals) are almost always involved with biologically important or "meaningful" life concerns, and the attentions and elaborations often serve to relieve anxiety about their successful attainment and preservation. Thus, before cutting down a tree in order to carve a canoe, a Yekuana feels that he must first commune with the supernatural power that controls the tree, negotiating its transfer of ownership. If this is not done, not only will the artifact be flawed but also the spirit accompanying it will be hostile and vengeful, leading to disease and possible death. As David Guss says, ritual tools are therefore as essential as physical ones for the accomplishment of any task (see also Dissanayake 1992, 92–93).

Meaning, as described in chapter 3, generally implies concern or care. And when people *care*, as they had to care about uncertain but biologi-

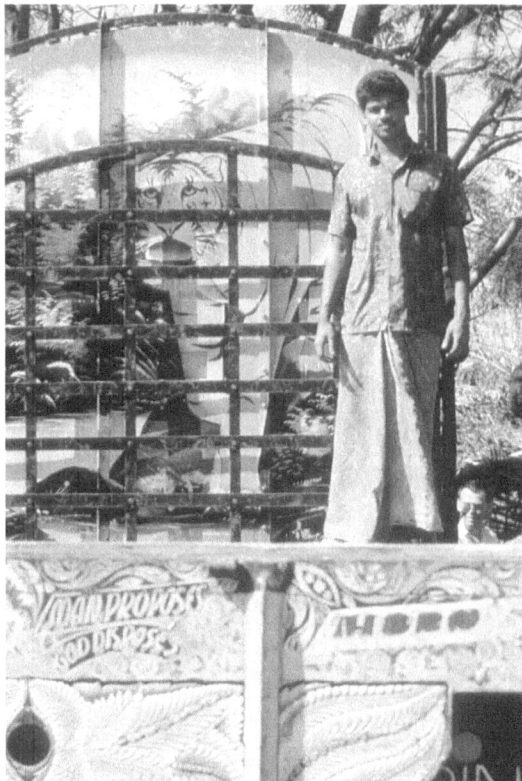

"Man Proposes God Disposes," decorated lorry, India. Photograph: Michelle Hankins.

cally significant and valuable things (such as assuring or restoring safety, prosperity, health, victory, or successful passage to a new state of being, or averting misfortune), they are moved—motivated—to exceptional, attention-getting, emotion-affecting, memorable activities. Such activities are a sort of "demonstration of serious regard" correlative to the biological significance and value of the things cared about. That is, the motivation to prevail, establish, or preserve—the "ultimate concerns" of religion—are felt emotionally and seem to demand a behavioral correlate, a special bodily effort.[5]

Although I have never seen it described this way, "ceremony" is, in fact, a one-word term for what is really a collection or assembly of elaborations (of words, voices, actions, movements, bodies, surroundings, and paraphernalia)—that is, of *arts* (chant or song, poetic language, ordered movement and gesture or dance, mime, and drama, along with considered and even spectacular visual display). It is as if the people who create and engage in these art-saturated ceremonies believe that in order for their efforts to succeed, nonhuman powers must be attracted and persuaded by displays of supreme beauty, skill, extravagance, and impressiveness. These qualities, which require an expenditure of time, thought, and effort, are unmistakable signs of caring and care.

The efforts and excesses of art may seem maladaptive in the capitalistic sense of minimum effort for maximum return on investment, but they apparently were not so in human evolution. Despite the negative cost-benefit calculations of effort by evolutionists or recent American congressional representatives, the shaping and elaborating of behavior and of the material world that we today call the arts have been *necessary* to the maintenance and continuity of human societies. While avoiding extremes of inappropriate effort and misperceived importance (the carved firewood and butterfly-wing sandals imagined in chapter 3), members of human societies everywhere have acted as if their serious and important concerns were better attained or assured when artifacts and actions associated with them were given rhythmic-modal elaboration. Whether or not a ceremony achieved its ostensible or immediate purpose every time—for example, averting misfortune or assuring success—there must have been other benefits that made such elaborations adaptive.

Elsewhere I have suggested (Dissanayake 1988, 1992, 1995) that group participation in a common endeavor would have strengthened the general cooperation and feeling of affiliation that in the ancestral way of life was essential in order for small, vulnerable bands to survive. Now I emphasize that what made ceremonies sensorily and emotionally gratifying (so that people were moved to perform them), as well as unifying (so that they contributed to the well-being of those who engaged in them), were elaborations of the rhythms and modes that initially evolved to enable mother-infant mutuality.

In this view, the arts evolved not as strategems for male competition (though like any other activity they can be used for such) but as physical correlates of psychological concern. The inborn rhythmic-modal sensitivities of mutuality, through cultural elaborations, became adaptive means for arousing interest, riveting joint attention, synchronizing bodily rhythms and activities, conveying messages with conviction and memorability, and ultimately indoctrinating and reinforcing right attitudes and behavior.

Since what is important to a society—its messages about order and meaning in the cosmos, in nature, and in social life, and about correct attitudes and behavior—can be thought of as its values, and since the arts enhance, preserve, and transmit these messages, art and morality are inextricable in traditional societies. As we saw in the case of the Yekuana (Guss 1989, 101), by simply making an artifact a person repeats the message encoded in the story of its origin. Kathryn Coe (1995) reminds us that the arts draw attention to essential ancestral teachings, crystallizing or encoding them in compelling and memorable forms so they can be passed through the generations—by women and elders as well as by sexually competitive men.

It is indisputable that a society's arts are integral to its moral order, for when they are lost or replaced by foreign arts (as has happened in so many aboriginal societies around the world), the entire culture breaks down. Throughout human history, a group's ceremonial elaborations (that is, its arts) have encapsulated the meanings that animate and perpetuate it.

Ethnographic studies of ritual and art sometimes seem to imply that these meaning-bearing messages are simply handed down like objects inherited from one's forebears or like information transferred—downloaded—from one generation to the next. It is important not to lose sight of the fact that ceremonies work by *producing changes in and structuring feelings*. As Radcliffe-Brown (1948 [1922], 234) remarked in his classic study of the Andaman Islanders, what ceremonies are intended to maintain and transmit from one generation to another are "the emotional dispositions on which a society depends for its existence." As rhythmic-modal sensitivities and capacities evolved to enable the emotional dispositions by which mothers and infants engaged in mutuality, so could elaborations of these sensitivities and capacities become vehicles for social coordination and concord, instilling belonging, meaning, and competence, which are feelings that comprise psychological well-being.

Thus humans' capacity to respond to the arts has been as crucial to their evolutionary presence as the desire or need to create them. The fact that we are emotionally and behaviorally susceptible to elaborated movements in time, visual compellingness, skillful execution, and the structuring and manipulation of our sensory experiences ensured that we would engage in socially reinforcing ceremonial behaviors, remember the information that these practices transmitted, and become emotionally convinced of their (and our) efficacy. Without the biologically adaptive reactions, the signals would not have arisen and been retained in human nature.

UNCERTAINTY AND CONTROL

From the time of Arnold van Gennep's writings (1908), students of ritual have been aware of its "liminal" character. That is, it marks a transition between one state and another—whether between life cycle stages, seasons, or existential states (see also Turner 1969). Some of these transitions are purely or primarily celebratory—think of such festive occasions as Carnaval, Mardi Gras, birthday parties, Thanksgiving, or the *naven* celebrations of a child's first accomplishments. They are motivated by the singular or special nature of the occasion that is being marked.

In most rituals, artful (special, exaggerated, compelling) features attract attention to biologically and socially important concerns that the rituals address. These features serve not only to recruit and direct people's attention but also to persuade them willingly to devote their efforts to these concerns—family, generosity, hard work, unselfishness, patriotism, and even sacrifice of one's life—which frequently go against narrow individual self-interest.

Rituals not only reinforce group one-heartedness (belonging) and like-mindedness (meaning). At the same time, they are age-old ways of addressing the uncertainty and liminality that are inherent in the human condition. Many ceremonies are motivated by anxiety—or may even generate it—and are structured so that they then deal with it in some way.

The sense of competence described in chapter 4 includes not only mastering physical skills and orderly, systematic knowledge in order to affect the world but also learning where and when to apply these skills and knowledge. Whereas other animals meet uncertainty or danger in the moment with a repertoire of three almost reflex defensive responses—fight, flee, or freeze—humans remember significant events in the past and anticipate what will be necessary or might come in handy later.[6] Our ancestors saw a promising stick or stone and brought it home to fashion it into a tool; eventually they stored food for the winter. Today we get flu shots, buy Christmas presents in July, purchase life insurance, save for retirement. Our high degree of memory and foresight means that humans are often anxious to forestall adversity—to control, or find the illusion that we control, uncertainty.[7]

Rituals are time-tested ways of addressing uncertainties and thereby gaining a feeling of competence. Psychoanalytic theory uses the term "ritual" or "ritualistic" to describe neurotic obsessive or compulsive behaviors that are unconscious manifestations of anxiety and attempts to control. In his study of early religion, Burkert (1996) characterizes ritual as entailing "fixed behavioral patterns marked by exaggeration and repetition, and often characterized by obsessive seriousness." My view is that ceremonial rituals may be better regarded as derived not from psychopathology but from the innate rhythmic-modal capacities used by mothers and babies in episodes of attunement. There exaggerations and repetitions are characteristic but are fluid, improvisational, and playful rather than fixed or obsessively serious.

Although some psychoanalysts have suggested that reenacting states reminiscent of infant security is soothing and reassuring, my own view goes considerably further than this simplistic explanation. Far from creating a state of soporific oceanic bliss, the elements of mother-infant engagements strikingly resemble the means used in rituals to gain attention, guide emotions, and reinforce memory. To repeat, both use (1) rhythmic, sequential organization of vocalizations, movements, and facial expressions in synchrony and antiphony (in ritual or art called chant, song, dance, and mime) and (2) cross-modal, or analogical, neural processing so that sense modalities of vision, hearing, and kinesics (touch, gesture, and bodily movement) are activated simultaneously and are experienced dynamically in terms of each other. In ceremonies these formal means become deeply affecting and meaningful (if not verbally describable) metaphors and symbols that emotionally conjoin those who experience them.

Additionally, rituals, like mother-infant interactions, use other devices that exaggerate or elaborate salient stimuli: repetition, accentuation, theme and variation, anticipation, surprise, and often (if not always) building to a climax with eventual resolution.

Burkert himself (1996, 19) mentions that ritual might be said to reflect a preverbal state of communication, to be learned by imitation, and to be understood by its function, but he does not go further with this association. Yet it seems clear that in rituals, as in mutuality, the rhythmic-modal devices just described contribute to the resolution of anxiety by coordinating and emotionally unifying the participants.[8]

Additionally, in a context of uncertainty about subsistence and survival, physical control—as formal composure, exaggeration, and repetition in modalities of voice and movement—might further provide a sense of emotional and psychological competence and control. In *Homo Aestheticus* (1992) I suggested as much.[9] Here I propose a mechanism for this sense of control. The same evolved neural mechanisms that "worked" in infancy to pattern and regulate emotional arousal, thereby enabling the sharing of emotional states with others, remain in place to be intentionally elaborated further, to similar ends. Expressing and regularizing movements and sounds with other people in rhythmic-modal ceremonial elaborations stimulates biochemical activities that both arouse and alleviate anxiety, give pleasure, and can lead to individual and collective emotional fulfillment.[10]

Anxiety, fear, and terror, Burkert (1996, 32) points out, have clear biological functions in protecting life, and the performance of ritual both grows out of anxiety and is designed to control it.[11] In his view, anxiety and danger are overcome by constructing or reconstructing a world of meaning (p. 128). I would add only that the constructing and reconstructing are accomplished through elaborations (arts), and that "meaning" inheres in the activity and its attendant emotions as well as in any artifacts or narratives that may result. As in mother–infant engagements, changes unfolding in the present create, and *are*, the experience (Stern 1995, 34).

In times of uncertainty, simply having something to do is reassuring. In humans, as in all other animals, an uncertain circumstance that seems significant stimulates the release of hormones (glucocorticoids and adrenaline) whose effects motivate us to seek a solution—to fight, flee, freeze, or, if we are humans, to otherwise forestall, deflect, or do something about it (Lopreato's [1984] "imperative to act"; Dissanayake 1992; Flinn et al. 1996, 128; Sapolsky 1992).[12]

Rather than doing nothing (or worrying), then, *doing something* in a stressful circumstance is adaptive. Indeed, psychologists report that doing (rather than thinking) induces high positive affect, whereas the reverse is true for negative affect, which can be induced more easily through thinking (Watson and Clark 1994). Activity helps to allocate energy resources to such bodily functions as immunity, growth, reproduction, muscle action, and cognition. Although, as with physical exercise, too much unrelieved emotional stress is not good, in reasonable amounts both exercise and stress are necessary and beneficial to good physical and mental health.[13]

The psychological rewards of *social* interchange are also indicated by a growing body of evidence that shows the relationship between social activity (of almost any type) and transient increases in positive mood to be "remarkably broad and robust" (Watson and Clark 1994). When physical exertion occurs, especially in social interaction such as sports or dancing, levels of cortisol and other hormones rise (Flinn et al. 1996), producing a feeling of pleasure associated with success and control. Again, simply doing something, especially with others, feels better than not doing anything. For males, winning a competitive game, experiencing a gain in social status, hunting, and moderate exercise all have been found to increase testosterone as well as cortisol—as does, of course, sexual or erotic stimulation. (In circumstances where men feel defenseless, their testosterone levels decrease: they are not stressed so much as depressed, which psychologically feels worse.)

That normal activities of hunter-gatherer life make people feel good should not be surprising. Sports, sex, and dancing—rhythmic, sequentially organized movements (and sometimes vocalizations) shared with others or another—are contemporary "rituals" that also make use of repetition, accentuation, theme and variation, anticipation, surprise, building to a climax, and resolution.[14] Although they still feel pleasurable and are good for one's health, they differ from premodern ritual ceremonies in being less integrated with the rest of our lives or less intrinsic to the making and transmission of cultural meanings.

It is easy to see how, during human evolution, ceremonial participation as a response to environmental uncertainty would have helped to relieve bodily stress and mental anxiety and provide a healthful sense of control. Although ritual practices can be viewed as simply superstitious and "explained" as means of brainwashing or social conditioning, the fact remains that they work, when people believe in them, because body and mind are inseparable.

Among the Yekuana, as described in the three previous chapters, anxiety-allaying ritual performances accompany every technological activity, both individual and collective, and use every modality—visual, vocal, and kinetic—in order to guarantee that the potentially dangerous and disruptive force in the original (natural) material will be safely incorporated or integrated into the made (cultural) artifact. Although the Yekuana are certainly an extreme example, ritual tools and activities can be viewed everywhere as ways of influencing or controlling uncertainty, even in cultures that are not so pervasively concerned as the Yekuana with decontaminating dangerous spirits.

Reviewing the four examples of ceremonial reinforcement of belonging described in chapter 2, we can see how these cultural traditions are ritualized ways of relieving anxiety and uncertainty as they also provide the rewards of socializing and the inherent sensory pleasures of experiencing and sharing artful behavior. Not only do the women lamenters in Karelia achieve mutuality and attunement with each other as they share the

feelings expressed in their songs, but also the very formalization and regularizing of their lamenting are the means to structure and relieve otherwise perhaps unbearable sadness. The young Medlpa pair who coordinate
their heads and bodies in swaying motions as their elders sing are given
"something to do" that is complicated enough to distract them from the
ambivalences and anxieties of courtship, yet their physical activity height-
ens the release of pleasurable brain chemicals as it furnishes the means for
each to assess the other's suitability as a partner.

The Kalapalo narrator and what-sayer develop their sung story for a
group of listeners who are caught up in dynamic interchange and forward
propulsion of the performance as they simultaneously and painlessly im-
bibe its moral messages. Everyone moves in temporal synchrony, achieving
the shared "high" of individual physical exertion within social interaction.
Something similar occurs in the Kaluli audience hearing the *gisalo* song,
familiar yet always different, enriched with multimodal metaphorical associations and the expectation of final, inevitable dramatic catharsis.

Thus the making and transmission of cultural meanings are expressed
and experienced through vocal, gestural, and kinesic actions that are exaggerated, regularized, and emotionally evocative—in other words, by
means of *the temporal arts:* chant, song, dance, and mime, whose rhythmic
and modal precursors are our first social experiences in early infancy and
perhaps are even reverberating echoes from our prelinguistic, prehistoric
past (Donald 1991; Oubré 1997).

THE PRESYMBOLIC ORIGINS OF ANCESTRAL ARTS

If my reconstruction is correct—if the arts of chant, song, poetry, dance,
and dramatic performance emerged during human evolution as multimedia elaborations of rhythmic-modal capacities that by means of these
elaborations gave emotional meaning and purpose to biologically vital activities—then prevailing ideas that equate art with symbol or image making will need modification.

The accepted notion in books of paleoarchaeology and anthropology is that sometime during the Paleolithic (usually around 40,000–
30,000 B.P.), "art" began to flourish.[15] Although the word "art" is rarely
defined in such contexts, it nearly always refers to the making of images
such as paintings, stenciled handprints, and other markings on cave walls,
engravings on bone or antler, and molded clay or carved figures. The usual
explanation for people's doing this sort of thing is that since image mak-

ing indicates "symbolizing ability," the painted or carved animal was a "symbol"—perhaps of the deity that people wished to acknowledge or the animal they wished to kill. Some prehistorians accept that not only images but also beads made from rare shell or bone are evidence of "art" (e.g., White 1989, 1993). Again, however, art is associated with the ability to symbolize, since the beads presumably were worn, or buried with certain individuals, to indicate differences in status.

With the ability to symbolize, it is then implied or stated, the genus *Homo* became truly human—that is, able to use language, think abstractly, and make "art." In other words, from this view art is evidence of something else, a by-product of symbolizing or related cognitive ability rather than a motivation in its own right.

I claim that a more useful and accurate way to think of the origin and nature of human arts is not as artifact or symptom but as intention and activity—that is, as the impetus to elaborate. While it is true that only humans make images and that images are symbolic, an image (or symbol) need not be elaborated any more than a tool or word or movement need be elaborated. If simply making an image or symbol was the point, then presumably any old rendering of the image in question would do. Thus images or symbols are not in themselves "art." Some Upper Paleolithic wall markings do look like irregular, even random, scratchings, and some Neolithic clay votive figures look as if they were turned out in a kind of mass production (like the little disposable, conical clay cups for tea that are used and thrown away by the thousands on railway platforms in North India). But it is of real interest to note that casually made or mass-produced images or artifacts like these are in the minority of human objects preserved from the past.

The remarkable fact about humans is not only that they began to make images or symbols but that they so frequently elaborated these images or symbols or used them to elaborate something else. Body painting is widely practiced by humans, but in some instances, even though symbolic, it may not be what is normally considered "art." For example, the Yekuana apply paint made of colorless resin protectively on themselves as well as on the objects they make—for example, canoes, baby swings, bows, arrows, baskets, and drums (Guss 1989). Magical herbs, prepared according to secret recipes, also may be applied to small incisions on a person's wrists or legs, to weapons, and to the eyes and nostrils of hunting dogs, or they may be worn in sealed gourd amulets for female problems with menstruation, childbirth, child care, or gardening. In some cases especially powerful mixtures of paint and herbs may be applied to the body for additional purification or preventive detoxification, but the act and fact of application itself seems to be more important than its visual impression: it is something like our own application of sunscreen or antibacterial ointment.

However, artful vocal elaborations usually accompany the Yekuana application of healing or purifying herbs and paints. Before sleeping in a hammock, playing an instrument, drinking from a gourd, shooting an arrow, or swinging an ax, individuals perform appropriate chants or songs that are made even more powerful (and elaborate) by being composed in a special secret language and performed in a special vocal style that uses interspersed short, rapid, blowing sounds. Purification of every part of a garden or house requires a longer and more elaborate ceremony—two or three days of collective chanting in a syncopated, responsive style.

Expanding our view of human arts to include rhythmic-modal activities like these, which accompany (or even precede) the making of visual symbolic images, opens new avenues for thinking about the importance of the arts in human evolution and, by extension, to human life in general. Temporal arts have been less discussed in evolutionary studies than images and marks because, obviously, they left no traces in the sites where ancestral humans once lived. Apart from footprints in a few French caves, perhaps indicative of dancing, and bone flutes from perhaps as early as eighty-two thousand years ago (Lau et al. 1997) (but certainly from twenty-two thousand to thirty-five thousand years ago in *Homo sapiens* sites in Europe and Asia), it is not known at what stage our ancestors began to move rhythmically, mime, and sing.

But such activities could have begun long before humans were able to make symbols. After all, even preverbal infants find precursors of these arts cognitively interesting and emotionally affecting. Well before they can make or use symbols such as words or pictures, children visibly respond to and participate in rhyme, mime, vocal play, singing, and moving to music. Even to modern adults, it is not only *symbolic* but *analogical* meanings in the arts that are affecting; we respond cross-modally and emotionally to the swoop and exuberance of a dance movement, the sense of hesitation or resignation and defeat in an actor's gesture, or the thick guttural innuendo in a jazz singer's voice, usually before recognizing or assigning symbolic "meaning" to the dance style or the spoken or sung words.

Even in visual objects, presymbolic associations of shape, color, and tactility attract and affect us. They make us want to look more closely.

Perhaps visual art originated for the purpose of marking and elaborating expressively moving (dancing, miming) or vocalizing human bodies, thereby accenting or drawing further attention to their meanings. In order to treat visual art in an evolutionary framework, Coe (1992, 219) has defined it as "color and/or form used by humans in order to modify an object, body, or message solely to attract attention to that object, body, or message."

The original messages enhanced by art in Coe's sense could well have been, and probably were in their earliest forms, nonverbal—as are similar "messages" marked on the bodies of other animals (for example, the colors or crests that indicate sex, age, and reproductive state). Apart from beads and deformed skulls (occurring in the fossil record from 70,000 B.P. [Trinkaus 1983, 146]) or intentionally filed or ablated teeth (from 17,000–19,000 B.P. [cited in Coe 1992, 224, with many other later examples]), body ornamentation, like song or dance, leaves no permanent trace. Shaped pieces of red ochre, a pigment used even today in body painting, have been found in archaic human sites as early as one hundred thousand years ago (Knight, Power, and Watts 1995).[16]

At some point our Paleolithic predecessors, perhaps wishing to succeed at a venture such as hunting a game animal or placating a powerful spirit, made a symbolic image of it. At the same time, however, and of equal or greater importance as an indication of their cognitive abilities, imaging was *not enough*. Additionally, great care was bestowed to make the image impressive, often with additional activities, just as important words (which are also symbols) might have been elaborated by saying them, as the Yekuana do when chanting, in a special voice.

Paleolithic cave images and symbols typically were put in special places—say, at the end of a long passage, often a winding and constricted tunnel, or, as at Cougnac (Gourdon, France), in a special place within a special place. Some of the cupules recently discovered at Jinmium and other sites in northwestern Australia (described in chapter 4) were carved in rows to accentuate natural passageways through rock (Taçon et al. 1997). The images of animals that have survived from the prehistoric past were not just casually scratched on bone or slapped onto cave walls, and it is unlikely that while the images were being made (or looked at), the makers (or spectators) talked and joked as if they were pouring (or looking at) concrete. In premodern societies of today, the people who make images (or who dye cloth or prepare paint for ritual use) frequently obey special rules of dress and behavior while performing these activities.

In premodern societies that have been observed during the twentieth century, painted or carved images are also rarely made idly or in isolation—"for their own sake" or to while away the time. Rather, the vast
majority are made for use in larger ceremonial occasions whose purpose
is to assure success and prosperity or to avert misfortune.

By equating the drawing or painting of images of animals with the
ability or desire to make a symbol, it is easy to ignore the crucial fact of
motivation, the desire to elaborate a place and an endeavor as a correlate
of emotional investment in the referent of the symbol, the wished-for
success of the endeavor. Moreover, the painted symbol was probably not
a lone icon but more likely the occasion for additional elaboration by special chanting. And the whole event likely was further elaborated by dramatic performance, dancing, and singing, thereby making the whole
participative and emotionally compelling.

Such a view seems to accord with what we know of symbolic behavior today. It suggests that "art" is not simply a kind of symbol making
and that it did not originate simply in order to make symbols. For example, the arts used in West African initiation societies (such as the Poro
society of the Senufo, the Ifa of the Yoruba, and the Bwami of the Lega)
are the means for taming and civilizing each generation and passing on
knowledge and skills through lifelong systems of tutelage, with distinct
stages of training and status. In initiation ceremonies, special carvings and
elaborate secret languages, songs, and movements are "orchestrated" over
time to be maximally affecting and effective (Glaze 1981, 87–88).

Art *uses* symbols, as it uses anything—systems, stories, objects,
events, ideas—as occasions for showing care and concern by elaborating.
A system, story, object, event, idea, or even symbol (whether word or image) is not "art" until it has been somehow elaborated. And the reason for
elaboration was not that people were finally capable of making symbols
but that human minds had evolved cognitively to a stage where they believed that extraordinary efforts would better assure good outcomes—a
capacity that probably preceded the ability to make symbols. Otherwise,
they could have simply scrawled their symbols on the cave walls, much
the way we draw when playing Pictionary.

Strictly speaking, scratching or marking on a wall *is* a sort of elaborating, making that wall special or different from the everyday. In a rudimentary sense we could think of almost any marking as an elaboration
and hence, in my sense, art. Yet for the reasons given in the preceding
paragraphs, I prefer to restrict the notion of art to elaboration and discard

the requirement of symbolization. When the markings are made with deliberation and care and with regard for their emotional effect—as was apparently the case with the cupules carved on the rock walls at Jinmium (Fullagar, Price, and Head 1996; Taçon et al. 1997)—one can certainly claim that they indicate "art" as well as symbols.

It might also be asserted that because of its extraordinary nature, the ceremony as a whole "symbolized" the extraordinary importance of the occasion. I find it more accurate to say that ceremonies (arts) of the ancestral past were *commensurate with*, rather than symbolic of, the importance of their occasions. And because of the biological (and hence psychological) importance of the occasions that were given symbolic treatment, the symbols were made artfully, that is, shaped and elaborated with care. Thus elaborating—drawing attention to and shaping knowledge *and feelings* about everyday necessities and facts of life (such as health, food, life stages, and social organization), thereby underscoring their biological importance—became a crucial element in the human repertoire, an essential feature of human nature.

Just as we in modern societies tend to think of the arts as being inherently symbolic, we also almost automatically think of them as separate and individual. If, however, as I have suggested, they originally occurred all together (as in mother-infant mutuality), then they were probably also experienced at once—visually, aurally, and kinetically—in terms of one another. This seems often to be the case in premodern societies of today. For example, in Senufo villages in Mali, Upper Volta, and the Ivory Coast, "art" objects are designed to be used "in a controlled time and motion sequence" (Glaze 1981, 198), and their full intellectual and aesthetic value is realized only in their dramatic appearance in a ritual (funeral or initiation) context. Similar observations have been made by anthropologists with regard to other celebratory events (e.g., Lawal 1996). It is probably always the case that music and movement go together: for the Andamanese, singing and dancing were "two aspects of one and the same activity" (Radcliffe-Brown 1948, 334).

Multimedia art forms exist, of course, in modern societies: opera, musical theater, and rock music concerts come to mind. But there are also more subtle ways of experiencing an individual art in multimodal or cross-modal ways, and indeed I believe this is a source of their often profound appeal and emotional effect.

Visual arts draw forth cross-modal sensations of tactility and kinesis with their emotional associations from color, form, and texture. Such sensory overlappings have perhaps always been implicit in the intentions

of visual artists, but they have become explicit in the twentieth century—
as in the blobs, spots, drops, strokes, smears, blurs, shimmers, and puddles
of abstract expressionist works, the dynamic equilibrium of horizontal
and vertical lines and the primary colors of a painter such as Mondrian,
the directed shapes and colors of Kandinsky (that for him explicitly referred to music), or the spreading mingled veils of Color Field painters.

Rather than imitating the look of the world, abstract painters like
these discovered that they could make choices based on constructs such
as the body's *felt* sense of bilateral symmetry, its movement in space, its dynamic relationship to time, its metaphoric and modal understandings, its
sense of inner coherence, and nonliteral image and kinetic motor patterns
common to all humans (Boothe 1996).

In contrast with the desire to copy external reality as one sees it, the
impulse to abstract involves all the senses, especially the sense of touch,
and is often provoked by materials—succulent, pliable, plastic, soft, hard,
malleable, diaphanous, translucent, shiny, oily, glittery—which are an
"essential and limitless source of inspiration" (Seelig 1992). Rather than
"overcoming" a material, artists can work with its intrinsic characteristics—for example, building up or taking away. Weaving, layering, and
laminating resemble sedimentation; carving, sanding, and filing relate to
erosionary forces (Seelig 1992).

At the time he first made them, Jackson Pollock's "drip" paintings
may have looked as though he were simply seeking gratuitous novelty,
flinging paint at conventional methods of making pictures and, simultaneously, at accepted taste. Yet one can also see that by allowing paint to
flow off the brush—by pouring it—Pollock was using the most direct
way to allow a line to have its own energy, to be independent of shape, to
express the integrity of its materiality as paint.

Even in mimetic works we may be moved by a surface that is richly
woven, brushed, colored, striated, or patinated. Svetlana Alpers (1988) has
noted how different ways of viewing Rembrandt's works are necessitated
by his choices in the application of paint—for example, the impasto tech-
nique highlights the paint's solidity and turns it into a kind of sculpture.
Rembrandt makes us *see* the qualities we know by touch—the weight,
pressure, and substance of things. Such sculptural quality is a "statement"
about vision, argues Alpers, quoting Mieke Bal (1994, 365): "Vision, then,
is a subcategory of touch, and paint is a solid object." In the 1655 version
of Rembrandt's *Slaughtered Ox*, the substance of paint as flesh affects our
viewing of it and makes it different from the relatively neutral brushwork
in the earlier (1643) rendering of the same subject (Bal 1994, 373–74).

Because the printed page allows only printed examples, I illustrate cross-modal or synesthetic experience of the verbal arts with a poem by John Gohorry about a musical performance. The reader is presented first with a sequence of strong visual images that seem to describe the appearance of the performers as they begin to play their instruments, but imperceptibly these become descriptions of the heard music and its movement. It is remarkable that even sounds, pictured images, and physical movements, along with less nameable sensations, can be conveyed from a poet's mind to ours by unspoken words immobilized in print.

The Iceberg Quartet

Their notes have the measure of sunlight
that the floe performs as a caprice.
Their tailcoats are the colour of seals

and the blue sash round the cellist's waist
is the clear blue of the clear blue sky
as she leans into the allegro,

the berg playing the score of itself
witnessed only, above sea-level,
by the inquisitive albatross

and, below, by omniscient whales.
A note at a time, the berg dissolves
but as night slips round the blue cliffs

the quartet begins what is not yet
its last movement, before the poles run,
whales drown, and music covers the earth.[17]

CEREMONIAL ELABORATION: TWO EXAMPLES

If, in Radcliffe-Brown's important observation, ceremonies are intended to produce changes in feelings or to structure them in order to maintain and transmit from one generation to another the emotional dispositions on which a society depends for its existence, then we should not be surprised at the association between elaboration and extraordinary effort and emotion. Let us look at two different examples, which I call "excess" and "overflow."

Elaboration as Excess: The Owerri Igbo Mbari

Sometimes elaboration has to do with excessive preparation time, physical effort of making, and cost of material, as well as with the extraordinary effect of the actual product. *Mbari* is a celebration of the Owerri, a southern Ibo group in Nigeria, which requires up to two years of preparation. Its general purpose is to enhance the group's prosperity and to inoculate against a broad spectrum of possible ills, such as famine, plague, death, or debilitating warfare (Brain 1980; Cole 1969a, 1969b, 1982).

Two years is a long time for a small village to exempt able-bodied adults from their normal work, yet during this preparatory period for the main *mbari* event, some thirty to forty people are secluded in a special enclosure where they must be provisioned and their usual tasks assumed by their families. As designated artists, they work full-time at constructing a

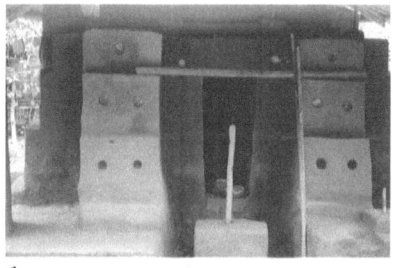

a

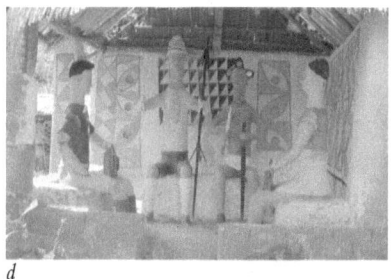

d

Stages of an mbari *house, Owerri Igbo, Nigeria. Photographs: Herbert Cole.*

a. *Unpainted mud wall and verandah in construction.*
b. *Artist painting molded clay figure.*
c. *Completed* mbari *house at night.*
d. Mbari *figures and outer walls start to crumble.*
e. *Further decay of paint and clay.*

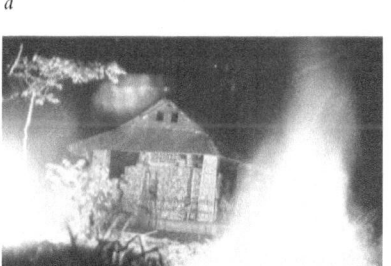

c

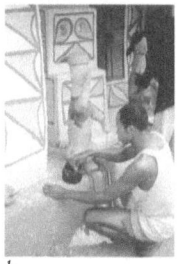

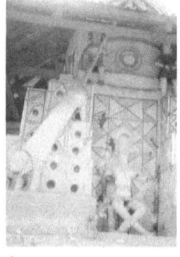

b   e

large, rectangular, two-story edifice of mud and decorating it with colored clay designs outlined with strips of raffia.

In addition, they make from three dozen to over a hundred large, three-dimensional painted figures and place them all around the "verandah" of the *mbari* structure. These are hand molded from the same clay-like anthill mud used for the walls, all collected at night and then specially pounded and puddled until it is of the proper consistency for handling. After the structure with its images is completed, the villagers are allowed to view the wondrous sight at a special celebration. For this they incur additional expenses, with new clothes, a great feast and dance for visitors, and animal sacrifices.

The culminating event and its preparations are elaborate in every way, yet what seems most extraordinary of all—at least to us in a society that is conscious of material costs and benefits—is that after the concluding celebration, when the *mbari* house and figures at last are viewed, they are then abandoned. Unrepaired and unrestored, they are allowed to crumble to dust or melt in the rain and ultimately fuse with the earth from which they were made. The largest mud figure, sculpted and painted last, is Ala, the major Owerri deity, mother of people, giver of yams, goddess of the earth. It is considered fitting that after the long preparation and celebration, the natural environment is allowed to reassert itself so that the entire *mbari*, event and objects, may become one with the very earth of which it was made and which, personified as Ala, called it into being. No need or desire is felt to preserve the ultimate material product of so much expenditure of mental and physical effort, time, money, skill, and ardor.

Throughout human history and prehistory, human societies have engaged in costly undertakings like this, some more and others less labor-intensive and spectacular. Within orthodox evolutionary theory, it is difficult to imagine that such herculean efforts could have contributed to the survival or reproductive success of anyone, individual or group. Few of us today believe that any ceremony would reliably prevent drought, flood, famine, or disease. The value of *mbari* becomes clearer, however, when we view it in terms of reinforcing the evolved psychobiological needs of belonging, meaning, and competence.

Mbari is overwhelmingly communal from beginning to end; even though there are designated artists, everyone in the social group "belongs" to the endeavor and joins in its realization. Simply deciding to hold the ritual in the first place requires formalized deliberation, as do selecting and engaging the workers. The villagers who participate in the initial decision making, and those who experience and enjoy the concluding festivities, are as much participants as the workers who manually construct the house and figures.

The figures and paintings on the *mbari* structure give focus to a variety of Owerri concerns, thereby emphasizing their individual and communal meaning or significance. Among the many extraordinary painted mud figures are some that are considered particularly beautiful or good: these represent the undeniably biologically and socially valuable virtues of hard work, prosperity, productivity, and fertility. Other images of spirits from the underworld, forces of nature, and mythological figures are regarded as terrifying—but are made tolerable by their context. There are openly sexual and even indecent images, which capture attention, although in everyday life they are forbidden. And there are entertaining caricatures of white people and depictions of bawdy scenes, which provoke laughter. All of these reinforce with their beauty or what I call "strikingness" the systems and stories with which Owerris comprehend, and feel themselves to be part of, their culture.

The ritual itself embodies competence, both the knowledge of what to do to ensure well-being and prosperity and the ability to carry it out. Careful activity is necessary long before and alongside the actual modeling and painting of the mud house and figures. During their seclusion, the workers' lives are regularized: they must wear special, nonordinary clothing and engage in special prayers, sacrifices, games, songs, and other activities. All these are highly stylized or "choreographed" in what might be regarded as a two-year-long multimedia performance.

For the artists, the manipulative pleasure of making continues over two years. The "hands on" interrelationship with the natural world is inherent in the material of mud and the makers' physical efforts, initially, and then in the active, bodily participation of the celebrants. When finally unveiled, the end result, the *mbari* house and figures, is a magnificent culminating emblem—material testimony to its makers' efforts. Being so splendidly extraordinary, it is ritually effective as an object and an experience. But there is no desire to preserve it, although every element of the long preceding constructive process was carefully considered and openly valued.

Throughout human history, ceremonial assemblages of arts—like *mbari* with its mixture of seriousness and frivolity, dancing and feasting, uplifting and startling but socially sanctioned images, all anticipated for months—suffused their participants with emotions that felt meaningful and were shared. Periodic reaffirmations of loyalty and reciprocity, fortified with arresting arts, mobilized and coordinated participants into a unified group, ensuring that members of the social group worked together in a common cause, believing in the validity of their worldview and the efficacy of their action.[18]

Elaboration as Overflow: The Temiar of Malaysia

The improvised duets of mother-infant mutuality predispose us to perform in and respond to temporally organized rituals of group belonging and bondedness. While I have just illustrated ceremonial elaboration and control with descriptions of the extravagant Owerri fabrication of *mbari* (and earlier with Yekuana ritual remedies for toxicity), it is important to realize that most occasions that unify individuals and reinforce their common cultural meanings do so with extensions and elaborations of the rhythms and modes of mother-infant mutuality—the performative and participative arts of music and movement. Even the Yekuana's applications of magic herbs and paint are accompanied by chants, and the *mbari* preparations have a formal temporal organization over many months. In societies in which the temporal arts are primary, however, the interwoven strands of rhythms and modes—as integrated means to integrative ends—are conspicuous, and their elaborated interminglings may produce a unifying sense of overflow (or overflowing sense of unity).

The Temiar, hunter-horticulturalists in peninsular Malaysia, hold ceremonies of singing and trance-dancing that integrate individuals with each other and with their environment while providing the means to heal. Using a kind of song-speech, the ceremonies both articulate and embody Temiar communal values of interdependence and reciprocity; the vocal activities themselves establish relationships, fulfill obligations, and coordinate effort (Roseman 1984, 1991). In their ceremonies, Temiar sonically intermingle their voices and express identity between groups by means of musical devices such as overlapping alternation between a singer and a group of choral respondents and alternated repetition of the same phrase by the singer and respondents.

Somewhat like the Yekuana, but to very different effect, the Temiar believe that all entities in the environment—animals, plants, and mountains, as well as humans—have potentially detachable souls that can be liberated as unbound spirit. A self (soul, spirit) does not end at an individual's own boundaries but rather, during dreams (and other noneveryday states such as trances, illness, danger, and singing ceremonies), may meet souls of other entities (for example, trees, river rapids, tigers, deceased humans) that express the desire to be the dreamer's spirit guide. Such a relationship is confirmed by the spirit guide's teaching a song to the dreamer, who then transfers his learning of the song to others in ritualized nighttime singing sessions. The song links the singer to the spirit guide and transforms him or her into a medium who can diagnose and treat illness.

Temiar have no word for "song": instead they use the word "path" or "way," which has multiple, linked (or cross-modal) associations referring to the visions bestowed by the traveling spirit guide and to the melody or song text, as well as to particular dance steps, certain leaves, and some performance conditions (such as whether the spirit prefers to arrive in light or in darkness). In transferring the taught song, the performer sings an initial phrase, which is repeated by a female chorus that follows the "path." The path may take variable forms: overlap between phrase and exact response, alternating overlap with a variant of the melody, or pausing and then responding with a series of melodically varied phrases with textual improvisation. Thus the leader-chorus distinction is collapsed by overlap and repetition, and the public performance of the revealed spirit-guide song moves the individual's dream revelation into the realm of community participation.

The sung speech uses a metaphorical, ambiguous language that is peculiarly adapted to elusive yet descriptive reference. The beguiling quality of this language derives from special terms received in dream revelation, from a preponderance of descriptive adjectives and expressives, and from poetic techniques of meter, rhyme, assonance, and reduplicative play.

Because parts of the environment (in jungle, field, and settlement) all have souls, the Temiar singers translate this environment and its resources into the culture as the inhabitant spirits emerge, identify themselves, and begin to sing in dreams or ritual performances, making networks of associations between humans and spirits. Swaying movements, fragrant and visually pleasing face paint, leaves, and flowers all entice the presence of spirit guides.

While the mediums sing, other participants dance slowly, bending and swaying, arms swinging more and more until they begin to lose balance, shudder, and stumble. As the chorus notices the unsteadiness and shuddery stumbling, it drives the tempo and intensifies the song by singing louder and an octave higher. At a certain point, one or another dancer breaks step and falls to the floor in a faint, when her soul is released into invisible movement. The flow from the individual to the collective is imagined as *kahyɛk*, a cool spiritual liquid like colorless plant sap, clear stream water, or morning dew. During singing, this arches in a watery thread from the jungles and mountains into leaf ornaments adorning the interior of the house where the ceremony is held. Singers and dancers draw this imagined flow from hand-held leaf whisks and hanging leaf ornaments, and it spreads into community members, linking humans and environment through the agency of the spirit guide, who is also simultaneously manifested in song (Roseman 1984, 1991).

Rather as Yekuana detoxify nature with special herbs, paint, and chants, Temiar transform the spirits of the natural environment into culturally constructed sounds in a performance that reframes or humanizes them. The individual feels personally transformed as well, so that healing can take place. "Knowledge constitutes the power to heal when it takes that which is unknown and defines it. . . . Singing enacts and demonstrates the power [appropriated from the spirit guide's 'way,' which the medium now knows] to take the chance out of illness. Singing shows what the medium knows. [Song is] speech transformed, sound humanized" (Roseman 1991, 148–50).

ELABORATION AND EMOTION

Although a mother's rhythmic-modal signals to her baby are "simplified," they can be described as elaborated. This is only an apparent contradiction. In order to attract and keep the infant's attention, she repeats (words, phrases, head movements, tongue-clicks, pats) and exaggerates (vocal contours, facial expressions, pauses, tempo, and amplitude). Although they serve the purpose of simplifying, both repetition and exaggeration are elaborations of normal or everyday sounds or movements. Elaboration gives salience.

Salience—prominence or emphasis—is potentially *emotional*. In the generalized, unremarkable state of ordinary consciousness in which most of daily life is spent, we do not experience emotion so much as what might be described as mood fluctuations like corks bobbing gently this way and that on a "stream of affect" (Watson and Clark 1994, 90) whose eddies are more or less good (positive), bad (negative), or indifferent. Emotion enters (or potentially enters) the scene when there is some discrepancy or change, provoking an interest. We "appraise" a salient or novel cue, anticipating what it means for our vital interests. Is that unusual sound a burglar? Does being called suddenly to the boss's office mean a raise or a reprimand?

Novelty (or change) is not in itself positive or negative—it may lead to anxiety, intense fear, relief, curiosity, or delight. But a novel event seems to trigger a readiness for emotion, if not a full-blown emotion (Ellsworth 1994a, 151). We are especially receptive to signals that indicate actual or possible harm, threat, or benefit.

Emotions as *felt* give flavor and pungency to our lives. Their ultimate biological purpose, however, is to motivate—to make us respond appropriately to the sorts of occurrences in the environment that could affect us for good or ill. Under their influence, we try to maintain or obtain what is good for us and to escape from, prevent, or modify what is bad (Ellsworth 1994a, 152; Frijda 1994).

Positive emotions are elicited by events that satisfy some motive (goal) that enhances a person's power of survival or demonstrates the successful exercise of his or her capabilities (Frijda 1994). Thus people typically feel joy and happiness from mastery and accomplishment, evidence of pleasing another, sensory pleasure, and satisfaction of a lack (that is, relief when something unpleasant has ceased) (Ekman 1994, 147). Joy and happiness have value as reinforcement, helping to assure that we want to do things that make us feel good—which in ancestral times were things that, on balance, were good for our survival. Negative emotions such as fear, displeasure, and anger alert us that some action should be undertaken to set things right or to prevent unpleasant things from occurring (Frijda 1994, 113–14). It is interesting that emotions are brought into play most often by the actions of other people (Ekman and Davidson 1994, 139) and may be intensified or enhanced when shared with others, as studies of mother-infant interaction make clear.

The early appraisals we make of novel cues lead to progressively more complex perceptions, beginning, for example, with a primitive sense of pleasure or aversion, or with a sense of uncertainty or certainty, and continuing through perception of, say, an obstacle or a reward, a sense of control or lack of it, and, eventually, attributions of agency (causality) and legitimacy (rightness) (Ellsworth 1994b, 193). These assessments contribute to the temporal course of how we feel, whether as gradual intensification or as ebb and flow.

Something rather similar occurs in the experience of mother-infant engagement, in which expectation is aroused through the manipulations and elaborations of salient stimuli that change in interesting but not fully predictable ways and, when all goes smoothly, cumulatively produce shared states of pleasure and delight. Mutuality and music are like capsule or prototypical examples of emotional experience, exercised for their own sake (although, unknown to the participants, mutuality contributes to each partner's reproductive success, and musical sensitivities predisposed us to engage in fitness-enhancing ceremonial rituals). They are like play, "not for real," although they have real benefits (Imberty 1997).

Over the course of human evolution, human societies have appropriated the capacities to respond to such elaborations—the repetitions and exaggerations of rhythms and modes that by means of change and novelty create expectancy and thereby engender and shape emotional trajectories—and have used them in ritual ceremonies and the temporal arts. As others have noted (e.g., Ellsworth 1994b, 195–96; Imberty 1997; Kivy 1990; Langer 1953; Storr 1992), some of the physiological and experiential sensations of emotional appraisals also seem to correspond to features of music such as crescendo and decrescendo, staccato and legato, accelerando and rallentando, and the ascending and descending melodic or intonational contours that have cross-modal associations as well as their own directed tensions and resolutions (Dissanayake 1999).

As participants or spectators we have evolved not only to respond emotionally to the temporal arts but also to be susceptible to the excesses that demonstrate seriousness of purpose and to experiences of overflow. In both we have access to an order of experience that is apart from and seems to transcend the ordinary or everyday. According to individual and cultural variations, this domain may be ecstatic or serene, extravagant or sublime, frequent or rare.

In societies that elaborate their cultural meanings with the arts of time (music, dance, performance), unusual states of mind and emotion occur in which people become worked up, overwrought, even entranced. Arresting rhythms, excitingly dynamic sounds of voices or other instruments, spellbinding drama, and colorful objects may unite to produce a suffusion of emotion felt as self-transcendence, an overflowing communion with other participants and with what seems to be an "other world" or a higher power. Such emotionally compelling states—felt as numinous and sacred—accompany and reinforce what is important to the social group, help its preservation and transmission, and unite the hearts and minds of those who participate and respond.

In *Instinct and Revelation*, anthropologist Alondra Oubré (1997) makes an intriguing case for the evolutionary importance in humans of an evolved capacity for states of transcendental consciousness, and she proposes neurobiological substrates, driven by acoustical stimulation, for such states (Oubré 1997, 177–78). Although these experiences are "indescribable," people from all parts of the world have nevertheless used comparable words, sensations, and images to convey a kind of mystical or numinous awareness that appears to be pancultural.

Some prehistorians suggest that visions of Paleolithic shamans in trance states are depicted in some of the painted and etched images on cave walls in South Africa, France, Spain, and North America (e.g., Lewis-Williams 1995; Lewis-Williams and Dowson 1988; Whitley 1994). Whether or not such a state refers to anything beyond itself is outside the domain of neurobiology or paleoarchaeology, but its adaptive value could well have resided in its reinforcing of communal truths, thus assisting group cohesiveness. It might also have provided a strongly felt individual sense of purpose or serenity, contributing to physiological and psychological health (Oubré 1997, 17).

The documented existence of various altered mental states in present-day people—for example, shamanism, different kinds of meditation, drug-induced rapture, !kia, glossolalia, or amokness—supports a claim that whatever the function of those states in evolutionary history, the human species is acquainted with paranormal or "special" realms of experience. If the cultures into which we are born value and encourage such states, they will be a normal part of our behavioral repertoire. One anthropologist (Bourguignon 1972) has judged that some 85 percent of human societies today acknowledge some form of transcendent experience and have "institutionalized" means for achieving it.

To rational Westerners, such states may seem the product of ignorant credulity or dementia. Yet the fact that they are so widespread and culturally important suggests that they had adaptive value. Archaeologist Brian Hayden (1987, 1993) has proposed that in early hunter-gatherer societies the intense emotions of ritualized ecstatic states helped maintain alliances when resources were scarce due to severe climatic fluctuations or other causes. Oubré contends that transcendental consciousness could have originated as early as a million years ago. Not only was it a product of human evolution, in her view, but it also affected human evolution, leading to the origins of symbolic thought, magical and social rituals, imaginative healing, and the emergence of metaphysical thought (Oubré 1997, 7–8).

Some societies (for example, Tukano [Reichel-Dolmatoff 1972], Fang [Fernandez 1972], and Cubeo [Goldman 1964]), though by no means

all, use drugs to induce altered states. Oubré proposes that such states originated in rhythmic singsong (chanting) used as a system of emotional communication long before speech developed. Hayden suggests that ecstatic
states were originally brought about by sensory deprivation, either in caves
or in states of near starvation, or by rhythmic drumming, dancing, or dramatic shock. David Whitley (1994) describes the aural effects of bullroar-
ers and flutes—roaring, whirring, ringing, whistling, or buzzing—that
serve as "portal" signals leading to altered states, which when achieved may
be experienced somatically as death, flight, being immersed or drowning,
or sexual intercourse.

Additionally, in studies by anthropologists there are many accounts
of ritual ceremonies that deliberately use pain, terror, and awe to induce
compliance, suggestibility, and commitment. Psychiatrist John Beahrs
(1990) has proposed that the dissociative state that is today called post-
traumatic stress disorder could well have been adaptive in ancestral times,
when life was physically dangerous but culturally and environmentally
more stable. The phenomenon called dissociation is a psychological defense against the immediate experience of painful, overwhelming events.
One sector of the mind, associated with the traumatic feelings, "splits,"
psychologically isolating the otherwise unbearable emotions and memories and thereby allowing the traumatized individual to retain a sense of
control.

It is known that persons who have undergone catastrophic trauma
are frequently especially susceptible, also, to hypnosis—another form of
psychological dissociation. In clinical settings, ease of hypnotizability can
be encouraged in patients either by interfering with their usual everyday
mental organization (often by altering the focus of attention) or by pro-
moting an affiliative bond, reminiscent of the symbiosis between child
and parent, between patient and hypnotist. Beahrs (1992) points out that
traumatization often elicits effects similar to those of the affiliative experiences of love and religious fervor: tightened bonding (even if conflicted),
confusion of boundaries, and resistance to reality testing (see also Freud
1979 [1921]).

In numerous premodern societies, percussive sound and movement
are utilized to achieve transcendence (for example, Sinhalese exorcists
[Kapferer 1983], !Kung San [Katz 1982], Haitian *voudoun* [Deren 1970],
Bering Sea Inuit [Birket-Smith 1950 (1927)], Balinese [Covarrubias 1937],
Kaluli [Schieffelin 1976]). But elsewhere, individuals achieve altered states
without drugs, trauma, physical exertion, or rhythmic sound, often by

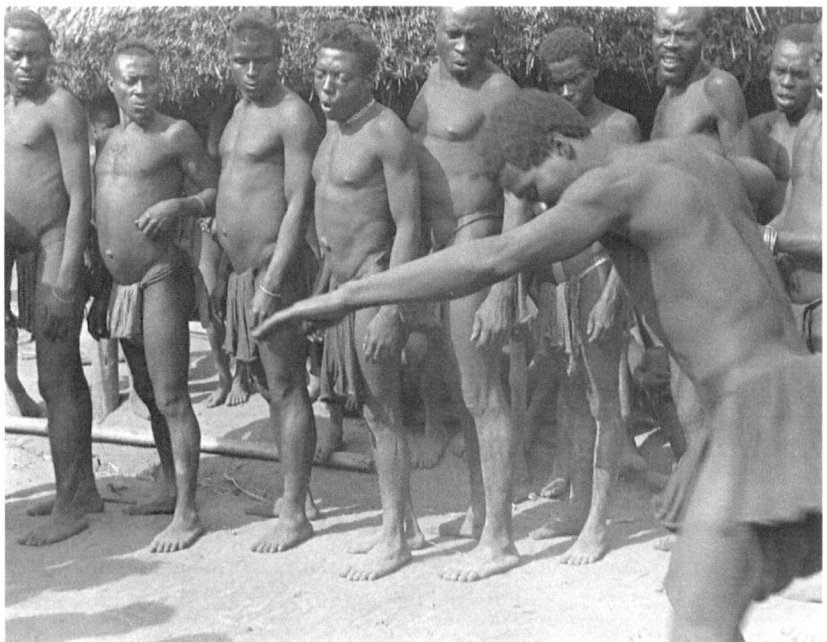

Dance rehearsal, Cameroon. Photograph: Paul Gebauer.

concentrating on "portal" (transformational) symbols—mirrors, gems and crystals, skrying bowls and pools, cave mouths, and doorways (Laughlin, McManus, and d'Aquili 1990)—or sounds (Whitley 1994), all of which could serve to focus attention and lead to a dissociative or reorganized mental state.

Neurophysiologist Walter J. Freeman (1995) proposes that activities such as group dancing, rhythmic clapping and chanting, and shared stressful events (as in sports, combat, and arduous initiations) release brain chemicals that promote affiliative emotions and brain states conducive to accepting and incorporating collective values. Laughlin, McManus, and d'Aquili (1990) describe how "transformational" symbols, as well as shared rhythmic practices, affect neurocognitive systems in the body by driving, tuning, and entraining brain waves. Whatever the physiological mechanisms, such restructurings of phases of consciousness apparently give rise to a range of similar experiences which then are interpreted according to the beliefs of individual cultures. Although the !Kung San transcendent state of *!kia* is attained and manifested quite differently from trance in the Temiar, one consequence of both is the ability to heal others.

Contemporary societies (apart from subgroups such as "charismatic" and evangelical religions) do not provide ritualized opportunities for their members to achieve trancelike states of self-transcendence. Yet varieties of these experiences are known to most people. A heightened and intensified state called "flow" (Csikszentmihalyi 1990) has been described when people "play" with total involvement, particularly in activities that require great physical exertion (for example, running and "working out"), sustained concentration (for example, artistic or intellectual creation), or both. Those who have felt "flow" may liken it to other transcendent states because of the felt loss of ego or self-consciousness, and the "high."

Moving together with others in time, especially in high-energy activity, does produce elation, as I can attest from personal experience with that characteristic late-twentieth-century ceremonial ritual, the aerobic exercise class. After performing repetitive patterned and coordinated exertions for an hour with some five or six hundred male and female students in the University of Edinburgh gymnasium, to the accompaniment of pulsating amplified music with a driving beat, I was almost able to levitate on the eight-block walk home. (See also McNeill 1995 about "muscular bonding" in military drill.)

Apart from experiencing the highs of entrainment to strong driving rhythms, more complex and subtle emotional experiences are also related to our evolved capacity to respond to rhythms and modes. Among these are the two states evoked in my title and in the introduction: intimacy or love, and art.

Although contemporary experiences of love, as of art, are based on universal human predispositions, I suspect that love today (or today's idea of love) is as different from its earlier manifestations as is today's art (or idea of art). In their current incarnations, both have become surrogates for the psychological satisfactions that once inhered naturally in human existence but are now, as described in earlier chapters, much less reliably addressed and met.

For most people throughout human history, intensely emotional and memorable experiences were engendered by participating with others in ceremonial events that were tangibly relevant to vital interests and evocatively resonant with the human condition. These experiences were satisfying and even healing, answering as they did to the inevitable existential uncertainty in subsistence lives and being suffused with the seriousness and shared belief that such lives require.

Today we do not lead subsistence lives, and in difficult times few of us are able to find solace or healing, much less transfiguration, in religious practices. Yet even in a nonreligious age, people still have a sense of the "beyond" and a capacity for heightened experience. In a provocative book, Charles Pickstone (1996), a British theological writer and pastor, suggests that for many people today, sex and art have usurped religion.

Experiences of the arts may be notably different from ceremonial occasions: for example, they may take place privately and not require active participation. Yet, at least implicitly, they too involve others or another—the artist, performer, composer, writer—with whom we engage intimately and profoundly. Such experiences of the arts, moreover, like the act of love, are composed of careful rhythmic-modal structurings and elaborations of aesthetic elements that focus, entrain, and repay attention. People who respond deeply to a performance of music, dance, or theater, or to a painting or sculpture, might say (or feel) afterwards, "I was taken right out of myself," or "I entered another world," or "it was perfection; time stood still." Philosophers writing about works of art may say that they "transport us out of the realm of the ordinary" (e.g., Heidegger 1971, 183). In Mozart's music, as I described in the introduction, Theodore Gombril, Jr., recognized a "pure and unsullied" passion. The overflowing fountains of sound revealed God.

Similarly, in the act of physical love, rhythmic-modal properties—as in the temporal arts and mother-infant engagements—are dynamically structured and altered to coordinate a pair emotionally and express their accord. Like the arts, such experiences may sometimes be profoundly moving, although also profoundly difficult to describe. After all, it is in writings about art and sex that one is most likely to find the use of "gossamer juggernauts of gorgeous waffle" (Lakeman 1997) or passages of "empurpled indistinction" (Hillman 1989, 228). Still, as Pickstone discerns, the referents of such imperfect efforts are usually themselves the nearest most of us come to knowing perfection.

In both love and art, slight expansions and contractions of temporal and spatial movement and intensity are the means of building, conveying, and sharing the anticipation and fulfillment of beginnings and endings, implications and realizations, antecedents and consequents, qualifications and subordinations—of entailment, contrast, redirection, opposition, pacing, heightening, and release. Thus described, a common emotional "grammar," based in infant experience, is part of our human heritage, to be employed in meaning-rich and sometimes transfiguring conjoinments—whether in ceremonies, love, or the arts.

According to Pickstone, sexual as well as religious or aesthetic experience may be creative and revelatory—a means to self-transcendence that can disclose the sacred in the familiar and ordinary. Humans' evolved emotional susceptibility to rhythms and modes, and their use of rhythms and modes for attaining states of self-transcendence, supports Pickstone's ideas, suggesting that heightened experiences of excess and overflow may be reached by many vehicles, although each journeys on the same long-established road.

6

Taking the Arts Seriously

WHILE WRITING THIS book, I happened to hear a congressman speak on television about government financial priorities. (His name is irrelevant, because I find his attitude to be shared by most of his cronies.) Asked about his position regarding loans to enable students to attend university, this gentleman said that he could advocate financial aid to people who were studying science or math, but not—and here he stopped to search his mind for a representative subject that was suitably undeserving. Having found it, he wrinkled his nose and curled his upper lip with disdain as he said, "but not *theater arts*," as if he were saying "making paper-clip chains." He obviously expected automatic agreement from the audience.

Readers of the preceding chapters will have learned that what we call today "theater arts" seems to have been one of humankind's early distinguishing activities—what we still identify in every society as ceremonial ritual. During tens of thousands of years before there was mathematics or science, there were theater arts. This is not to say that the activities of math and science are unimportant, but it *is* to say that one might presume that theater arts (which include all the arts—performance, visual display, music, dance, and elaborated speech) are not simply to be dismissed.

The lack of science and math in prehistory and in premodern societies did not preclude lives that were emotionally rewarding and "meaningful," although they were certainly not so materially easy as ours today.

Perhaps the relative paucity of "theater arts" in modern societies is correlated with our oft-expressed sense of nonmeaning or emotional impoverishment. This is a question worth examining.

The superior technological ability of modern societies has wiped out aboriginal populations both directly and indirectly for hundreds of years. What we know of their lives comes from travelers' tales, missionaries' and anthropologists' accounts, and what we can surmise from a few artifacts that have been preserved in museums. Because vanished societies' ritual practices did not protect them against the mechanical might of others, it is easy to dismiss them as superstitions—as we dismiss our own arts as "frills."

Yet the five preceding chapters should have made clear that as part of our biological adaptedness, humans evolved with certain psychological requirements, summarized in the titles of my chapters. To repeat, we evolved to need mutuality with other individuals, acceptance by and participation in a group, socially shared meanings, assurance that we understand and can capably deal with the world, and the opportunity to demonstrate emotional investment in important objects and outcomes by acts and experiences of elaborating.

These psychological necessities were instilled, expressed, and felt by means of what I have called rhythms and modes, which themselves are inherent in our biological adaptedness. They appear spontaneously in the engagements of mothers and babies, as well as in the materiality of handling and making. Unbound from their origins and elaborated as components of ceremony and, much later, as independent arts, rhythms and modes throughout most of human existence encapsulated and transmitted group meanings that further confirmed individual feelings of belonging, meaning, and competence and united individuals into like-minded, like-hearted groups. Their objective truth, convenience, and cost-effectiveness were of less importance than their emotional convincingness.

If we repudiate these evolved avenues to transcendence and meaning, what do we do instead? Can we expect our species to prosper if its evolved abilities are not fostered and its evolved needs are not met? A society that devalues making and elaborating forfeits a critical component of its members' birthright. The care or control used to fashion and embellish a thing is correlative with the value one gives it. Treating vital interests with respect and care and acknowledging their significance in a socially shared endeavor is another universal human practice. Without such manifestations of personal and group investment, what avenues do we give ourselves and our children even to articulate, much less achieve expression of, our values, individually or collectively?

At the ends of chapters 1 through 4 I described "legacies" of each ancestral need that affect contemporary lives, despite the very different world into which modern people are born and must make their way. In this final chapter I describe some of the legacies of the human need for elaborating, an activity that is today called "art." As such, it is loved and feared, esteemed and reviled, glamorized and dismissed, but rarely accepted even by its advocates as a normal, natural, necessary—if dormant—attribute of every person.

DISMISSING THE ARTS

Before making a case that might convince even the dismissive congressman to take the arts seriously, let me first examine some of the oft-cited reasons for regarding the arts with suspicion or repudiating them outright. Although stated in various ways, these criticisms of the arts are really variants of two general attitudes that appear contradictory but on closer examination are seen to be subtly interrelated: (1) artists and their arts are deviant and dangerous, and (2) art is superfluous and elite. My treatment will be necessarily abbreviated, since an analysis of either theme could be the subject of another book. One may rightly scoff at such superficial assumptions about art and artists, but I find that often it is makers and lovers of art themselves who, deliberately or unwittingly, contribute most to their persistence.

Artists and Their Arts Are Deviant and Dangerous

In many premodern societies the arts are associated with magical powers, and their makers are regarded as special kinds of people because they have access to these powers. Shamans and visionaries use artful means to attract spirits and to convey their messages to an audience: these techniques may be bizarre, manipulative, frightening, and even harmful.

In other societies, however, such as the Temiar, Medlpa, Kaluli, Ba-Benjellé, and Kalapalo, the arts are not restricted, and every normal person engages in them without complication. For the Yekuana, it is the world untreated by the arts that is dangerous. Although it has a long history, even appearing in the writings of Plato,[1] the generalization that artists are by nature dangerous or deviant has no more substance than to say the same of doctors or politicians. Anyone who commands power can misuse it.

Today the only artists who command power in modern secular, pluralistic, market-driven societies are the popular-culture superstars who neither need nor request government patronage. Artists who are not celebrities or otherwise commercially successful are not respected by the general public, and even though they are specialists, like shamans, few among the citizenry want to hear their messages. Choosing a calling over lucrative employment is less admired than it once was.[2]

At the same time, for those who do value them, artists and their imaginative products have become a repository for what remains of human spiritual longing and emotional expression in a nonreligious world founded on technological and rational solutions to human problems. Yet even if artists are poor and socially marginal, they are *potentially* a source of trouble, since stirring up emotions and unfamiliar modes of thought can interfere with reasoned, pragmatic problem solving or challenge fundamentalist dogmas within the status quo.

Nevertheless, since the Enlightenment (and with roots of the idea discernible from the Renaissance) the poor, unessential artist has been assigned or allowed to assume the rather romantic or glamorized role of outsider—prophet and visionary, rebel and revolutionary, social misfit (whether eccentric, naive, reclusive, insane, or just plain odd), or misunderstood genius (see Cubbs 1994, 77–78). Certainly today, when expanding profits, high consumption, and cost-effectiveness are valued above everything, the person who takes the time and trouble to elaborate (rather than mass-produce or at least customize) *is* anomalous and has little reward but to conform to, and even take pride in embodying, the idea of the free artist-outsider. The role has been socially tolerated because in most instances it has no important consequences, and in some cases it even sells. After all, audacity, nonconformity, and arrogance characterize successful insider traders as well as outsider artists. And in any case, the art market has strong reasons to perpetuate belief in originality, uniqueness, and rebellious genius.

For over a century, artists have been accused of not knowing how to draw or paint (or tell a good story or compose a decent melody or intelligible verse). Still, although their works were considered grating or empty or ugly by the masses, they seemed harmless enough, and since the cognoscenti claimed to find serious purpose and deep insight in them, they could be allowed to exist in their own limited sphere—like any specialized irrelevant pastime or sideline. *Chacun à son goût.*

From about the time of Pop Art, however, many artists' works have become harder to ignore. Their makers no longer appear to be exploring the limits of paint or space or spirituality, as their predecessors claimed to be doing, but rather the limits of credulity and decency. So long as the arts appeared high-minded and venerable, or at least enigmatic and evocative, society could tolerate them no matter how weird. But today even sympathetic members of the public often feel that artists have let them down, denying them the spiritual and emotional nutrients that the arts have immemorially provided and—what seems even worse—deliberately deriding, insulting, and offending their minds and sensibilities. *Chacun à son dégoût!*

There are, of course, reasons within the art world itself, as in the larger society, for this stalemate in which no one wins and both sides feel cheated. The general populace is largely unaware of recent trends in the art world that have specifically set out to destroy or minimize the outsider aura of artists, along with attendant claims for their works' originality and uniqueness. The results—insubstantial, impermanent, incoherent, often deliberately trivial, derivative, or ugly works—only confuse a public that is not au courant with these efforts to demystify, democratize, and even collectivize art making. Works of cryptic subjectivism or hermetic abstruseness, "conceptual" or "authorless" works that cannot be appreciated without a knowledge of the history of art, or unapologetic transgressions of "community values" add to the impression of art-world chicanery and further compound public mistrust.

My own view is that it is unfair to censure today's artists and arts for being complex, confusing, and contradictory when the larger society itself is rife with complexity, confusion, and contradiction. Moreover, where business and government are devious, ruthless, and unconcerned with human well-being it seems disingenuous to accuse artists of these same faults—a case of pots and kettles if not beams and motes.

However, with regard to the common accusation that art today feeds and thrives on excess—danger and immorality—more remains to be said. In the previous chapter we saw how, in their origins, religion (a society's sacred beliefs) and the arts (its ritual practices) developed together symbiotically. The precariousness and hence seriousness of ancestral life called forth correspondingly serious demonstrations of care that, it was hoped, would ensure protection and prosperity. Seriousness and importance found psychological equivalents in exaggeration, so that *excess* has never been far from ceremonial elaborations, as was illustrated with the example of *mbari*.

At the end of chapter 4 I described children's susceptibility to video games as a response to what ethologists call "supernormal signals"—exaggerations of features that in normal circumstances indicate harm, threat, or benefit and thereby attract attention. Something that is supernormal (that is, *larger* or *more*) automatically suggests greater importance and thus compels greater regard. It is then to be expected that the human desire to affect positively the serious circumstances of life often expresses itself as *creating* (not just responding to) supernormal signals. Hence the tendency to excess in ritual elaborations, where words, voices, actions, movements, bodies, surroundings, and paraphernalia are made as elaborated and exaggerated—as impressive or beautiful or costly—as possible.

For example, the *mardayin* (sacred law) of the Arnhem Land Yolngu of Australia comprises ceremonial songs, dances, paintings, sacred objects, and ritual incantations associated with ancestral beings (Morphy 1992, 186) that allow Yolngu to become directly involved with the ancestral past. Some of the paintings are made on men's bodies with blood drawn from their inner elbow and are additionally highlighted with white plant down stuck onto the blood. Ceremonial blood-letting gives the men a feeling of lightness, joy, and happiness that they interpret as power. The emotion resulting from this exaggerated action is further reinforced by seeing the shimmering painted design, which itself is considered to be a manifestation of ancestral power.

Such supernormal exaggerations and elaborations can become quite outrageous and overwrought. At Hindu religious festivals in Sri Lanka, we saw men expressing their devoutness by piercing their tongues or cheeks with metal skewers. Some rode swaying from a bracket, suspended by meat hooks through their back muscles, on the bed of a slowly moving truck. Others used the occasion to fulfill a previously made vow by rolling in the dust three or more times around the perimeter of the *kovil* (temple).

Walter Burkert (1996) lists some of the extreme actions that have been sanctioned by religious belief throughout history: animal and human sacrifice (often of the purest and best individuals), internecine wars, inquisitions, witch burning, *fatwa*, mass suicide, and sacrifice of valuable possessions, even parts of one's own body—as in the flesh sacrifice of the Santee-Yanktonai Sioux Sun Dance ritual. Said a devotee, Mato-Kuwapi, about his own sacrifice:

> A man's body is his own, and when he gives his body or his flesh he is giving the only thing which really belongs to him. . . . I might give tobacco or other articles in the Sun Dance but if I have these and kept back the best no one would believe that I

was in earnest. I must give something that I really value to show that my whole being goes with the lesser gifts; therefore I promise to give my body. (cited in McLuhan 1971, 39)

Horrific sights, loss of blood, feelings of pain, exhaustion, fear, and loss of consciousness can be shaped and contained by custom and used to reinforce an individual's and a group's sense of purpose and belonging. They can also instill dangerous beliefs that promote fanaticism and violence, as when expressed in groups who feel themselves to be at risk from identifiable others. Excess as tribalism, factionalism, and vandalism seems to satisfy its proponents' needs for belonging, meaning, and competence at the expense of others who belong to different groups and adhere to different meanings.

States of passionate intensity can work for good or ill, bring enlightenment or monomania, and make people capable of superhuman or inhuman actions. In small, homogeneous ancestral societies, susceptibility to excess would not have persisted unless it was generally advantageous, reinforcing belief and unification within a like-minded group—as among the Yolngu or Owerri or Temiar of today.[3]

Excess, then, is not restricted to the arts, in our own time or in the past, and in itself need not be dangerous. It can be hedonic, as expressed in the saying "Too much ain't enough," or jubilant, as in Mae West's "Too much of a good thing can be wonderful." In human elaborations, excess has signified not only hype but hope, not only contest but concord, the human best as well as the worst.

In the arts, excess has been most commonly manifested as extraordinary or ideal standards set for skill, beauty, purity, perfection, sacredness, and seriousness, which then understandably became the mainstays of Western classical and idealist aesthetic theories. As such, no one considered art or artists dangerous and disruptive.

Today, however, excess is typically manifested as shock or shockingness—a way to gain notice in a world bombarded with competing claims on people's attention, a way to protest against privilege and oppression, or simply the standard against which the "ordinary," the unshocking, is measured. It would be difficult for a contemporary artist to outdo the "shock ads" of the Italian clothing company Benetton in 1997. In one Parisian newspaper, *Liberation*, a centerfold displayed genitals, in many shades of skin color, of adults and children. Other ads that year included images of a dying AIDS sufferer and a victim of a Mafia shooting.

Some artists in the West today have atavistically revived the old excesses of premodern rituals, utilizing forbidden language or substances (blood, semen, mother's milk, excrement), sexual license, pain, mutilation, and occasionally even actual danger unto death. They have also made art that is excessively decorous and pure, excessively large or small, excessively banal or trivial, excessively esoteric or cryptic, excessively vulgar, or even excessively boring or meaningless.

In truth, while it may be called dangerous by those who are offended, most of this excess falls into an indifferent and bottomless maw. The nonhuman powers that really affect our lives and that many contemporary artists address with their arts—global economic trends, proliferating technologies, geopolitics, weapons manufacturers, media conglomerates, polluters of environments—are more uncaring and heedless of human suffering and desire than any tribal ancestors or gods ever were. They are certainly more dangerous than any creation by a mere mortal artist, and what is more, enjoy generous and unchallenged federal support.

Art Is Superfluous and Elite

To say that artists and the arts can be dangerous at least accords with the seriousness of their origins and customary uses. To say they are superfluous and only for an elite requires a lack of acquaintance with the arts of other societies as well as an unwillingness to accept their manifold forms in our own. This parochial view is, however, held by most people in America today, including many members of the art world who thereby support the very philistines whose attitudes need to be changed.

The charge of elitism is one of the biggest obstacles to taking art seriously, and it feeds into the belief that art is superfluous. If art is valued only by those who are wealthy and leisured enough to pay attention to it or educated enough to appreciate it, it follows that everyone else should be able to manage without it. The charge of superfluity can be applied both to the arts themselves and to the activities of people who make, do, or appreciate them. In the first instance they are "mere" ornament and decoration, and in the second they are "merely" pastimes, hobbies, or sidelines. Neither—product or process—is considered to be essential.

Calvinists and Puritans believed that the mind of the churchgoer would be distracted from thoughts of God by the beauty of music, stained glass, and other sensory delights. Other of our American forebears may have been less pious but also had reasons to deprive themselves of conspicuous arts, because many came from the most desperately poor com-

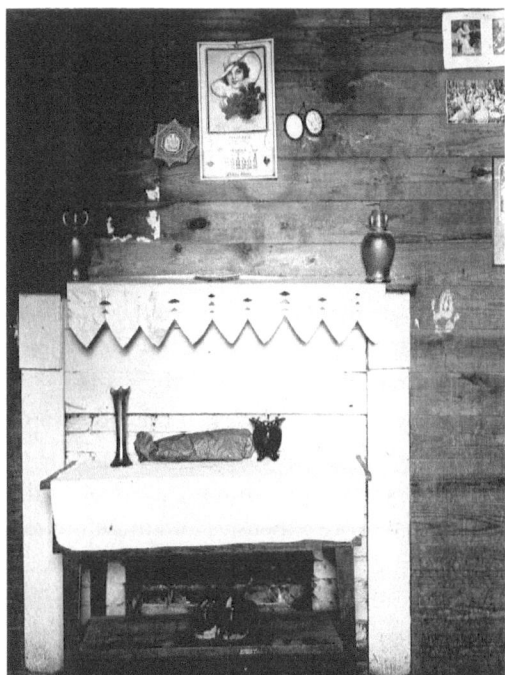

"Pinned all along the edge of this mantel, a broad fringe of white tissue pattern-paper which Mrs. Gudger folded many times on itself and scissored into pierced geometries of lace, and of which she speaks as her last effort to make this house pretty" (Agee 1941, 163). Photograph: Walker Evans. Library of Congress

munities of Europe and found everything but basic food, clothing, and shelter a luxury. Even when elaborative or artful activity was present in their lives, as in social or religious contexts, it was too humble or tied to tradition to be considered by others or themselves as "art."

To be sure, among the settlers of our country, women—motivated perhaps by notions of gentility—did put pictures on the walls, curtains at the window, embroidered covers on the pillows. James Agee (1941), in *Let Us Now Praise Famous Men*, describes the lacelike paper cutouts made by a sharecropper's wife to decoratively edge her mantelpiece. And young ladies of the 1920s, going out to work or aspiring to become proper housewives, learned from books like Harriet and Vetta Goldstein's *Art in Every Day Life* (1926) how to dress themselves and furnish their homes with good taste (Gorman 1997).

These are acts of decoration, and like tending babies, cooking, and cleaning, they have generally been considered the province of women.[4] As women and their work have been disparaged and disregarded, so have, perhaps by association, artists—for similar reasons: they are traditionally more concerned with appearance ("making things nice") and involvement with other people and their emotional needs. A more onerous resemblance between women and artists is their use of artifice to trick and deceive: they can't be trusted, and what is more, this unnecessary concern with how things look depletes the hard-won capital of responsible, hard-working males.[5]

Decoration and ornament in many societies are hardly superfluous and dispensable but are instead essential to a thing's effectiveness (Dissanayake 1992, 102–6). The efforts of twentieth-century women to beautify themselves and their homes may be directed by mass-market fashion more than culturewide ideas of participation and custom, but the women are nevertheless taking pains to elaborate themselves and their surroundings as humans everywhere have done without being considered vain or frivolous.

Aesthetes who are disdainful of convention-bound ideas of home decoration themselves follow fashion, if more expensive and therefore exclusive, in other realms. And as described in the previous section, the art world, at least that part of it that is influenced by the art market, certainly has a stake in keeping the arts esoteric: artists make unique products, and only the most discerning (whose wealth allows the leisure to learn about esoterica) buy them.

Historically, privilege has been an integral part of the development of the arts, but that should not be surprising. "History" of necessity began only with the invention of writing, which itself originated as a way to keep track of surpluses in settled agricultural societies that had become socially stratified.

Among hunter-gatherer and other small-scale societies, however, the arts have been much more democratic. Even in "big man" societies (as in Papua New Guinea or the Northwest Coast of North America), in which prestige was an important motivation for the arts, the entire society participated. For tens of thousands of years these oral cultures were preserved and perpetuated by means of the arts. For only ten thousand years, and even today not in all parts of the world, have the arts been associated with an elite.

That, however, is the world we—artists, art lovers, and their critics—know and use as the model for arguments both for and against the arts. To say that the arts deserve support because they "enrich" or "enhance" our lives implies that they are superfluous—added or extra—rather than intrinsic. To say that the arts are "good for you" suggests that they are cosmetic or palliative—superfluous or elite—rather than essential and universal.

In recent decades, nonelite and nonmainstream groups of many types have become outspoken in American social life. Long-established elitist and exclusivist ideas about art, with their assumption of western European cultural dominance and superiority, have been challenged with some success, especially in university art departments. As in this book, arts and artists in non-Western cultures as well as nonelite artists in Western societies are generally included in discussions of what art is, how it works, and what it is for.

In this spirit, the latest academic entrant to the art discourse, "visual culture," wishes to replace the idea of a history of art with a history of *images*, which is considered to be more inclusive and useful. Certainly a world of photographs, films, television, and CD-ROMs requires a recognition of the power of images and their problematic representations of or relationships with reality. Rather than considering made objects and performances as "art," which immediately places them in a superordinate (or elite) category apart from other things seen, visual culture studies examine them for what they "mean" or represent in particular individual, social, and historical contexts—for example, how they reflect attitudes toward and interpretations of gender, race, or class, or how they are related to other aspects of a society or historical period.

To take images seriously, however, requires more than exploring what this or that image has meant in this or that context. It is also important to recognize that people not only make images in various contexts for various purposes but also, at a more fundamental level, in certain circumstances (where people are serious about something), they elaborate them (for example, use care in their fashioning, put them in a special place, use them to make something else special, conjoin them with other arts and participate with them). The present-day emphasis on images and vision is reminiscent of archaeologists' preoccupation with prehistoric "symbols" and consequent neglect of the motivations for and emotional concomitants of making images and symbols in the first place.

Visual culture studies' interest in images in their contexts is fine as far as it goes, and many interesting things can come from it, just as interesting things came from the emphasis on art works and their historical place or the concern with aesthetic quality by art history and art criticism—the predecessors of visual culture studies. But for assessing the vital necessity and value of the arts as a human activity (rather than simply particular results or contexts of that activity), neither approach suffices.

Both visual culture studies and art history and criticism have assigned privileged status to images and vision—that is, looking and interpreting—

and thereby have overlooked making and doing.[6] First and foremost, however, the arts are things that people *do with their bodies*.[7]

Human patterning and picturing grow out of natural predispositions to use the hands, as described in chapter 4, just as singing and dancing arise from natural elaborative (repeating, regularizing, exaggerating) movements of the vocal tract and the body. In infancy these unlearned rhythmic-modal capacities, as precursors to the arts, are the behavioral means—the doings and makings—by which we are acculturated. Conceptually separated and "solidified" as specific arts—particular images, songs, performances—they become the embodiments of a culture. Although studies of the arts are generally concerned only with these individual manifestations, to take art seriously we must be equally aware of its unlearned precultural and performative origins. These are real and important, and it is unlikely that they are less psychologically and emotionally important to people today than they were to our ancestors a quarter of a million years ago.

UNLEARNED PRECURSORS OF THE ARTS

Being a baby means wanting to participate in patterned, multimodal, emotionally communicative improvisations with other people, to imitate their sounds and activities, handle things, and play with vocal sounds and physical materials. As described in earlier chapters, these impulses or needs are primary and pleasurable; they are among the abilities that make us cultural, able to socialize and talk, find and share meanings, and develop competence in our lives. They make us human. Babies do not have to be trained to learn them in the way that lions must trained to jump through hoops or elephants to dance. Without prompting, they are ready, emotionally motivated to try to do those things. They *need* to do them or they are not normal babies and will not be normal adults in their societies.

Being a child means wanting to investigate the material world with one's hands. As even adult artists know, materials have seductive power and can themselves compel the urge to handle and use them (Carroll 1997; Seelig 1992). Earth and water, as mud, seem to demand touching, marking, and shaping. Children naturally collect and even organize materials, finding them in the most unlikely places and transporting them home to play with or simply keep.

Even very young children love to make marks, and when given the opportunity to draw they will scribble energetically, if at first randomly. They will make marks on any surface—clothes and shoes, skin, walls and furniture. The continuity, effort, pleasure (self-motivation), and endless repetition that characterize the earliest motor activities also inform drawing. Both the kinesthetic pleasure of scribbling and the natural affinity for finding uses for materials continue to fund acts of drawing and artful making throughout childhood (Carroll 1997).

Children learn to draw with "orderly growing complexity" (Fein 1993). Initially they are motivated not to draw what they see but to follow what might be called an inner imperative to form. Their scribbles evolve naturally and inevitably into meanders and labyrinthine forms, then spirals, and eventually into increasingly refined geometric shapes and variations and combinations of those shapes: circles, concentric circles, concentric arcs, circles with radials, and quadrisected circles. Children notice these forms emerging roughly from their scribblings and then spontaneously go on to repeat and perfect them conscientiously, as if they find

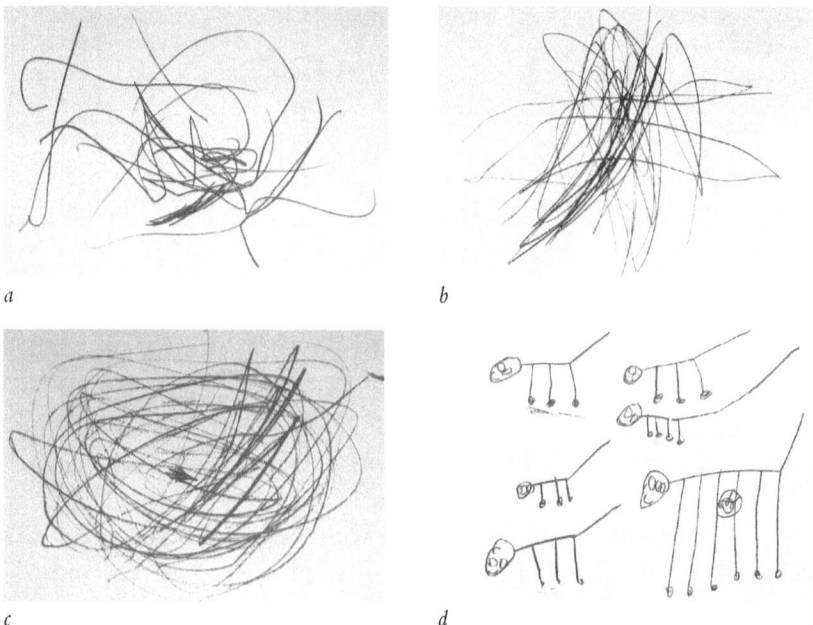

a

b

c

d

Children's early drawing. From First Drawings: Genesis of Visual Thinking, *by Sylvia Fine (Exelrod Press, 1993).*

a. *Age 2 years: controlled arm and hand movements within paper's limits.*
b. *Age 2.5 years: centering and clustering lines.*
c. *Age 3 years: large arm movements make circles around central mark; fewer broken lines.*
d. *Age 4 years 3 months to 4 years 8 months: horses, one pregnant.*

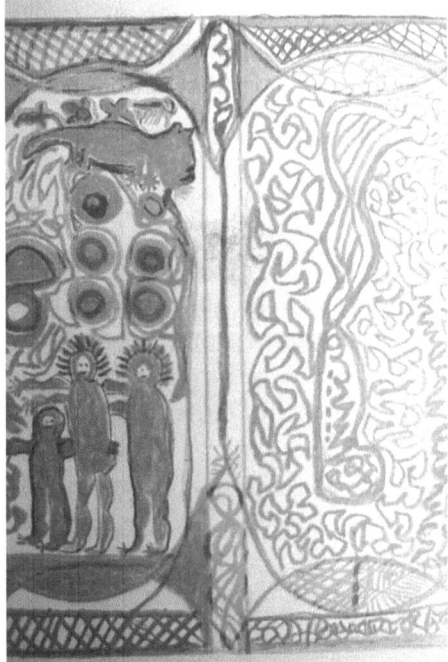

Drawing of First Couple wearing feather crowns, with offspring. "Songs" at right. Tukano, northwest Amazon, Colombia. Photograph: Gerardo Reichel-Dolmatoff.

them inherently attractive. Although with adult prompting children may label their drawings family members, flowers, suns, or animals, the images at first all look remarkably alike.

Human minds seem naturally to organize objects visually according to geometric prototypes. Eventually the building blocks of representational form emerge from only four figurations—perpendicular, parallel, and oblique lines and the circle. Children discover these spontaneously between ages three and four and use them as the fundamental elements of their first drawings of humans and animals.

To begin with, the child is playing with form, in Alexander Alland's felicitous phrase (Alland 1983), and not attempting to make faces or bodies. Always in early drawings structural integrity is more important than "realism," so that at a certain stage arms and legs may emerge from a circular head, or an animal might have six or seven legs to fill in extra space on a long torso. Balance, coherence of form, formal logic, and pattern are the imperative guiding principles of early drawing, and the child's self-discovered, autonomous, shapely forms eventually become elements of adult decorative pattern-making (Fein 1993). To assign "meanings" to our children's early works (or to those of people from unfamiliar cultures) on the basis of their apparent postures or details may be automatic and irresistible. Even when they are accurate, however, literal intepretations may obscure our awareness of the imperatives of underlying universal formal structural principles in human picturing.

Young children may express cross-modal associations in their drawings, as when they "hop" the marker across the page to show a rabbit hopping or make a truck sound while drawing a line to indicate the truck's moving. These are action representations rather than graphic images (Winner 1994). Drawings by Tukano men in the northwest Amazon seem to represent "songs" in a similar manner, as vocal/visual contours that rise. In a prehistoric Australian rock painting, a female figure is depicted with dashes placed around her mouth and the club she holds, possibly to indicate sound and motion.

Indeed, it seems reasonable to assume that our ancestors learned to draw as children do, and the commonalities among people's pictures all over the world support this assumption. Sylvia Fein (1993) has compiled a persuasive pictorial collection of the similarities in artistic structure to

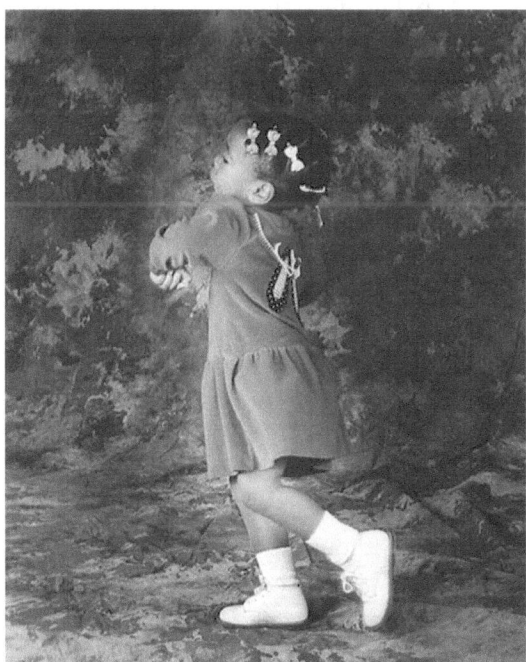

Waiting for her photograph to be taken, a little girl dances in her own world. Photograph: Elizabeth Leeor.

be found in the drawings of children, prehistoric and traditional people, and contemporary artists in modern societies.

The fascinating developmental trajectory presented so graphically and convincingly by Fein makes clear that refining or regularizing and repeating fundamental forms—that is, spatiotemporal patterning and elaborating—are innate and early parts of the human repertoire. Indeed, patterning and elaborating, recurrence and variation, occur in other modalities of movement, including vocalization, as precursors of what will become dance, song, and poetry.

Even eight-week-old infants play with their own vocal sounds by prolonging them; between four and six months, they produce substantial vowel-like sounds, bilabial trills, squealing, and growling. Between six and ten months, true babbling begins and occurs more when the baby is alone (Locke 1993).

Such activities are vocal scribbles and meanders. They lay the groundwork for later, spontaneously initiated speech activities—sound play, word play, distorted speech, and solitary monologues—that are unlike anything children hear from their elders (Kartomi 1991). In the Southern Highlands of Papua New Guinea, Kaluli parents consider such antics to interfere with proper development of language and specifically terminate it if they overhear it. Nevertheless, Kaluli children, like all other children, persist with manipulations of pitch, prosody, timing, and turn-taking (Schieffelin 1990, 99). The same applies to patterning and elaborating movements in games and dances, which children everywhere also invent and enjoy.

It is not too much to say that this shaping and elaborating of ordinary behavior and objects beyond the requirements of nature is as defining a characteristic of humans as their manual dexterity.[8] Like geometrical abstraction, repetition and pattern seem to be impelled by inner need, related to control—a way to order the chaos of experience which, unordered, is like a scribble or growl or stumble. Making something orderly and controlled and then doing a riff on it is fascinating, spellbinding, irresistible.

Just as children naturally draw, sing, dance, and play with words, they also spontaneously like to make believe, dress up in costumes, and adorn their possessions and surroundings. Although these characteristic and universal activities can be called "play" and thereby dismissed, it seems clear that they predispose humans to ceremonial participation. They may easily be channeled into appropriate ritual and artistic elaborations, just

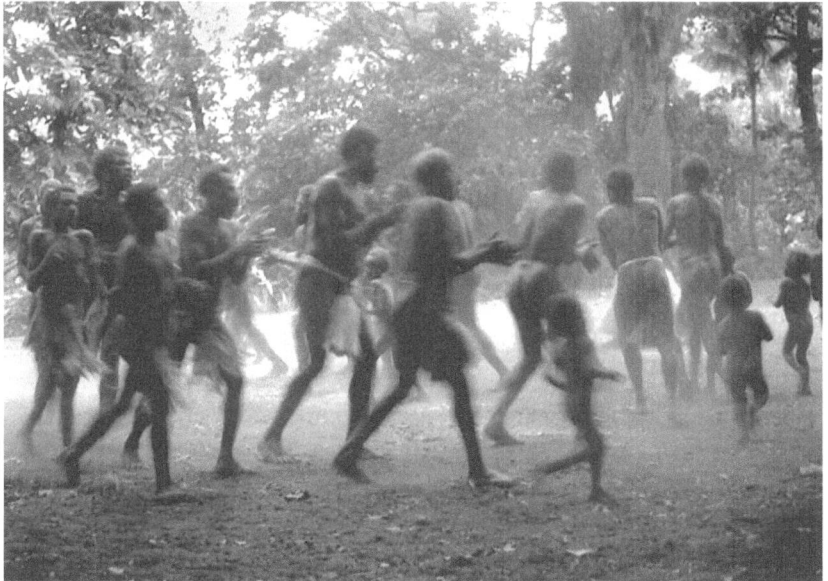

Males of all ages participate in Kastom dancing, Tanna Island, Vanuatu (western Pacific). Photograph: Janet Fullwood.

as children's play with objects and wish to imitate adults' practical activities develop into ordinary subsistence activities.

Today's Western children eventually show embarrassment about singing or dancing spontaneously, and they usually cease drawing when they reach the age of comparing their work with that of others and finding it inferior. In premodern societies, however, people of all ages unselfconsciously dress up, sing, dance, and do whatever painting or decorating of their belongings is customary. It was a surprise to me at a Papua New Guinea *sing-sing* (a Melanesian pidgin word that refers to an integrated art form of song, dance, and costume) to see strong, tough, adult men wearing body paint and feathers, seriously cavorting around in imitation of cassowaries and pretending to throw spears, all in a way that no American male past elementary school age would dream of doing. But I realized that the potential for such behavior must surely be there and will persist if encouraged by the social group. Young Melanesian boys must practice and yearn for the day when they too can publicly dress up and pretend to be cassowaries, as in the United States they practice baseball and basketball.

TAKING THE ARTS SERIOUSLY

The preceding five chapters each described an evolved psychobiological need and some of its manifestations. First was mutuality, our earliest acquaintance with love and the seedbed for the rhythmic-modal capacities that enable expression and satisfaction of the other needs. From the fifth need, elaborating, come the arts, which are inherent in and develop from the rhythms and modes of mutuality. In this scheme, love (mutuality) gives rise to art (elaborating).

These five needs and the rhythmic-modal means for their expression and satisfaction evolved for a way of life very different from the lives we now lead. In premodern and traditional societies, people were able more spontaneously and straightforwardly to experience community and reciprocity, assume an acknowledged place in a group and join with others to do things perceived as important, accept and affirm a worldview in shared systems and stories, learn to make useful things from the natural world for their subsistence, value their own efforts and know that they were valued by others, and acknowledge their emotional investment in important objects and outcomes by taking pains to make these things and events special.

It would be foolishly naive or monomaniacal to believe that all the world's problems—famine, war, the iniquity that spawns them—could be solved simply by practicing or experiencing the arts. Nor will art alone save a human soul. Yet in a world that shows increasing evidence of unmet primary psychobiological needs, it seems well worth describing, as I have in previous chapters, how the arts have addressed and satisfied these needs in the past. It is also worth proposing, in the remainder of this chapter, that they can do so again.

A recent survey of twenty-four American artists, men and women from a range of ethnic groups and economic levels who make their living as dancers, actors, directors, painters, sculptors, writers, composers, weavers, and photographers, bears out many of my evolutionary conclusions. The results reveal that "the creative process" fulfills needs for belonging, meaning, and competence, although the researchers (Nemerowicz and Rosi 1997) did not conceptualize their interviewees' responses in these terms. I would summarize their findings this way:

Art is a behavior: the artists reported that they conscientiously focused on the process of creating (that is, problem finding and solving), not on the final product;

which is interactive: the process was described as a series of encounters between the artist and "others"—the self, the environment, and materials and ideas;

hands-on: the process was in part a communicative interaction between the artist and the materials of his or her discipline;

emotionally rewarding and psychologically meaningful: the process itself was often characterized as a "high" ("exciting," "addictive," "intoxicating") and as having a satisfying physical as well as emotional effect; the artists said they were guided by basic principles and beliefs about themselves and the intrinsic value of the creative process;

communal: the artists valued the role of collaboration in their work, and although some collaborated more than others, nearly all wished they could do it more; they mentioned the importance of feedback from others, the need for an audience, and the sense of community;

and supportive of identity: most had their identity as artists formed early in life by positive reinforcement and acknowledgment from significant people, usually parents and teachers.

Several of Nemerowicz and Rosi's findings reflect American society's common attitude toward work and art. The artists felt guilty, anxious, and depressed if they did not work; many worked on several projects simultaneously. Some had felt lonely and isolated as creators in childhood, but later, after finding a community of people all pursuing the same artistic endeavor, they felt comfortable with their identity as artists. Although they received support for their artistic pursuits, most also reported receiving mixed messages about the desirability of becoming an artist. And women artists revealed more self-doubt and doubt about the worth of their art than did men.

The needs of professional artists are important, but it will become clear that I am interested in advocating more than government sponsorship of individual artists and organizations, although I believe this should be continued and expanded. Taking the arts seriously means arts for everybody, not simply as enrichment or appreciation but—in schools and communities—as encouragement and opportunity to participate from the first years of life and throughout life, as was the human birthright. To advocate broad support of the arts among everyone does not mean diluting the contributions of professional artists and their work.[9] On the contrary, a larger audience should be available to value and want to support them. Participant knowledge of anything, from cooking to tennis, enhances appreciation of its finer points and its virtuosos.

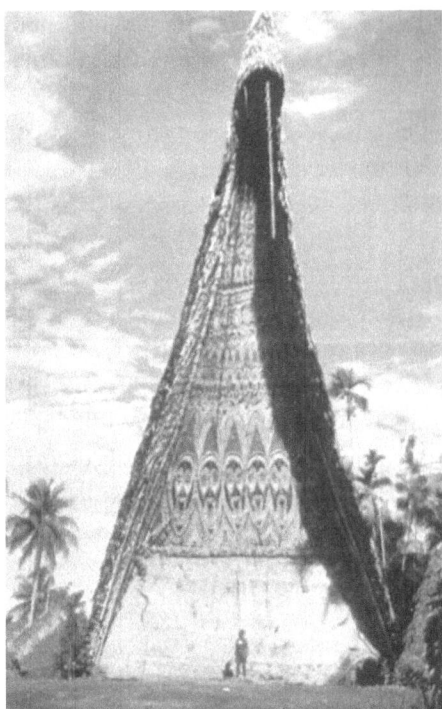

A Sepik River area Haus tambaran, *built entirely by human hands. Papua New Guinea. Photograph: Maureen MacKenzie.*

The Arts and Belonging

In the Sepik River area of Papua New Guinea, Arapesh and Abelam men build gigantic structures in which to hold *tambaran*, a complex of male initiation rites (Thomas 1995, 51). Because clan prestige is indicated and expressed by the size of the *haus tambaran*, the men expend almost super-human efforts of technological expertise and physical coordination in its construction—for example, the ridge beam alone weighs a ton. To fur-ther enable successful achievement, they hold special preliminary feasts and rites of purification. When the building is completed, the men are rightly amazed by the product of their joint effort and consider it to be magical.

And in a sense it is. Collaboration can produce wonders. The arts have frequently been described by members of premodern societies as a way of activating human "vital force"—not simply encouraging partici-pation but *creating* it (Lawal 1996; Zemp 1971). Individual success may feel good, but our evolutionary history has ensured that successful *group* effort feels even better, as was evident in the elation expressed by the collabo-rators in the successful Rover landing on the planet Mars in July 1997.

Today it is common to speak of finding "identity," meaning individual, self-created identity. But individual creativity and accomplishment, even to those who are fortunate enough to achieve them, are seldom enough. Despite (or because of) their self-interest, humans do much of what they do *for* other people—for their approval and admiration, or in order to receive good things in return. It is well to remember that we evolved to do things *with* other people also, for everyone's mutual interest and benefit. "Fellowship is life, and lack of fellowship is death," wrote William Morris (1886–87). Self-actualization requires social actualization.

Typical in traditional societies are "rites of passage" in which at prescribed times young people leave one identity and, through art-filled ceremonies, assume another. Although the elaborated insignia, dress, paraphernalia, and behavior of today's armies, clans, gangs, teams, and fraternities confirm that the arts still display and build collective identity, not everyone finds such a group. This is in contrast to traditional societies where everybody belongs.

In contemporary society we have traded the securities (and constraints) of group solidarity for the excitement and possibilities of diverse and unfixed identities. Our initiations—joining sports teams or fraternal groups, graduating, joining a profession, becoming part of a corporate "culture"—offer some of the satisfactions of teamwork, but these are more piecemeal and precarious. There is no guarantee of permanent membership. Although there is more "choice," these choices too often are confined to choosing among various consumer goods, pastimes, and "life-styles"—which do not really, or fully, address the requirements ordained by our evolved psychobiology.

Belonging and a sense of identity are, of course, in the very nature of collaborative arts such as musical ensembles and the "theater arts" so scorned by the congressman. Even today theater reveals the traces of its origins in ritual ceremony. As in *mbari*, there is preparation—a preliminary period of choosing, planning, constructing, and rehearsing. Both players and audience accept what Brian Hansen (1991, 4) has called an implicit "performance contract" to enter and abide by the requirements of the special imaginary world of the play. There is a formal opening and closing (the rise and fall of the curtain) upon an area specifically set apart (the stage). There are traditions and superstitions, from saying "Break a leg" (or "Take wings!") on opening night and not whistling in dressing rooms to expected audience behavior—the hush as the curtain opens, the curtain calls with applause and cheers.

In contrast to sports events, which can also be a kind of theater, a drama production is a noncompetitive, collaborative "team effort" in which spectators, cast, and crew are interdependent and *all win*. All roles are important, including that of the audience, which helps to create the performance and then appreciates its co-creation. Ideally, something remains afterward to affect the lives of the participants. Members of the production, as they return to their ordinary lives, talk about it among themselves, analyzing and revisiting the "run" in memory for its unique moments and a recovered sense of the unity it created. Theater people I know have told me that each production is "like a family."

Like theater, dancing or making music together also builds community. Regular rhythm, attained with others in coordinated movements and sounds, is a sign of good working order, so it feels good. Irregularity and unpredictability too, within limits, feel good—they let people know that they can fit in, can anticipate and understand what is happening in their world. Synchronous or matching actions are unifying, creating as well as indicating collaboration, exchange, and concord (McNeill 1995). The Gèlèdé festival in Nigeria facilitates social interaction and artistic collaboration among Moslems and Christians as well as adherents of traditional Yoruba beliefs—"people who would otherwise have been at loggerheads with one another over religious or other differences" (Lawal 1996, 80).

John Nunley (1996, 137) has described how, at the end of the Second World War, the island of Trinidad experienced an economic recession, due in large part to the departure of American sailors who had been stationed there. The economic problems spawned an accelerated street life of gambling, prostitution, and crime accompanied by the proliferation of a new type of street music. Performers—largely underemployed, lower-class young men—had converted empty fifty-five-gallon oil barrels into tuned percussive instruments that produced a unique melodic and rhythmic sound: the steel band. Although much of the middle-class establishment viewed the musicians and their music as contributing to the disorder, a few community leaders persuaded the government in 1950 to sponsor a steel band association in order to "eliminate violence, coordinate competition, provide financial assistance, and maintain a standard of excellence." Steel band music has become a world-admired folk art that acknowledges both individual improvisatory ability and group communal creation.

Practitioners of the visual arts, too, can become involved in collaborative endeavors—making a neighborhood playground, as in the Kwanzaa Project in Columbus, Ohio (Daniel 1995), or inviting members of the community to donate materials and labor for a collaborative garden/

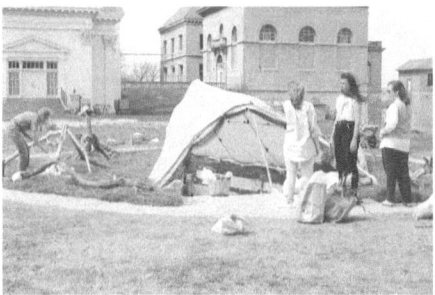

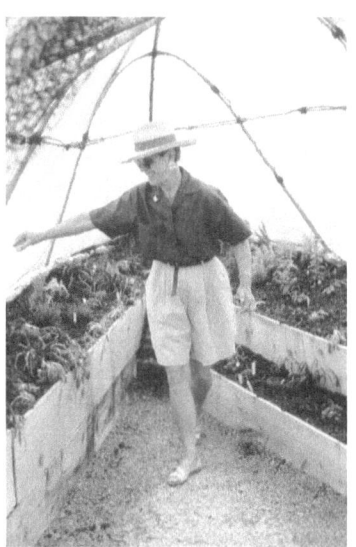

"Celebration of Renewal," collaborative garden project on the banks of the Ohio River, designed by Julie Schweitzer with the assistance of Kathleen Everhart and built from recycled and community-donated materials and services. Coordinated by the Louisville Visual Art Association, Louisville, Kentucky, spring 1995. Photographs: Louisville Visual Art Association.

installation at the Visual Arts Center in Louisville, Kentucky (Gorman 1995).[10] Participants attest to the satisfactions of joint accomplishment.

Even some "gallery art" today emphasizes group endeavor. The Italian artist Giuseppe Gabellone (b. 1973) designs works that cannot possibly be made by one person. In one example, a long, cylindrical, ropelike piece was constructed by wrapping pieces of fiber around and around bunches of the same fiber, a task that required not only time and coordinated labor but also skill and strength. The whole rope was then itself wound around a central pole. The many layers of the completed piece, and its immense length and unwieldiness, became a testament to the collaborative effort necessary for its fabrication.

Another planned Gabellone work, a steel cylinder with a total diameter of ten meters, is meant to be assembled from seventy-nine separate but identical sections. Because each section weighs sixteen kilograms, the completed ring requires that seventy-nine people work simultaneously, coordinating their labor in order to connect the pieces, fitting the tongues and grooves smoothly together. Each single part, requiring one worker to place it, is essential to the stability of the entire structure (Bonami 1996).

Engaging in collaborative activities like those just described goes beyond popular ideas of art as individual expression and creativity. Although the projects provide the satisfactions of group and individual effort and achievement, they are much more than self-esteem therapy. Participants

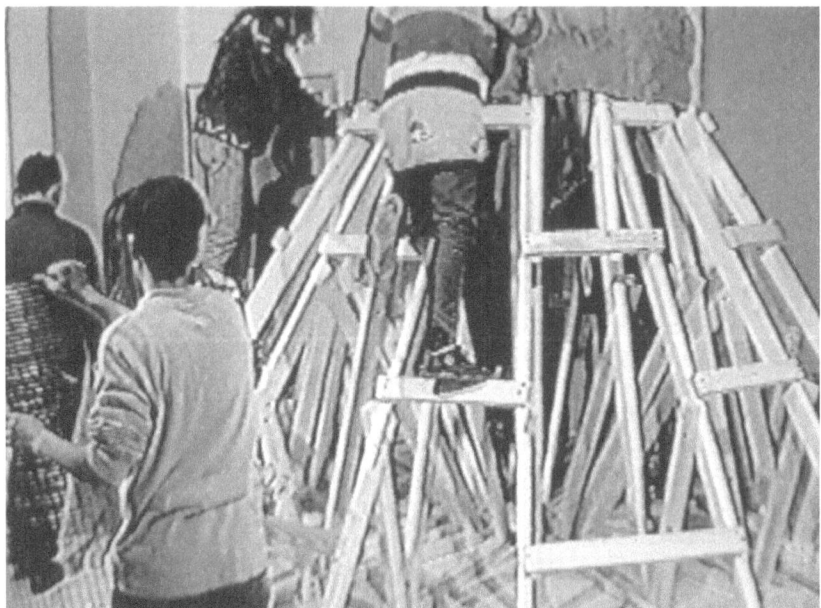

"Vulcano," mixed media, 1995, collaborative art project designed by Giuseppe Gabellone, Brindisi and Milan, Italy. A five-hour video, also titled "Vulcano," documents the construction of a volcano from clay over a wooden armature. The artist asked the collaborators to carry out their work in total silence. Gabellone is interested in the physicality of materials because it is there that the energy of the people who make his works is manifested. After the project was completed, the volcano was destroyed. Photograph: Studio Guenzani, Milan.

are made aware of their common humanity and hence become more fully engaged—body and mind—in life.

The Arts and Meaning

Human psychobiology predisposes us to seek and make meaning. Because values cannot manifest themselves as essences, elaborations help us recognize, express, and celebrate these meanings concretely. But where should contemporary people find meanings to elaborate? With the superabundance of images in the world and the plethora of possible ways to approach and discuss them, it would seem that *any* meaning, like any point of view or interpretation, is as good as any other meaning, point of view, or interpretation.

Despite the emphasis in this book on prehistoric and premodern people and on infants, I am well aware that art and life in contemporary societies are different from and more complex than in premodern societies, and that adulthood is very different from infancy. Obviously there are more possibilities, more choices, more information, more influences, more opportunities for good and ill, and no discernible way to discriminate among them. Today's discontents respond to no simple remedies, if ever they did. We can elaborate any meaning we wish, or no meaning, or we can forgo elaborating altogether.

I would point out, however, that despite today's unprecedented and profuse complexities, it remains true that beneath the teeming, meaning-rich and meaningless surfaces of contemporary life we continue to be affected by the same abiding concerns that premodern ceremonies such as *mbari* treat—concerns that people have always been moved to elaborate because of their biological importance.

In all their myriad social contexts, human meanings continue to reside in the same perennial and universal interests and verities—the natural world (earth, water, weather, stone, wood, fire), everyday artifacts (shelter, clothing, utensils), and subjects treated immemorially by human rituals, among them birth, death, attachment, desire, loss, change, hope, helplessness, the mysterious and unknown, memory, gratitude, awe. To seek, find, and celebrate meaning in these vital subjects is not simply or only cultural programming or wishful thinking. Although our specific formulations of these meanings may be socially constructed, the human importance of acknowledging the concerns remains real and unchanging.

For today's seekers of meaning who are elaborators or artists, what has changed are other things such as the purposes, intentions, and justifications for elaborating, one's fellow humans' endorsement and responses to elaborative activity, and the larger society's lack of regard for any kind of occupation or result except that which receives, for whatever reason, monetary reward.

The makers of the *mbari* house and figures knew that what they were doing was valued; their purpose and intention was nothing less than to bring prosperity and well-being to themselves and their community, which in turn not only wholeheartedly endorsed and responded with pleasure and satisfaction to the finished work but itself initiated its making and participated in its consecration. In comparison, present-day elaborators understandably feel lonely and faint of heart.

Caught up in the tedious or disorderly daily routine, we can forget that beneath all the flotsam and jetsam, our lives and concerns are deeply serious. "Resonance" by the larger society to these serious concerns is mostly trivial or stereotypical, so that we may discount our own inner conflicts and insights or else force them into the superficial culture's Procrustean beds of cynicism, wisecrack, and psychobabble.

Still, I suspect that most people hunger for a more profound life. The arts—ours and those of others—are *ways of treating the inner life seriously*, embodiments of our affective experience. The former American poet laureate Robert Hass observed that people die every day from the lack of what is in poetry. I assume he was referring to a sense of meaning, of connectedness, seriousness, the validity and momentousness of one's sense of being. If our society does not sufficiently provide such things, our arts—at least some of our arts—can. They allow us to show how much we care, to "take pains" rather than "get by." They put us in touch with our better self. They encourage attention to and involvement with the most abiding and affecting parts of human life and allow us the experience, in Thomas Berger's memorable phrase, of "outcrops of transcendence."

The Arts and Competence

The contributions of the arts to needs of competence are legion. We evolved to use our hands and bodies in the natural world, and as any teacher will confirm, using the natural world for raw material and for observation and eventually for make-believe and imagination is a tried and true source for emotional, cognitive, and manual satisfaction. Readers may accuse me of oversentimentalizing the man with the hoe, but I find in his labor a kind of dignity that is lacking in the worker at the computer terminal.

The arts help people to care and realize that they care about the natural world. People in every culture, at any age, find and have always found fascination and sustenance in the growth of plants and in wild animals, caves, the elements of earth, air, fire, and water, unusual stones, storms, blood, and skin—and have used or celebrated them in their arts. They are subjects of perennial and infinite metaphorical possibility.[11]

As well as aiding learning about the world, the arts are intrinsically motivating to the activity of learning itself: they reinforce probable success. Hands-on practice gives immediate sensory gratification and allows direct incremental assessment of what needs to be done. Like an athlete perfecting a movement or skill, a person engaged in the arts is aware of improvement achieved by direct effort in the here and now. One of the chief tenets of the arts and crafts workshop in the Industrial Home for Destitute Boys in Victorian England was that art and skill were latent, ready to be drawn out of the least superficially promising of people (MacCarthy 1994, 175–76).

In one of his many public lectures, "The Art of the People" (1879), William Morris proclaimed: "That thing which I understand by real art is the expression by man of his pleasure in labour. I do not believe he can be happy in his labour without expressing that happiness; and especially this is so when he is at work at anything in which he especially excels" (MacCarthy 1994, 420). For those of us or our children who do not receive such pleasure or happiness from job, sports, or schoolwork, the arts may be a more promising route to this delight in our own ability and achievement, popularized as "flow" (Csikszentmihalyi 1990).

The arts can also reduce anxiety and uncertainty, as described in chapter 5, by uniting people in focused, patterned physical activity. Visual art, music, dance, and drama also provide a form for feelings and allow the expression of what cannot be said in words. To anyone who has seen a skilled practitioner work with a troubled subject, the value of the arts as therapy is unquestionable.

With regard to the notions of art as "therapy" and as instilling a sense of competence, I was interested to learn of the importance of the European "high art" tradition to the population of Sarajevo when the city was under siege in 1992–93. An Edinburgh composer, Nigel Osborne, who

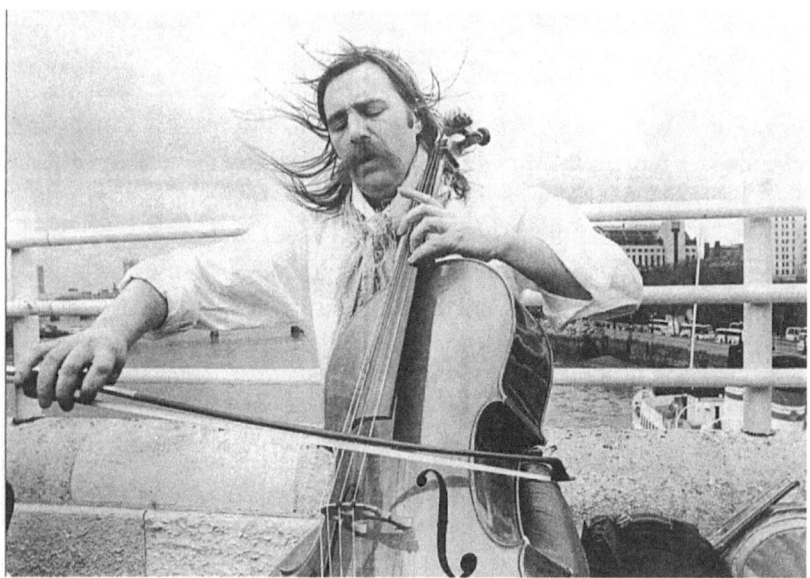

On a bridge in London, cellist Vedran Smailovic recreates his performance from the streets of Sarajevo in 1992. Photograph: Edward Webb, The Independent, *April 2, 1994.*

was deeply involved with the people there related in a newspaper article the words of one artist: "I think art did quite a lot for the city. Art gave people some energy, the feeling of still being civilised, and perhaps a little bit of self-respect."

He could have been referring to one instance reported by Osborne when, after the breadline massacre in May 1992, the cellist Vedran Smailovic put on his white tie and tails and played the Albinoni adagio in the middle of the street. According to many, this marked the start of the civil resistance movement. The image of Smailovic with his instrument, among the ruins and subsequently in the graveyards under sniper fire, became an icon for a city that chose to see itself as dignified, cultured, and European rather than barbaric and brutal like its assailants.

When the former Obala Theatre, destroyed by shelling, became a public shortcut to avoid snipers, its director decided to turn the ruins into an exhibition space.

> Often objects and images were created from the materials of destruction, like Mustafa Skopljak's stalagmites of shattered glass and dolls' faces buried in sand, or Ante Juric's installations of debris, mud, and water. . . . This has nothing to do with fragmentation, deconstruction, or the atomic blast that scatters meaning and reference. It is integrative and reconstructive: an almost sacred act of nurturing and healing. (Osborne 1994)

The "Witnesses of Existence" exhibition, as it was called, was itself wrecked by mortar fire on Christmas Day 1993, but the artists rebuilt it, and with the help of the United Nations it was later exhibited elsewhere in Europe and the United States (Gambrell 1994). In Sarajevo during the siege, there continued to be an excellent children's choir, music education went on despite everything, and the Sarajevo String Quartet gave concerts throughout, predominantly at matinees and informal ad hoc occasions.

Osborne (1994) concluded his article:

> It seems to me that something very strong has come from my colleagues in Bosnia. While the world stood by and watched a holocaust on television, and while Western art floundered in a colossal imaginative recession, the artists of Sarajevo were the frontline of European civilisation, creating a new inclusive art, refined in hell-fire, tough enough to deal with anything, and absolutely necessary.

The Arts and Specific Concerns in Lives Today

It is a measure of how different our lives today have become from the sorts of lives for which we evolved that the arts must be defended against our leaders' dismissive sneers, that they require justification and advocacy. But in addition to their contributions to belonging, meaning, and competence—that is, to the quality of our emotional lives—it is also possible to point to bottom-line benefits that the arts can bestow on America's economic standing.

A number of advocates of the arts have reported specific contributions that the arts make to education for the changing world and workplace of today (e.g., Chalmers 1996; Eisner 1995; London 1994; Simpson et al. 1997; Wilson 1997). They show, with support from empirical studies, how ways of thinking that characterize art making and experience can also enhance thought and learning in other, more academic subject areas. The Getty Education Institute for the Arts in Los Angeles sponsored (and now distributes) an eighteen-page special supplement on the subject, *Educating for the Workplace through the Arts*, which appeared in *Business Week*, October 28, 1996.[12] Corporate America's awareness that the arts might be good for business is probably the best option they (both the corporations and the arts) have, and the Getty organization should be commended for getting the word out to the right people in the right places.

Rather as our body's physiology is better adapted to process fresh vegetables, fruits, nuts, and wild game than dairy products, sugars, alcohol, oils, and fatty meats, so our natural mental aptitudes indicate abilities that were crucial in the lives of hunter-gatherers. They are, provocatively, the very abilities that are also integral to the arts: visuo-spatial assessment and memory; manual dexterity and mechanical insight and improvisation; kinesthetic control, grace, and economy of movement; storytelling and other verbal-persuasive skills; musicality; and social sensitivity. In schools, such aptitudes frequently take a back seat to those for reading, writing, and mathematics. Not surprisingly, since hunter-gatherers had no use for them, aptitudes for the three Rs are rarer in the pool of human talents today than are the other, "nonliterate" abilities. Yet in schools, the more "natural," common (and artistic) abilities are rarely fostered or rewarded, so that even those who have them to a high degree may be considered by others (and themselves) to be "dumb" or "lazy."

Yet by using these natural aptitudes, good teachers can help all students to understand new information and concepts. In some instances, knowledge from the arts transfers directly to other, more traditional subjects, as from ceramics to the chemistry of heat, music to fractions (counting), Picasso to geometric shapes,[13] sculpture or dance to understanding the law of gravity. Singing and piano lessons apparently even improve spatial reasoning in three-year-olds (Rauscher, Shaw, and Ky 1993; Rauscher et al. 1997). But the arts develop the mind and senses in more subtle and interesting ways as well. I will describe some of these bonus benefits that pertain to my subject here and refer the interested reader to more detailed and comprehensive statements elsewhere.[14]

Even when a student is natively good at the sequential analytic skills of reading, writing, and mathematics, art making develops additional intellectual abilities and instills habits that contribute to learning and problem solving in general. The arts give practice in using trial and error to get something right; relying on one's senses, intuition, and critical judgment to make creative choices and decisions; understanding how images and other nonverbal modalities are used both literally and metaphorically to create meaning; holding several possibilities in awareness and being open to change; recognizing that there are many ways of getting from here to there and that (unlike in spelling, arithmetic, grammar, or computer programming) there is more than one solution to a problem. Making artistic connections and seeing aesthetic relationships gives experience with solving complex problems and understanding systems in a variety of contexts. Through the arts, one learns that many problems (such as important life decisions) have no clear-cut method for solution but that an awareness and exploration of possibilities is the first step in addressing them.

The experiences of meeting challenges, solving problems, thinking new thoughts, and recognizing deeper feelings keeps art makers coming back for more, testing and pushing beyond the limits of their knowledge, awareness, and expertise (Carroll 1997). Art making helps to instill qualities of "character" such as discipline, patience, and delay of immediate gratification. Watch small children making pictures and note their seriousness, concentration, and immersion in the task at hand.

Today, when discipline and decorum are increasingly viewed as interfering with one's "freedom," it is well to remember that they have sustained human individuals and societies for millennia. Although standards of considered behavior may well enforce a repressive social control when imposed from without, as inner guides they indicate the value that we attach to a thing. When we make or do something, no matter how humble, it mirrors us back. Our skill and talent, or their lack, and the extent of our caring are there to be seen. If we care, it shows, as it does if we do not care.

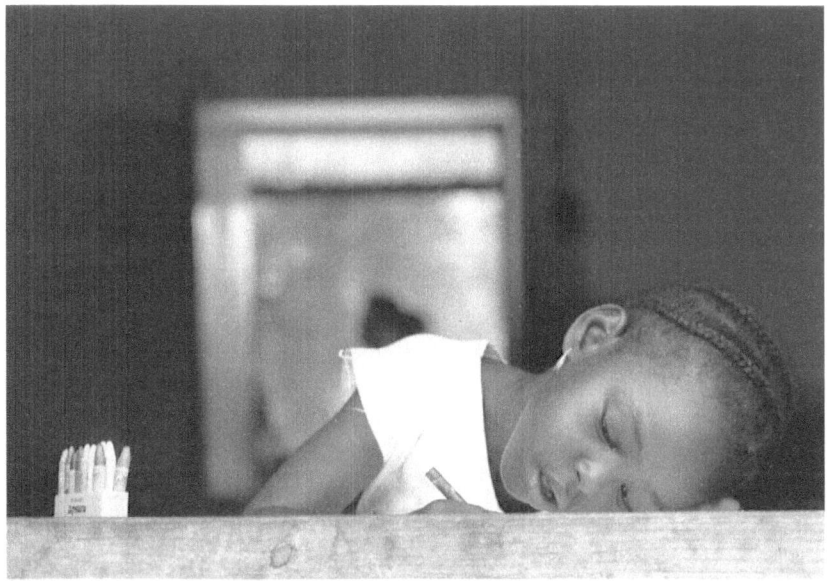

Absorption and pleasure in drawing at a girls' primary school in Juba, southern Sudan. Photograph: Maria Antonietta Peru, UNICEF.

The arts can teach discrimination, the awareness that small differences can have large effects. By paying attention to subtleties of qualities, people's powers of observation and judgment are trained. Through experience of the arts we discover the intrinsic satisfactions of complexity. We recognize that the goal is not always to arrive at a destination but to enjoy the journey, and that the journey can become a way of life.

In my experience, artists are ever alert to details and connections that arise unexpectedly in daily life and contain the promise of elaboration and further connection to other things and to feelings. Although busy lives conspire against noticing ordinary things, the arts encourage openness and curiosity, seeing possibilities in unpromising material, and paying attention to the moment. Using nature as material or subject matter encourages recognizing one's connection to place, to the environment, to Life as well as one's own life.

The arts can be an antidote to the hyperverbality, linearity, meta-analysis, and mediated knowledge that pervade complex technological societies but are themselves unprecedented in, and even disadvantageous to, earlier ways of human life. Indeed, the arts reconnect us to the more global, synesthetic, emotion-suffused, analogic or metaphorical, often nonverbal kinds of thinking that we had as children and that have characterized our species for hundreds of thousands of years. The arts, in their cross-modality, foster associational or relational thinking, whether we are makers or participants. Although commonly considered to be impractical, this sort of mentation is pervasive and satisfying, as is demonstrated in myths and arts from all over the world.[15]

Rational, analytic thinking provides us with high-powered mental spectacles with which to narrowly focus and clarify the world. Used exclusively, however, they can give us mind-strain. Electronic and print media tint and even distort the lenses. It is healthy from time to time to remove them, take in the world as we were born to do, let thoughts and sensations roam as the arts allow. Rather than encouraging useless, self-indulgent fantasy that destroys logical thought, such ideation may well enhance it. Analogy and metaphor give practice in connecting the unlike but similar, fostering and rewarding imagination and "creativity," the ability to conceptualize and cultivate possibilities from thoughts and feelings that would not otherwise emerge.

Awash in the deluge of a ceaseless and unrelated superabundance of images and messages, where pretense and reality are hard to distinguish, we can find a kind of elementary sanity and satisfaction in what hands can do—including ordinary, workmanlike, even repetitive actions of scraping, sanding, beating, turning, weaving, stitching, knitting, hatching, and polishing that are traditionally parts of making carefully. The arts' rhythmic-modal fundamentals are always grounded in the life of the body and of nature, providing a kind of engagement with the physical world that some artists, in their concern with "ideas" and "concepts," may forfeit. There is the irreducible materiality of handling, and the pleasure of working according to natural body rhythms and of having, like the child, an undisputable effect on the world.

The arts help to shape and control, thereby reducing anxieties and uncertainties. Describing in words, finding expressive movements, or creating visual images and forms for one's own loves, hates, fears, fantasies, and aspirations can become a way of articulating the inner world and then imagining extensions or alternatives to it. By enabling the searching out and expressing of one's own feelings and the exploration of others', the arts expand awareness of what it means to be human.

The arts of the past contain the treasures of humankind. In many cases they are the only records we have of past cultures. Throughout human history the arts everywhere have addressed common needs of belonging, meaning, and competence; they have elaborated the things people care most about: their bodies, possessions, and surroundings, their human relationships, their relationship with the verities and immensities of nature. The arts not only teach us about individual cultures but also, through the universal elements they use and our own responses to the universal concerns they address, tell us of our common human heritage. But this way of looking at arts must be taught: it is not immediately evident in culture-bound traditional curricula (however, see Chalmers 1996).

TAKING LIFE SERIOUSLY

In this book I have described how the arts may have originated in human evolution. Their precursors are unlearned rhythmic-modal aptitudes that predispose us—babies, children, and adults—to partake of and participate in artlike behavior. These aptitudes were available to our ancestors when they began to address, in ceremonies, matters of serious concern, matters such as health, prosperity, and fecundity that affected their survival. Because people really cared about the results, ceremonial elaborations were not performed casually.

This origin suggests that if we want to take the arts seriously, it is necessary to take life seriously—that is, to expand our field of life concerns beyond a succession of heres and nows, the momentary preoccupations that most people take all *too* seriously. Existential seriousness is an endangered property these days, as much by default as by deliberate design. There is little in the contemporary job-and-market-shaped lives of most of us to encourage a considered or serious, as opposed to a "work hard, play hard," attitude toward those lives.

My position and tone in this book may at times have seemed overly solemn and earnest, as if I were unaware of the humor, whimsy, and delights that, to be sure, are as characteristic of the arts as utility and gravity. I do not much like to be perceived as a humorless grump or scold, but it seems that someone must speak plainly. After all, the advocates of Money, Self, and Fun can be heard loud and clear, as can their repressive and reactionary enemies, in the interdependent "McWorld vs. Jihad" so cogently examined by Benjamin Barber (1995).

It is fair to say that today a preponderance of the people in American society have been born, more than at any other time in human history, into a social milieu whose ideals are entitlements to personal ease, sensuality, and gratification and to spontaneity, novelty, informality, irreverence, telling it like it is, and letting it all hang out. These are the reverse of traditional society's hard work, conservatism, moderation, respect for authority, conformity, and similar straitlaced virtues that most people are glad to exchange for their opposites when given the choice.

Although in extreme cases they can be repressive and oppressive, it is well to remember that the old and duller principles have characterized human societies far longer than our present exciting new ones, and humans evolved with the former as the norm. For hundreds of thousands of years, ancestral ways of life satisfied human needs; fulfilling these needs was what life *was*. Today "the good life" (which in traditional societies meant many children, good health, long life, prosperity, and cosmic and social harmony) is often conceptualized as the sweet life, *la dolce vita*, or "the American Dream," where plenty of money transforms the old "sins" of human nature—gluttony, lust, sloth, pride, anger, envy, and greed— to eating well, love affairs, holidays, prestige, power, competitiveness, and possessions. Yet the limitlessness and irresponsibility we extol can only characterize people whose lives are *not* serious.

I realize that few people in modern societies actually live a sweet or, except for the unemployed, idle life. And as I said earlier, it is difficult to be serious when one's days are spent in job-work rather than work-toward-one's-life. Most of us have little choice about how we occupy our days.

Yet it remains true that despite the maladies of the quotidian, for most of us, most of the time, the sources of our values are not existential—at least not until the X-ray shows a blot or we confront our very own hurricane or devastating flood. For our distant (and even recent) ancestors, and for populations of faraway people who face famine or enemy annihilation, ease, fun, and irreverence are not choices of life-style. The sicker forms of humor and disengaged cynicism that come from being "with it" and having "seen and heard it all" are incomprehensible to people who have been with and seen and heard real misfortune or atrocity.[16]

Rituals, with their associated arts, are prominent in societies that are close to elemental realities, the hardships of disease, scarcity, and death. Because we are less immediately aware of these, our need for propitiation and intervention is less. Citizens of contemporary societies are burdened not by the demands of primary subsistence or the dangers of untamed nature so much as by the dictates and distractions of trivia, by a surfeit of information and sensory assault, and by the imperatives to earn and spend.

Even so, the needs and meanings of our common human species nature remain, despite their increasing neglect, devaluation, and even irrelevance to a competitive, technocratic, pragmatic, materialistic, efficiency-oriented society. If humans evolved to demonstrate their serious concerns in excessive ceremonial elaborations, one might presume that people today still require such experiences and make or seek them. How are contemporary elaborations the same and different from those in more traditional societies?

Observers of contemporary Western society have described the "ismitis" that afflicts us—our secularism, materialism, instrumentalism, consumerism, narcissism, skepticism, and cynicism, along with our increasing alienation from each other and our overfilled, fractionated, and frantic lives. There would appear to be little time for elaborations, but they are there, if in secular, materialistic, fractionated (and so forth) forms. That is, although holidays are often a time to sleep or work or shop, our social and personal elaborations are still largely attached to life concerns—religious, political, therapeutic (Lippard 1994, 14)—and are to be found where our communal and individual values are.

Like ancestral and traditional people, we continue to mark and elaborate important life stages—birthdays, weddings, memorial services for the deceased, graduations (commencements), promotions. When we do something as common as dress carefully for a job interview or a big date or plan festive details for a holiday celebration, when we design a garden or attend any ritualized event, when we admire the "rightness" of an athlete's movement and laugh appreciatively at a witty turn of phrase, we are making choices and exercising judgments as "artists" do.

Yet these are fragmentary scraps of making and recognizing elaborations. Although they are perhaps better than nothing, compared with the place of the arts in traditional societies they resemble the unintegrated spasmodic movements of a creature that has been mortally injured or taken from its natural life-sustaining element. In a quite real sense, like zoo animals we have been removed from our natural environment and show the exaggerated consequences of this displacement in the fitfulness of our artistic ventures as well as in more unsavory pathologies of unmet needs for belonging, meaning, and competence—gangs, addictions, anorexia, bulimia, self-mutilation, clinical depression, suicide, attention deficit disorder, random violence, serial killing—which, if not altogether absent, were socially shaped and managed in hunter-gatherer societies.[17]

The collective excesses that most engage us today are the elaborations and spectacles of rock concerts, blockbuster films, television extravaganzas, and athletic contests. Our *mbari* ceremonies on which extraordinary communal (creative and financial) effort is lavished are advertisements and the events or products they enhance. In the most vivid, attention-grabbing ways, message, event, and product promote and promise youth, sexiness, status, power, knowing the score, getting the most for the least—which, whether we are aware of it or not, are easily recognizable as selective advantages. Entertainers urge us to have fun and be "in the know" as we admire their wealth, glamour, and skill and vicariously partake of these by purchasing what they wear or endorse.

Distractions and vicarious experiences have then become the ceremonies by means of which a secular, market-driven society articulates its version of such perennial human concerns as acquiring the needs and goods of life, caring for and beautifying the body, finding love, achieving and preserving status and security, and sharing a worldview. But these specific "goods and services" elaborated by modern media are more important to the health, fecundity, and survival of the international marketplace than to that of human individuals or populations.

We can look at corporations and "the marketplace" (and even contemporary proliferations in science, technology, and business) as modern amplifications of our evolved short-term instrumental interests, supported by human appetites and physical necessities but having no intrinsic commitment to the survival or betterment of either individuals or groups.

Interestingly, such unrestrained expansion is not inherent in the satisfaction of instrumental, physical appetites and needs, as is evident in small-scale societies, which could and did remain at a minimal level over millennia. In contrast, the long-range interests of the individual and group—the appetites and needs for social integration and communal meaning—were too important to be indicated only once, in a given modality, in terms only of immediate conditions.

Thus the arts have always traditionally exhibited emphasis and reiteration and, in ancestral societies, could not afford to be minimalist. As the very warp and weft—the supporting fiber and constructed design—of the moral integument, the arts in their traditional role had to be as redundant, all-encompassing, sense-, body-, and mind-involving, impressive, and seductive as possible. Tailored to our human responsiveness, art in its origins had as *its* bottom line an overriding concern with the human quality of life. Its celebration therefore acted to ensure our survival and betterment, without—as today—putting all our eggs in the basket of direct subordination to immediate physical desires. Today, we've got it backwards.

Although we are living today in ways that are almost entirely opposed to those in which we were evolved to live, some developments in the current art world have put us more in touch with those origins and our fundamental nature. For example, the emphasis on cultural diversity has wisely expanded the study of art to include its manifestations in all societies, reminding us of its communal and performative aspects, its multimodal nature in which song, dance, performance, and visual spectacle all combine, its integration with the lives of its practitioners, and its multiformity. This is well and good, but as it stands, not enough.

It is, I believe, more important to learn what we have in common than to show one another what our particular culture does differently or better. If it is recognized that the arts everywhere address the same human concerns that have been part of the human condition for millennia, then we have a means of bringing people together rather than dividing them. Just as cradleboards, baby sashes, and car seats are all ways of transporting babies, so can we recognize that Navajo sandpaintings, Temiar songs, and Yekuana baskets are ways of dealing with illness. Body decorations are indications of identity and status in every culture of the world. Ceremonies of thanksgiving, of renewal, and of marriage and death, and expressions of adoration and wonder and gratitude, occur everywhere.

Because of their importance, elaborations evolved to be intrinsically satisfying, emotionally and intellectually. The arts help us take life more seriously because they encourage us to show that we care about important things. In addition, they are age-old ways to pass on culturally important values in stories, to celebrate culturally important events, to enhance and enrich the environment, to articulate and deal with anxiety, to mark and affirm individual and cultural identities, and to join individuals in common endeavor, providing them the opportunity to become part of a larger whole—that is, to enlarge the individual's sense of being.[18] If our government, schools, and communities consider these achievements a waste of time, they are saying that what was essential for 99.9 percent of human history is a waste of time today. What else is more important?

I cannot do better than to end this chapter with some impassioned words from Robert Hughes, which come from a quite different approach to the arts but echo uncannily the message of this book:[19]

> One of the ways you measure the character—indeed, the greatness—of a country is by its public commitment to the arts. Not as a luxury; not as a diplomatic device; not as a social placebo. But as a commitment arising from the belief that the desire to make and experience art is an organic part of human nature, without which our natures are coarsened, impoverished, and

denied, and our sense of community with other citizens is weakened. This may sound like rhetoric, but after twenty-six years of writing in America I know it to be true—I know it in my heart, my sometimes mean and irritable writer's heart. The arts are the field on which we place our own dreams, thoughts, and desires alongside those of others, so that solitudes can meet, to their joy sometimes, or to their surprise, and sometimes to their disgust. When you boil it all down, that is the social purpose of art: the creation of mutuality, the passage from feeling into shared meaning.

Appendix
TOWARD A NATURALISTIC AESTHETICS

WITHIN THE PROTECTIVE walls of the academy, art and biology occupy widely separate precincts. It is therefore somewhat surprising that
despite marked differences of aim, method, vocabulary, and style, they
reach rather similar conclusions about art: the arts are products of culture,
not biology; art practices and experiences are contingent and relative, not
inherent; and aesthetic judgments are sham or delusory—that is, they are
really statements about something else, and they serve (usually unwittingly) individual interests.

Reasons for these conclusions are generally good ones, and I do not
deny their validity. I do claim, however, that they—reasons and conclusions—do not go far enough, primarily because they arise from our society's restricted and impoverished view of art and aesthetic experience.
That the arts are variable and mutable seems obvious. Who, looking at
most of the pet dogs in the neighborhood, would ever believe that genetically they are essentially the same as wolves? The arts in the modern world
generally appear in such confounded, domesticated, ineffectual forms that
their ancestral kinship, viability, and potency can scarcely be imagined.

Once we accept and truly appreciate the message of this book, that
the antecedents of the arts—rhythmic-modal experiences—evolved to
enable our human way of life in relationship with others, it becomes possible to enlarge and amend the customary dismissive ways in which our
society thinks about art.

Yet even this larger view—that art, as making and elaborating, is innately predisposed and universally present in humans—appears to entail the same relativism as orthodox evolutionary or art theory. For if humans everywhere are art makers and experiencers, are there grounds for declaring that one example or experience of art is better—of greater human value or quality—than another?

This is not simply an academic question, for all of us are at one time or another puzzled if not affronted by the array of stuff that goes by the name of art today. Okay, it's all art, but is there not a more satisfactory way of approaching it than the extremes of "Anything goes!" and "If you have to ask, you don't know"? To conclude this book, I specifically apply its biological view to contemporary aesthetics as an additional contribution to taking the arts seriously. By sketching the outlines of a naturalistic basis for judgments about experiences of art, I hope as well to suggest new possibilities for reconsidering and even reinstating the relevance of currently fraught words such as beauty, quality, and transcendence.

HOW AESTHETIC JUDGMENTS CONCEAL
SELF-INTERESTED AGENDAS

Certain enduring words and ideas in Western aesthetics have become discredited today because of their implicit elitism or presumption of superiority. Attributions of quality assume the presence in art works of differences or subtleties that make one experience more notable ("better") than another. Under the pervasive influences of multiculturalism and poststructuralist theory, those in the art world or university have accepted that standards of beauty, taste, judgment, and aesthetic value are not real in themselves but are products of the norms and ideologies of individual societies. Even more, it is said, they depend on particular entrenched interests that those in power wish to use and reinforce in order to preserve their dominance.

Such cultural authority explains why post-Renaissance, European-influenced cultures considered painted female nudes in poses of delectability and availability to be appropriate subject matter for "art" and yet thought of sculpted images from India or Oceania as ugly heathen idols. Similarly, chamber music and opera were deemed superior to Gershwin songs, African cross-rhythm drumming, and the performances of Barbra Streisand. "Art" (paintings and sculptures) was distinguished from "craft" (whether ceramics, photography, textiles, or glass), and consequently each occupied different museums, commanded different prices, and enjoyed different social status.

Over recent decades, and for what seem like good democratic reasons, we have learned to shun terms such as "beauty," "quality," and "transcendence" and deny the ideas they embody. While these words were staples of Victorian conversations about the elevating effects of art, they have become as unmentionable and taboo in contemporary art discourse as "breast" and "thigh" were to the Victorians. With their residue of patriarchy, privilege, religiosity, and European dominion, the very words now imply a kind of unexamined self-satisfaction, self-interest, and ultra-conservatism that has become widely suspect.

For their part, evolutionists find notions of beauty and quality only too easy to explain.[1] While art theorists consider judgments of beauty and quality to be facades behind which lurk people's feelings of social superiority, evolutionary theorists see them as screens that conceal individual adaptive interests. Orthodox evolutionary theory conflates aesthetic value with adaptive value (Thornhill 1998) and views value terms such as "beautiful" or "good" simply as indicating choices or judgments that in ancestral environments tended to lead to greater survival or reproductive success. (This position will be described in greater detail in the following section.)

Evolutionists realize that people do not usually make choices based on conscious calculations of survival or reproductive advantage. To take obvious examples, we do not engage in sexual intercourse only because we wish to produce offspring, nor do we eat chocolate eclairs because we want to keep our caloric intake high—even if, in a bottom-line sense, this is why sex and creamy (fatty) sweet foods are pleasurable. Our finding beauty, pleasure, and value in anything are the "proximate" reasons—the tricks or illusions—that motivate us to do what is ultimately beneficial.

Insofar as "art" is considered to be a by-product of large brains or a concomitant of symbol-making ability, the evolutionist view of aesthetic quality echoes that of cultural constructivism: our choices are culturally influenced and thus "relative." Because the life circumstances of Owerri, Temiar, Kaluli, Kalapalo, and others vary from one another, their art creations and experiences can be understood as culturally (even individually) unique. This is a logical conclusion.

However, if we view art not as an accidental by-product of big brains but as the active human capacity and motivation to elaborate and respond to elaborations, we can go beyond the simplistic assumption that "aesthetic" evaluations are nothing more than enticements of our adaptive interests. Early in chapter 1 I distinguished between lovemaking and copulation, dining and feeding, and killing game animals with respect and with indifference. It is universally human to recognize and actively create such distinctions, even if the arenas in which we do so vary.

Such distinctions, or differences in behavior, reflect emotional dispositions that transcend the simple satisfaction of an appetite. When evolutionary theorists regard art as only adaptive preferences, they provide little explanation for why humans should have evolved the capacity to experience a stronger or more elevated state than the ordinary pleasurable satiety felt (presumably by other animals also) after the satisfaction of hunger or sexual deprivation.

Practically speaking from the viewpoint of an evolutionist, the emotional rewards of all individual consummatory experiences of mating or eating (or anything else) should be roughly similar if they serve the motivating purposes—reproduction, survival—for which they were designed. Apart from ultimate adaptive valence or cultural conditioning, evolutionary psychologists give us no criteria for explaining why some experiences are generally received by their percipients as qualitatively more meaningful, valuable, pleasurable, or desirable than others—that is, as aesthetically superior.

Previous chapters of this book have clearly shown that ideas of beauty or quality and routes to transcendence—like specific art practices and objects—do vary among human cultures and have to be learned. They are contingent and self-interested. Nevertheless, it is also true that people in all societies have criteria of beauty (that is, what is an especially fine, superior, or desirable example of a thing). They make distinctions and note differences of quality. And in most if not all human groups, experiences of the beautiful and excellent may lead to valued and desired heightened emotional states.

I contend that in a naturalistic aesthetics, learned criteria of quality and learned responses to beauty will nevertheless rest upon evolved universal predispositions, and some aesthetic experiences and ways can be demonstrated to be qualitatively superior to others. Aesthetic experiences may begin with evolved responses to signals that indicate adaptive immediate self-interest, but they are affected even more by evolved predispositions to elaborate and respond to the elaborations of others. In their more elevated forms, aesthetic experiences transcend simple short-term self-interest, making us aware of our embeddedness or participation in an expanded frame of reference that is larger than ourselves.

NATURALISTIC CRITERIA FOR AESTHETIC QUALITY [2]

As the etymological roots of the word indicate (Greek *aisthetikos*, "of sense perception"), a naturalistic aesthetics begins with sensation. An aesthetic experience is perceived with the same sensory equipment that is used when a person engages with anything. However, one can think of the aesthetic stance as a way of "taking" the world, not only as a source of sensory stimuli that have informational content but also as an occasion of receptiveness to relational tendencies or "play"—elaboration, exaggeration, emphasis—that can be found in (or made from) the stimuli. The redness of a fruit is appreciated not only as a signal of its ripeness and hence edibility but in another, more feelingful, less constrained way.

In a naturalistic aesthetics, a "good" or successful work (whether composed of material, sound, movement, words, or ideas) will address and satisfy human psychobiology as it evolved to live and prosper in the world. I offer four successive criteria for assigning aesthetic quality ("aesthetic success") to an event or occasion. They are usually experienced as a whole, though I separate them for easier description and analysis.

1. *Accessibility coupled with strikingness.* The initial entry to an experience of art comes, like any other perceptual experience, from its accessibility to our evolved sensory and cognitive dispositions—our visual receptivity to a certain range of colors in the spectrum, say, or the acuity with which we hear a specific array of pitches, frequencies, or intervals. Such parameters of access are both biologically given and developmentally affected, as when our ability to distinguish a specific speech sound or musical interval becomes sharpened with experience.

As well as being comprehensible to human senses and interests, the elements of the aesthetically successful work will be generally considered particularly striking or fascinating—either in their attractiveness or beauty or in their intimations of humanly relevant uncertainty or even hazard.

The arts everywhere make use of intrinsically emotionally captivating and cognitively interesting colors, shapes, and sounds that ancestrally were (and may still be) relevant to vital interests and subject matter of biologically important concern—male-female relationships, life transitions, the mortal body, feelings of hope or helplessness, and so forth. Movements that are strong, vigorous, and controlled, or graceful and fluent, are associated with vitality, youth, health, and competence, as are vibrant tones and entraining rhythms. Clear and true colors, firmness, and glossiness visually indicate freshness and ripeness. (Their opposites, signs of weakness, decay, or disease, are disliked and considered to be ugly.) Eye motifs, zigzag lines, and other cues of possible danger are also immediately compelling (Aiken 1998; Üher 1991), as are intimations of violence or death.

Such features and themes in themselves provoke sensory and cognitive interest and often gratification. They are "good to look at" (listen to, move to, read about) because they are subliminally (or overtly) associated with their wholesome and biologically useful or important referents, easily embodying them and provoking emotional response. Or their unnerving and disturbing associations, in the "not for real" context of an artwork, may provide frissons and the pleasurable relief of safety. Elements that are sensorily and cognitively boring, incomprehensible, or emotionally irrelevant will not be aesthetically "accessible" or "striking."

In her well-argued, evolutionarily informed study of how art evokes emotion, Nancy Aiken (1998, 67) demonstrates how stimuli that evoke adaptive responses "can shape our emotions, and, because of their emotion-shaping qualities, these stimuli are used in art" (see also Coe 1992). Although Aiken's study does not set out to account for all aesthetic responses or the totality of an aesthetic experience, it provides a welcome contribution to understanding their underpinnings and their universality.

It is these signals of adaptive interest that to date have been the sole subject matter of proponents of "Darwinian aesthetics" (see, e.g., Thornhill 1998). Although Aiken deals, as they do, with unconscious or reflexive emotional responses to certain adaptive visual and auditory images, she does not discuss aesthetic quality.[3] Aiken correctly claims that sensory preferences and subject matter that appeal to adaptive interests compose *part* of the emotional response to art.

As evolutionists point out, what people call "beautiful" typically refers to aesthetic elements at this initial level,[4] and most normal humans should respond similarly. For example, a contemporary person would probably also consider "beautiful" the pieces of fossil coral I mentioned in chapter 4 (see figure, page 113), which archaic Homo sapiens carried from a distant source to a dwelling site in present-day Swanscombe two hundred thousand years ago (Oakley 1981).[5] These manuports had no obvious use, but their all-over pattern of "stars" is regular, intricate, and even dazzling—visually and cognitively satisfying and pleasing.

Yet while accessibility rests upon vitally relevant sensory and cognitive signals of things that were beneficial (or otherwise required attention) in other evolutionary choices, and strikingness emphasizes this accessibility, such signals are not in themselves art but *ingredients* of art. They can and do exist in nonaesthetic contexts as well. That is, accessibility and even strikingness are necessary but not sufficient conditions for aesthetic *quality*.

This insufficiency is made emphatically apparent by a recent survey carried out by a marketing research firm for the Nation Institute and two Russian émigré artists, Vitaly Komar and Alexander Melamid (*The Nation*, 14 March 1994, 334–48; Danto 1997; Komar and Melamid 1997). A thousand and one adult Americans were surveyed for their attitudes toward the visual arts, including favored subject matter, colors, and other details. The findings—which later proved surprisingly similar to results of comparable surveys in nine other countries, including Russia, France, Turkey, Kenya, and China—are test-case examples of evolutionary psychology's predictions (Appleton 1990; Kaplan 1992; Orians and Heerwagen 1992), although the investigators were unaware of this potential application of their study.

The most preferred features were then incorporated by Komar and Melamid into a single painting of figures in a landscape, titled *America's Most Wanted*. The savanna-like landscape contains a reassuring source of water—a placid lake—beyond which are distant, gently sloping hills. Dark wooded cliffs in the left background provide an intriguing sense of mystery, which is ameliorated by the serene clouds and open vista in the foreground. Of the spaced trees, one is of a size to climb into if sudden danger should require it. The figures include a benign animal food source (a pair of deer), humans in their reproductive prime (three young people in casual summer clothing), and a strong male leader (George Washington). All that the painting possibly lacks is appropriate emphasis on the young female's low waist-to-hip ratio. Yet *America's Most Wanted* turns out to be memorable not as a picture but as a provocative stunt that in itself—as a "performance piece" with polls, publicity, paintings, exhibitions, focus groups, and a book—raises interesting questions about art and life today (Dissanayake 1998; Komar and Melamid 1997).

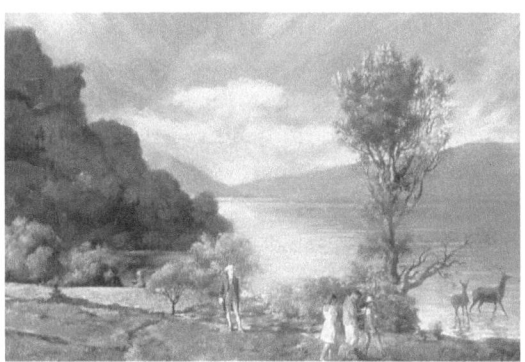

America's Most Wanted,
by Vitaly Komar and Alexander Melamid, 1994. Oil and acrylic on canvas, 24 by 32 inches. Photograph: D. James Dee, courtesy Ronald Feldman Fine Arts, New York. © Komar and Melamid.

Elsewhere (Dissanayake 1995) I have claimed that adaptive signals like those of the Darwinian aestheticians can be usefully regarded as "*proto-aesthetic*" features. In aesthetic experience, we not only notice and are attracted by naturally enticing and striking features that set apart an event or object from unenticing or ordinary events or objects. Something additional is done to the qualities, events, or objects: they are additionally patterned and exaggerated or otherwise emphasized so that they become more colorful or vivid, complex or elaborate, harmonious or unified, compelling or moving than their nonaesthetic counterparts. I would say that when strikingness is deliberately added by intentional emphasis, the aesthetic enterprise begins (see also Coe 1992).

A red fruit growing on a tree is less aesthetically striking than a red fruit placed on an offering tray with other fruits, carefully stacked shaped rice cakes, and shiny variegated leaves. Emphasis and intensification (through rhythmic-modal repetition, elaboration, and exaggeration, or other indications of special care) enhance accessibility—additionally marking importance. Skill, which indicates competence and care, additionally attests to the seriousness of the maker's intentions. Rare or costly materials appeal because of their novelty and the knowledge that they are difficult to obtain.

The quality of brilliance or dazzle, as responded to two hundred thousand years ago by archaic *Homo sapiens*, can serve as a representative proto-aesthetic and adaptive preference that remains accessible and striking today. Sheen is valued by the Wahgi of Papua New Guinea (O'Hanlon 1989), who rub themselves with pork fat and shiny body paint. Costumed Kaluli dancers in the Southern Highlands of Papua New Guinea move so that they will shimmer like a waterfall (Schieffelin 1976). Cattle-keeping Nilotes of the southern Sudan (for example, the Nuer, mentioned earlier, as well as the Dinka, Atuot, Mandari, Anuak, Pokot, and Maasai), like other pastoralist peoples, make no art objects and have no tradition of visual art. Yet they respond protoaesthetically to dazzle when, in poetry and song, they liken the coats of their display oxen to new grass, the sun, moon, gold, and an ivory bracelet (Coote 1992, 252–53)—all desirable things, since for them glossiness indicates health and the state of being well nourished. Their word for beauty is "dazzling array," meaning visually stimulating.

2. *Tangible relevance.* The naturally accessible and striking (protoaesthetic) elements of an aesthetically successful work will additionally have a tangible context in the particular life-world of the recipients—that is,

clear connections to their vital interests, the important things relevant to satisfaction and survival in their environment. They pertain to or are about the things that people care about and consequently address universal human needs for belonging, meaning, and competence.

The Aboriginal Yolngu of Australia, mentioned in chapter 6, have no systematic or explicit theory of aesthetics. In their *mardayin*, or sacred rites, however, they are clearly concerned, like any "artists," to utilize naturally striking protoaesthetic elements to produce effects on the senses by means of which the success of their work can be judged (Morphy 1992, 182). Since paintings are covered up or destroyed within hours or even minutes of completion, their power and beauty inhere to a great extent in the *activity* of painting, which has three stages: making the correct design (in basic outline), making the design ancestrally powerful (by painting it), and making a painting that enhances or beautifies the object it is painted on (pp. 187–88)—the human body as well as bark and wood.

Mere painting is not enough in itself but requires additional brilliance or dazzle, which is achieved by adding white or yellow dots or by affixing white plant down to the painted surface. The visual effect of shimmer or scintillation (called *bir'yun*) engenders feelings of lightness, joy, happiness, and power.[6]

Because Yolngu (like people in other traditional societies, some of whom were mentioned in the foregoing examples) consider people who are plump and sleek to be healthy and thus believe that fat is "good," it is not surprising that their criteria for artistic success (apart from correctness, which is assumed) include qualities of glistening brightness and clarity and that these are associated with ancestral power and beauty (Morphy 1992, 188–89; Taçon 1991).[7] Morphy likens the emotional response to *bir'yun* to "the effect of heat on skin" (193), rather than its being a product of aesthetic contemplation and interpretation. Yet this almost automatic effect arises not "simply" from the feature of dazzle and its perhaps universal association with sheen and well-being but additionally from its cultural association with ancestral presence, which embodies health, joy, and happiness, hence sacredness. Because the protoaesthetic quality in itself is humanly accessible, attractive, and striking, it therefore lends itself easily to added cultural meaning when further elaborated (or given an aesthetic context).

Similarly, Trobriand canoe prows are carved in intricately complex patterns which, when aesthetically successful, dazzle beholders (Gell 1992, 44), thereby manifesting the culturally relevant magical ability of weak-

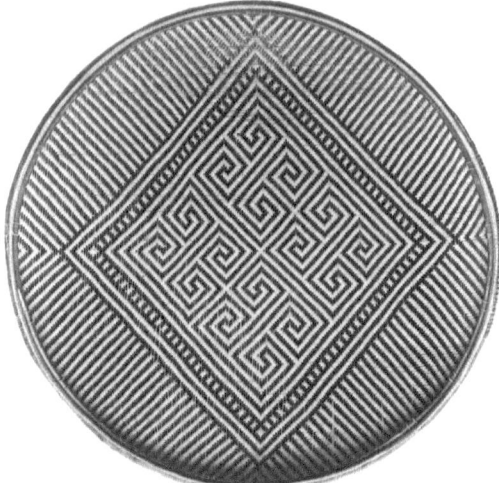

The awidi, or coral snake, design, like other of their basket designs, reaffirms the Yekuana's preoccupation with deadly poison. Designs always emerge diagonally from the corner of the square within the circle, presenting an image that is implicitly ambiguous. To keep all the elements in equal focus at the same time is nearly impossible, with image and counterimage endlessly competing for attention. This kinetic play of forms exists in all of the abstract basket designs; it is a metaphor for the inseparable dualism in Yekuana philosophy (Guss 1989). Photograph: Bobby Hansson.

ening possible enemies as well as enabling the canoe to travel fast, even to fly over the water.

The Nilotic Sudanese songs that evoke brilliant things are about the central subject of that culture: cattle. To the Yekuana, as described in chapter 3, a woven black and white eye-dazzling design of a stylized poisonous coral snake on a basket is linked in the mind with other instances of cultural control of material danger. In our own Western aesthetic tradition, a radiant rose window evokes the order and splendor of the Christian worldview. Participants and recipients find personal and social relevance— belonging, meaning, and competence—in experiencing these activities or entities.

Aesthetic features may be used to address and engage the interests of any group. The permutations and intricacies of the contemporary art scene are intensely fascinating to its aficionados. Those who lack instruction and familiarity, however, can hardly be expected to respond to endless explorations of, say, the nature of representation, which is a subject of tangible relevance to only a numerically small group. In the case of art works in an unfamiliar tradition, we may well respond to the accessibility and strikingness of their protoaesthetic elements—their pancultural attractiveness, such as true color, melodious sound, dazzle, exciting aural intensity, arresting subject matter. But without appreciating a work's tangible relevance to the cultural tradition in which it exists, we cannot expect to experience fully its emotional power. It is also obvious that personal preoccupations manifested in cryptic or maudlin private revelations will have limited relevance to and hence appreciation by others.

3. *Evocative resonance.* In addition to the context of tangible pertinence to vital cultural or individual interests, other associations or overtones to one's world or concerns may be evoked by experiences of the arts. There will be "more than meets the eye"—a complexity or density of meaning embodied in the work and further revealed through its creator's or performer's artful and insightful manipulations. In Nilotic Sudanese cattle poetry, for example, the scintillating things to which an ox is likened—new grass, the sun or moon, gold, and ivory—have inherent additional modal properties and common features that enrich the core feature of dazzle and its association with well-being.

In warrior societies, tangibly relevant ancestral designs carved and painted on a shield invoke not only protoaesthetically fearsome and fascinating natural creatures—for example, praying mantids, bats—but also powerful beings that can protect a man in battle. In Gothic cathedrals of Europe, a rose window evokes more than rich color and visually satisfying pattern: it also evokes manifold ideas and sensations associated with light—for example, illimitability, inaccessibility, transfiguration. Such associations and revelations may well call upon and be embodied in pan-culturally appealing ideas or motifs, but outsiders to the culture will probably respond less deeply to them than insiders.

While the criterion of tangible relevance applies to culturally relevant matters of subsistence and hence vital interest, the criterion of evocative resonance recognizes the nourishment and power of complex and less obvious (that is, disguised, mysterious, subtle) references to individually or culturally important things. For example, Frankenstein's monster and the story of Dr. Jekyll and Mr. Hyde are both protoaesthetically and culturally scary and fantastic but, as conveyed by Mary Shelley and Robert L. Stevenson, additionally carry inexhaustible implications—evocative resonances—for the human condition.

In contrast, while the attention-grabbing special effects of contemporary video games and action films may similarly ignite evolved protoaesthetic responses to excitement, activity, danger, and fantasy and may even seem tangibly relevant to the otherwise unrewarding lives of the adolescents who partake of them, they do not resonate beyond their immediate shock value or adrenaline surge and are of lesser aesthetic value. At best they direct fantasy or provide escape or time-killing, but these are neither vital nor generative of further meaning.

4. *Satisfying fullness.* At the "highest" or greatest level of perceived aesthetic value, the respondent feels as if something has been accomplished by the work or activity, and a sense of completeness or sufficiency is felt—rightness and even perfection, as in Gombril's "pure and unsullied" experience of Mozart's music. Ibrahim Poudjougou, a Dogon sculptor in Mali, told Rachel Hoffman (1995) that occasionally he made an object that made everyone who saw it "stop breathing" for a moment.[8]

Not every aesthetic experience, of course, has supreme closure; such epiphanies may occur only once or twice in a lifetime. Yet in works that strongly manifest the three other characteristics (accessibility with strikingness, tangible relevance, and evocative resonance), a high, if not sublime, degree of fulfillment is usually also felt. Such fulfillments arise when life interests are touched, experiential depths are sounded, greater possibilities are evoked, and the works that embody these have been constructed and composed with care and commitment—but, I daresay, not otherwise.

To illustrate the relationship between successful (satisfyingly full) aesthetic achievement and the care expended upon making and using art, I refer to a study of Kominimung carvers in Papua New Guinea (Smidt 1990:95), whose designs on warriors' shields are drawn from an elaborate system of coded visual symbols of clan affinities and emblems (described and commented upon by Dutton [1994]). Warriors protecting themselves with shields are not just human beings holding planks adorned with designs that signal adaptively relevant colors, forms, or even motifs.

To begin with, the men are protected by a culturally "tangibly relevant" ancestor of their clan depicted (with "evocative resonance") on the shield, with whom they identify and even "merge." (When holding the shield, its reverse upper half remains plain and unpainted and rests against the warrior's shoulder, as if he could almost literally get under his ancestor's skin.)

Additionally, although a warrior's belief in the protective potency of his shield is a motivating factor in his success in combat, it is not simply the presence of the correct (relevant), evocatively resonant designs on the shield that convinces him of his power but the evidence that they have been carved with skill and care. Dutton (1994) reminds us that because Kominimung men's lives depend on their shields, their making requires an intense devotion to getting both the design and the construction right. Thus the carver's devotion to the shield bearer's protection is intrinsic to its effectiveness and consequently to the work's aesthetically satisfying fullness.

According to one carver, Pita Mangal: "A woodcarver must concentrate, think well and be inspired. You must think hard which motif you want to cut into the wood. And you must feel this inside, in your heart." For the Kominimung, Dutton emphasizes, good carving is a matter of both technical mastery and of *feeling*—of "meaning it" (Dutton 1994:5). The carved shields manifest and transmit the "emotional dispositions upon which society depends"—in Radcliffe-Brown's (1948) phrase—trust in ancestral protection and in the carver whose commitment and care are unmistakable, clearly evident in his workmanship.[9]

In most instances the quality of emotionally satisfying fullness does not inhere in a work's contribution to immediate survival but is nevertheless profoundly memorable. As such, it has a kind of *sufficiency* that distinguishes it from the temporary thrills of pastimes and diversions, which generally leave one empty, wanting another fix—another video game, another televised sports event, another porno film, another hand of cards, another amusing one-liner—rather than replenished and transfigured, as happens with full aesthetic responses, which can last a lifetime.

Psychologist Gerald Clore (1994) suggests that the felt intensity of an emotional response (to anything) may be directly correlated with the amount of cognitive restructuring that the experience engenders. He gives as examples the death of a spouse, learning that one's beloved has had an affair, and reinterpreting close personal relationships in therapy.[10] In each of these events, few aspects of one's life are untouched, so that much mental content must be restructured (Clore 1994, 391–92).

Such traumas seem quite different from experiences of the arts, but Clore points out that a musical or other performance, in which we are sufficiently involved to generate an elaborate model or expectancy of what is occurring and fully attend to it, progressively transforms its content, setting up and resolving ambiguities or problems and thereby restructuring the mental world of the perceiver. Although Clore includes experiences of jokes and sports events as examples along with music and drama, I was struck by his statement that we react not simply on the basis of the amount of raw stimulus change but that *one new fact* may alter what came before (Clore 1994, 393).

Such possibility of transformation suggests careful planning or structuring on the part of the creator of the temporal sequence and close familiarity with the tradition being manipulated on the part of the percipient. Just as one traumatic event can require the restructuring of a lifetime of habit, so one astutely placed element (in an ongoing sequence) can restructure aesthetic expectation and create an intensity of feeling that surpasses one's reaction to successive gratuitous plot twists, special effects that just happen, or even a summating succession of thrills.

Clore wonders whether intensity of feeling is the experience of cognitive reorganization itself, or the experience of physiological arousal triggered by such change. (I myself wonder whether the two are not, for all practical purposes, the same experience.) And he contrasts the experience of profound disappointment with that of profound amazement, finding the former affective and the latter nonaffective. Aesthetic amazement, however—as in the preceding example of responding to a performance—can be profoundly affective. Rilke's "You must change your life!" is occasioned by contemplating an archaic Greek marble torso but occurs in the context of a web of experiences in life and art, as does the tribal initiate's life-changing experience during the amazing revelations of a carefully structured dramatic ceremony.

MENTIONING THE UNMENTIONABLE

As I have repeatedly asserted in this book, artful elaboration in traditional societies has been used to draw attention not to just anything but to important life concerns that people rightly cared about. "Protoaesthetic" elements, subliminally associated with their biologically relevant referents, naturally provoked sensory interest and gratification—which increased when the elements were made additionally striking or beautiful.

When Trobrianders believed that a garden would grow well only if it "looked right" (Gell 1992), they took special care and did not go hungry. Through especially affecting and interesting stories, cultures passed on socially valuable moral precepts such as reciprocity or respect for elders.

The words "right" and "especially" in these examples imply that mere strikingness for its own sake is insufficient and that value judgments—judgments of quality—are relevant. Some things are better and others worse, according to an aesthetic or moral standard. This sort of appreciation requires more than simply being able to *see* (or hear). Unlike peahens, which respond automatically to the beautiful detailed elements of peacocks' tails in motion, humans can *learn* to appreciate qualitatively the accessible and striking details—in canoe prows or calligraphy—especially as they are perceived and even transformed in new and different contexts—that is, within a tradition.[11]

In order to exercise judgments it is necessary to make distinctions. All living things discern subtleties in sensory features that are biologically important, such as the odor, texture, and taste of food. Humans, even babies, possess exquisite perceptual and emotional sensitivities to the smallest differences in shapes and proportions of human faces and facial expressions and to subtleties of human voices.

Evolutionists have esteemed this ability to note small, subtle differences—such as recognizing the difference between *p* and *b* in a spoken word, or detecting possible signs of deception in a face or voice—for its practical importance in later life. But although these are obviously critical adaptive skills, it is important to point out once again that the earliest exercising and developing of infants' discriminatory sensitivities occur in what are essentially *aesthetic* contexts, that is, co-created improvisatory interactions with caretakers. In these encounters, sensitivities to rhythmic and dynamic change are manipulated in order to coordinate the mother-infant pair emotionally and express its accord. Although inborn capacities for discrimination contribute to an infant's subsequent development of cognition, language, and sociality, they also predispose it to respond to emotionally evocative, resonant, and richly satisfying aesthetic experiences.

There are endless examples of the human appreciation of subtle qualititative difference, some more and others less based on learning. New Jersey photographer Leon Yost has made a collection of plumb bobs, the small weights of iron, brass, or lead that builders suspend from a long string to indicate verticality (or perpendicularity). Although plumb bobs generally conform to a regular plan of "head, shoulders, and body" that tapers to a point, the minute differences among their proportions and shapes carry surprisingly distinct modal associations—say, of plumpness and hence friendliness, or austerity, elegance, clumsiness, and the like.

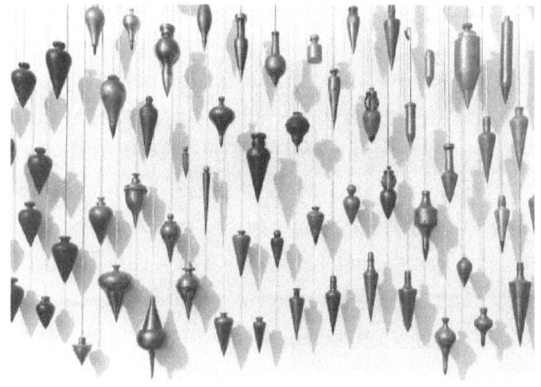

Collection of plumb bobs.
Photograph: Leon Yost.

A designer of any visual object, from an automobile to a bowl, knows the difference made by a few degrees of an angle or several millimeters of length. From acquaintance with potters I have learned that a teapot—a utilitarian vessel with spout and handle—is infinitely variable. Effective phrasing or "expression" in music performance relies on minute attentions to proportion in dynamics and duration of tones in their relations to one another.

The Chinese art of writing, what we call calligraphy, is similarly "modal" but requires diligent cultivation for full appreciation. It is composed of marks in space that address the eye, yet like music it unfolds in time, and like dance it develops a dynamic sequence of movements, pulsating in rhythm, reflecting the writer's mood, sensibility, and personal character as well as conveying the meanings of the words it ultimately represents (Leys 1996). Those who are familiar with this art and understand its varieties find in it infinite opportunity for appreciating complex associations and distinctions of quality. Yet novices see pretty much only brush strokes. It's all Greek (or Chinese) to us.

Qualitative judgments characterize evaluations of the things that are important or even customary parts of our lives. People who live in France, where bread, like all other food, is important, know a good loaf when they taste it. Any Sri Lankan over the age of five can pass judgment on chicken curry or *seeni sambol*. Members of youth subgroups display meticulous visual discrimination of style in attire and possessions (see Crow 1996, 20). Young American boys who can barely read and write will know the distinguishing features of an amazing number of makes and models of cars or bicycles. Sudanese keepers of cattle pay scrupulous attention not only to the sheen of an ox's hide but also to the animal's particular horn shape, body dimensions, and unique color configurations. Evans-Pritchard (1940, 41–44) noted ten principal color terms used by the Nuer, multiplied by at least twenty-seven further terms for their configurations.

Most specific sensory qualities have, like the visual shapes of plumb bobs or calligraphic marks, modal associations, which become the metaphors and similes of poetic language. Sudanese find endless stimulation for poetic description in the various features of their cattle. In songs they may, for example, liken ox horns to masts of ships or the overflowing of a boiling pot. They even use the words for cattle colors to describe features of their environment (Coote 1992, 254). The reverse seems more natural to us—for example, to name a horse "Lightning" or "Storm" rather than give these meteorological phenomena the name of a type of coat coloration: "Golden Tannish Beige" or "Intense Gray with Black Splotches."

In my naturalistic aesthetics scheme, considerations of aesthetic quality can apply at any of the first three levels, and the (generally rare) feeling of satisfying fullness will be inseparable from awareness of high quality. Judgments of adequacy, beauty, and interest will be almost automatic at the first level, where elements instantly are appraised and recognized as more or less appealing—striking as well as accessible. At the second level, also, members of a culture will generally judge quickly how relevant the aesthetic work or occasion is to their particular tangible life concerns.

It is at the third level that assignments of quality will be most exacting and most dependent on variations among percipients, whose personal sensibilities and breadth or depth of knowledge will affect how much is brought to bear on experiencing the resonances that inhere in the aesthetic event.[12] As Denis Dutton (1994, 4) has remarked, the world of art and its uses is one of making connections—of marking and tracing relationships and influences. (This is so, even when we make or experience something that deliberately breaks with tradition.) Inevitably, as societies become more stratified and diverse, ideas about what is beautiful and excellent also become stratified and diverse, and the arts of any one group may not be appreciated or even recognized by the others. Yet our reasons for assigning value to particular entities are not merely capricious or purely individual, because others who are well acquainted with these works usually feel similarly about them and often for the same reasons.

It is then more than genre or style or creative intention that distinguishes a multimillion-dollar sex-and-violence blockbuster, advertising campaign, or best-selling suspense novel from the dark depths of the Beethoven opus 131 quartet or the passionate intensity of *The Brothers Karamazov* (see Dutton 1994). The latter works embody a degree of seriousness, commitment, resonance, and fullness that simply does not inhere in a slasher film, beer commercial, or page-turner, skillfully made (and interesting for social analysis) as it may be.

To recognize qualitative differences between these sorts of works need not imply that thrills are worthless or that only transfiguring experiences are worth having. It is worthwhile, however, to point out that in a milieu of affluence and overconsumption one can easily mistake "impact" for "import" and then wonder later why nothing is ever enough. Material abundance spills over into expectation of experiential abundance, so that we ask of each meal, each party, each sexual experience that

it be uniquely memorable or climactically overpowering, desiring to convince ourselves of a superlative, overheightened good time every time. (Or
is this not the reason that standing ovations have become routine, when
they were once a rare indication of an audience's being moved especially
deeply by an artist's musicality, or perhaps a way of honoring an eminent
performer at his final appearance after a long, distinguished career?)

Impact is wow, import is wonder. Impact is rapture—do it again!;
import is raptness—that is, absorption, full engagement, even to the point
of being unable to breathe, speak, or move. Impact is more bang for the
buck; import is "less is more." Impact is celebrity; import is consequence.
Ironically, insistence on instant, constant, maximum gratification—the
ever larger and longer orgasmic thrill—coexists with the contradictory
democratic claim in art and literary theory that every experience, being
culturally constructed, is ultimately equal, including experiences of transcendence.

In *The Varieties of Religious Experience*, the American philosopher
William James (1941) upheld the validity of the "poor man's" experience
of ecstasy (admittedly a description that would not be used today) when
he discussed the variety of transcendent feelings that every human has at
some times and places of life—responses to the beauties of the arts and
nature, the birth of a child, a religious insight, the finding or giving of
love. James said that for everyone these experiences stand as a "high-
water mark," a supreme experience of sublime value.

Even though he championed the unassailable worth to each person
of his or her own high-water mark, James did not reach the politically
correct conclusion that each mark is therefore the same. Introspection
will reveal to each of us that tastes not only change but qualitatively mature: satisfied with soft white bread or yearning melodies at sixteen, one
learns to value the subtleties and complexities of sourdough baguettes and
Brahms trios—and will not consider the experiences equivalent. The
same is to be said for the differences between eating to fill one's belly and
dining, mechanical sex and considered lovemaking.

To be sure, the first morsel of dry bread to a previously starving man
may be exquisitely unforgettable, and there are times when half a loaf seems
better than none. But we are not normally so starved of food or companionship that anything will do. On the contrary, life generally consists
of a meandering river of transitory physical and sensory satisfactions and
dissatisfactions, more and less memorable, with the occasional high-water
mark that remains as a touchstone of transcendent perfection.

In the late nineteenth century, some people, such as Walter Pater (in Carritt 1931, 187), claimed that life existed for the sake of having these elevated experiences and recommended that one devote oneself to perfecting them. While that might seem like the height of elitism, humans in societies everywhere have recognized and cultivated experiences that to them were tangibly relevant, evocatively resonant, and satisfyingly complete.

Because quality resides in caring enough to make emotional and physical investment—to use an old-fashioned phrase, to "take pains"—a person's or group's creation reflects the seriousness of their lives and concerns: their heart, character, and experience. Until quite recently, the arts have been a way of treating the inner life and its concerns seriously, requiring development, cultivation, and maturation, a lifelong acquisition of insight.

In countless traditional societies, maturity of judgment about moral and aesthetic matters (which are considered inseparable) is cultivated over a lifetime.[13] For example, the Dinka notion of *dheeng* refers to such personal characteristics as nobility, beauty, handsomeness, elegance, charm, grace, gentleness, hospitality, generosity, good manners, discretion, and kindness. As an adjective, it is also applied to singing and dancing, personal decoration, initiation ceremonies, marriage celebrations, and any demonstration of an aesthetic value (Coote 1992, 266). The social background of a man, his physical appearance, the way he walks, talks, eats, or dresses, and the way he behaves to his fellows are all factors in determining his *dheeng*.

One might translate *dheeng* as "virtue" or "class" (as in "that [person, occasion, behavior] has class!"). However, in an academic milieu of cultural and individual relativism (not to mention a milieu of general philistinism in the broader society), virtue or "class" is as unmentionable as beauty or quality, immediately associated with a false and unacceptable "superiority," snobbery, and elitism. These charges cannot, however, apply in ancestral or small-scale unstratified societies, where standards are communally created and expressed.[14]

Today it seems easy to question a claim that humans have innate capacities for the development and display of *dheeng*, or for making judgments of beauty and quality, when on every side is the ugliness of much of contemporary American life—state roads with their strip malls and parking lots, the sprawl of housing developments, carelessly worn T-shirts and shorts on flabby bodies, the shabbiness or defilement of unloved neighborhoods. Yet human history reveals that appreciation for beauty, excellence, and skilled workmanship is inherent, like a taste for wholesome food, and needs only direction and reinforcement. In all but a few small-scale traditional societies,[15] ritual paraphernalia, utensils, textiles, and many other items are inarguably well made and beautiful.

In such societies, which of course are not affected by market incitements to perpetual novelty, individuals grow up surrounded by time-tested designs and shapes, proportions, and color combinations, so that these become almost automatic standards for judgment. People in our own society who are born into a family of professional ice skaters or violinists unconsciously acquire a connoisseur's appreciation of the fine points of ice skating or stringed instrument playing, even if they themselves are not skaters or violinists of the highest rank. Similarly, if we had grown up in an Ainu (Japan) or Kwakiutl (North American) village two centuries ago, or in a Gejia (Guizhou Province, China) village today, we would almost effortlessly make, use, wear, and fully appreciate exquisite subtleties in artifacts and clothing that only specialist connoisseurs are able to appreciate today.

If artful elaborations have been used traditionally to emphasize important life concerns that people rightly care about, it seems clear that in order to have beauty and quality, we must ourselves care. And when a society cares mostly about money and fun, that is where the distinctions will be made—in the fine print of legal contracts or the subtle signs of being "with it" in fashion, vocabulary, and other fast-changing emblems of material and social success.

The "values" that suffuse our lives are additionally affected by the fact that the primary avenues for elaboration—advertisements and popular entertainment—have to compete among themselves for our attention. Because their ultimate aim is to persuade people to buy something, often things they don't need, advertisements must entrap potential customers rapidly and surreptitiously, hitting the brainstem with supernormal stimuli and skirting the reflections of the neocortex. Big, bright, and fast replace small, subtle, and mindful.

Certainly ads and amusements can be appreciated for their beauties, and some are notably better and others worse. Some are even subtle and insinuating. But the *purposes* for which their beauty and quality are enlisted are mostly trivial—persuasion to spend beyond our means and distraction from the serious and real.[16]

Yet it is serious and real—"ultimate"—concerns, not only in the bi-

ological but also in the *religious* sense (see chapter 5), that have characterized human life for millennia.[17] Religion (or what we today call religion)
together with the arts (or what we today call art) addressed these concerns
and compellingly transmitted the sense of belonging, meaning, and competence that evolved as integral to human nature because these ensured
that humans would find life, and life with others, worthwhile. Forsaking
the means—religion and art—as superstitious and superfluous, we for-
sake the ends—the psychological certainties and emotional satisfactions
that we are born to require.

It is not surprising that the certainties of "religion" and the profun-
dities of "art" seem outmoded and obsolete today, when the Hubble tele-
scope reveals every sort of wonder except the pearly gates, or when home
computers coolly access details of the Sistine Chapel ceiling for a school
project. It would be as ludicrous for us to return to hunter-gatherers' answers to life's ultimate concerns as to resume their means of livelihood.

Yet who would dispute the present human hunger for the profound,
the longing of the "thirsting millions" (Danto 1997, 187–88) who nevertheless continue to feel the lack of what was once abundantly to be found
in religion/art. For after the fun and ease and spontaneity pall, when every
subsistence need is filled, the ultimate concerns remain. Politicians and
business people may tell us that making and experiencing the arts is un-
economical and irrelevant for addressing immediate practical problems,
but for coming to terms with the human condition we could do far worse
than to take the arts seriously.

Notes

1. The discussion here should not be taken to mean that the kinds of emotional interactions that individual parents have with their children will specifically improve or dampen those children's sensitivities to either love or the arts. Although there are certainly effects of ontogeny (individual development and experience), my argument in this book is from phylogeny (evolution).

2. These and other definitions in the book are from *Webster's Ninth New Collegiate Dictionary*, 1987 (Springfield, Mass.: Merriam-Webster).

3. In ancient Greek music, "modes" were particular tonal patterns—like scales or ragas—that were believed to imitate and produce specific feelings. My use of the term is far less precise, although it too has to do with feeling.

4. Genders, ethnicities, religions, and ways of life are "veils" or "wrappings" in the sense that had a baby with your (or my) exact DNA been exposed to another hormonal environment in the womb, or born into another culture, it would be different from you or me, as we know ourselves today, but would still be human, would have recognizably human needs and abilities. Such a view of human nature is an axiom within evolutionary psychology—for example: "The social and cultural are not alternatives to the biological. They are aspects of evolved human biology" (Tooby and Cosmides 1992, 86).

5. The two views are not mutually exclusive, although looking through one lens or the other does tend to bias one's assessment of the whole picture. I will say little about human selfishness and competition here, not because they do not exist but because they already are well established and have ample advocates.

6. Daly and Wilson (1995, 1273) suggest that selection favors discriminative mechanisms of parental psychology that allocate "parental investment" in infants. They note (p. 1282) that the newborn's precocious social response may be an adaptation for "advertising quality and eliciting maternal commitment" (but they do not refer to its capacity for the kind of interactive mutuality described in the

present book). Not only in the remote past but even today in societies that experience scarcity, mothers may withdraw care and attention from some infants in order to protect the survival of other family members who are vulnerable—a practice that has been termed "benign neglect" (Scheper-Hughes 1987, 14).

7. This viewpoint has been called "mismatch" theory. See, for example, Bailey (1996).

8. My source for teen suicide statistics is *The 1996 Index of Social Health* (Institute for Innovation in Social Policy, Fordham Graduate Center, Tarrytown, New York), as reported in the *Seattle Post-Intelligencer*, October 14, 1996.

9. On the basis of his examination of fossilized female pelvic bones of *Homo erectus*, and calculating the size of an infant skull that could pass through the opening (one-third the size of an adult brain, as is the case in *H. sapiens* infants today but not in ape infants, whose brains at birth are one-half adult size), Richard Leakey (1994, 48) concluded that intense parental care had begun to develop at least some 1.7 million years ago.

10. "According to the most popular view in the field [of evolutionary psychology], many other important human activities are spandrels [that is, nonadaptive features], including art, music, [and] religion" (Pinker 1997). Most books about human evolution do not discuss art, or they treat it as evidence of another cognitive ability such as symbolization (e.g., Mithen 1996, 155). "Darwinian aesthetics" (e.g., Thornhill 1998) treats adaptive preferences for signals that indicate good mates or safe environments but has little if any application to art (see the appendix and Dissanayake 1995, 1998).

I. MUTUALITY

1. The psychologist Erik Erikson is well known for using the term "mutuality," which in his scheme was the origin for later critical stages of individual psychosocial development. I have not been specifically influenced by Erikson, nor have I consciously borrowed from him, but I am sure there are commonalities in our thinking.

2. Evans-Pritchard (1940, 19) found that among the Nuer, even the subject of girls led inevitably to talk about cattle, the central focus of Nuer social and economic relations.

3. Strictly speaking, since human infants' eyes and ears are open at birth, they are *secondarily* altricial (Martin 1990, 426; Portmann 1941), a special development from the precocial primate pattern.

4. In this chapter and elsewhere in the book, I refer to the baby as "it," in order to avoid having to use the unwieldy "he or she" or "(s)he." In the German language, "baby" and "child" are "neuter" nouns, so that the pronoun ("it") used in English for inanimate objects or nonhuman life does not sound demeaning, as it might to an English reader here. I apologize but believe my choice makes for smoother reading.

5. In this book I use the term "baby talk" specifically to refer to the interactive behavior between adults and nonverbal infants under approximately six months of age that I describe in the present chapter. I do *not* use it in the linguistic sense, as imperfect speech directed at older infants and toddlers (for example, "get your blankie and let's go night-night").

6. The majority of studies of early interactions have taken place in North America and western Europe. Not surprisingly, differences have been found among the practices of different socioeconomic classes and ethnic groups in the United States (Fajado and Freedman 1981; Feiring and Lewis 1981; Field and Widmayer 1981) and among different nationalities and socioeconomic classes in Europe (Lewis and Ban 1977). Variations have also been observed among different Native American societies—Hopi and Navajo (Callaghan 1981) and Maya (Brazelton 1977)—and different African societies (Lewis and Ban 1977). Some of these

societies, and others, are described in more detail in chapter 2. For the most part, the differences are small, having to do with the proportion of time spent looking, smiling, and vocalizing by mother or infant and with the pace and intensity of the encounters. For Japanese "heart-to-heart (inter-*jo*) resonance," see Nakano 1996.

7. Leakey (1994, 48) claims that *H. erectus* of 1.7 million years ago showed intense parental care (see note 9, Introduction).

8. Another suggestion is that the size and shape of a human female's breasts are a signal to males of her reproductive potential: immature, ripe and promising, pregnant, lactating, past prime, postreproductive (Coe and Steadman 1995, 213).

9. Even deaf mothers use a "baby talk" version of sign language (simplified, exaggerated, and repetitive), which a deaf baby prefers to adult-oriented signing (Masataka 1996).

10. There may, of course, be "misattunements," as when one or the other member of a pair is unresponsive or when a mother is "intrusive," unable to read the baby's signals of overstimulation and its wish to "tune out" or disengage.

11. Howard Gardner (1973) called such properties "vectoral," which is how I referred to them in earlier work (Dissanayake 1988, 1992). An observer of interactions between deaf mothers and deaf babies concludes that six-month-old infants are as predisposed to attend to slowed presentation, exaggerated hand and arm movements, and frequent repetitions of signs as hearing infants are to attend to their counterparts in speech (Masataka 1996).

12. Since 1997 the journal has been called *Evolution and Human Behavior*.

13. For good summaries of infant abilities see Friedrich 1990, Begley 1998, and Grunwald 1998.

14. At thirteen months, most words have to do with (1) parents, (2) requests/ refusals, and (3) greetings (Hauser 1996, 338). See also Simon Baron-Cohen (1995,

132): "The drive to schmooze is not linguistic but lies in the development of the mind-reading system [that is, the 'need to communicate about a shared reality' (p. 44)]."

15. Chimpanzees hunt cooperatively and actively share meat with others in the foraging group, but they do not appear to transport any food back to stay-at-homes (Stanford 1996).

16. In 1989, *Webster's Ninth New Collegiate Dictionary* defined "bonding" as "the formation of a close personal relationship (as between a mother and child), especially through frequent or constant association." In the *Oxford English Dictionary* of the same year, however, the meaning of the word—as in earlier American and English dictionaries—had to do only with building (for example, bonding courses of bricks), electricity, pledging to repay money, or storing goods in bond. In Longman's dictionary of 1991, the first meaning of "bond" (as intransitive verb) was "to hold together or solidify (as if) by means of a bond or binding; cohere," and the second, "to form a close emotional relationship with another individual." The previous (1985) edition of Longman's did not give this second meaning.

Konrad Lorenz used the term "personal bond" in 1966 in his popular book *On Aggression* in reference to pair formation in geese, and Lionel Tiger, in *Men in Groups* (1969), introduced the term "male bonding." A decade later M. H. Klaus and J. H. Kennell published *Parental-Infant Bonding* (1976), and in 1980 an academic paper was titled "Of Human Bonding" (DeCasper and Fifer 1980). Other scientific papers about attachment used "bond" and "bonding" in the late 1970s, but the term seems to have entered popular discourse only in the 1980s. It is now, of course, extremely common.

2. BELONGING

1. Detachment as a coping mechanism for intolerable physical or psychological stress is, of course, known—as in

abused children or in some symptoms of what in adults is called post-traumatic stress syndrome. Children whose attachment needs are severely interfered with may become sociopathic or psychopathic, lacking in empathy, and unable to form close emotional bonds with others. (See Talbot 1998 for a chilling account of the "behavioral and biochemical fallout of early neglect" found in many children reared in East European orphanages and later adopted by North American parents.) In ancestral times, pronounced asocial tendencies would have been eliminated. (See also note 5, this chapter.)

2. Conflicting identities are a source of psychological discomfort in modern or modernizing societies. I remember a student acquaintance at the University of Papua New Guinea, whose home was in the Eastern Highlands. Although he was a typical university student, familiar with libraries, schedules, and weekend beer parties, during vacations he would go home and live in the men's house, eating and dressing in local style — even becoming involved in intertribal disputes (to the extent of getting painted up and going with the other men to a neighboring village to belligerently confront their enemies). Although he could see that these traditional behaviors were unsuitable to his new Westernized self, it would have insulted his father and uncles if he had refused to join them. This was a source of conflict for him, although he admitted that he enjoyed the camaraderie of the men's house.

3. Humans lived within such limits for a hundred thousand generations or more, depending on one's starting point in gauging when ancestral hominids became "human."

4. It is worth noting that psychiatric illness is largely concerned with a person's relations with others. For example, schizophrenic patients hear others who are not physically present, delusionally believe that others are out to harm them, or are unduly disconnected from other people. Manic patients maladaptively presume

that power, entitlements, and responsibilities that others display belong to them. In depression, the patient feels little worth compared with others, and phobic or panic patients are typically relieved if another person is nearby (Gardner 1996, 16).

5. Mealey (1995), in a sociobiological model of sociopathy, suggests that two evolutionary mechanisms give rise to two developmentally different etiologies. In "primary" sociopathy, a small, cross-culturally similar and unchanging frequency of individuals who are born unresponsive to the cues that normally encourage socialization and moral development will display chronic, pathologically emotionless antisocial behavior throughout most of the lifespan and in a variety of situations. In contrast, "secondary" sociopathy is displayed differentially by individuals who are exposed to social and environmental conditions related to disadvantages in social competition. Frequent (but not necessarily emotionless) "cheating" is adopted by some at-risk persons and will fluctuate according to age, hormone levels, status within a referent group, and changing environmental contingencies. In other words, only a few sociopaths are "born"; most are "made" by circumstances, and Mealey suggests that the frequency of the latter in a population can be decreased by social programs that reduce social stratification, anonymity, and competition; by intervention in high-risk situations with parent education and support; and by increasing the availability of rewarding, prosocial opportunities for at-risk youth. My statement in the text refers to secondary sociopathy.

6. Historian David T. Courtwright (1996) asserts that "violence and disorder occur most often in groups of armed, touchy, bigoted, intoxicated, undisciplined, unparented, unmarried, and irreligious young men."

7. Other group-living animals such as chimpanzees, lions, and wolves hunt (and kill) in comradely groups. They demonstrate and reinforce their sociality in daily

life by playing together and sharing food (in the sense of allowing their associates to eat from the same carcass). So far as I am aware, they do not choose to die for one another.

3. FINDING AND MAKING MEANING

1. I do not address here the phenomenon of overromanticizing primitive life and other symptoms of nostalgia that are shown by many people in modern societies. However, see Dissanayake (1992, 6–8) for a discussion of the modern attraction to "the primitive" and Dutton (1991) for a critique of some of its critics.

2. Apart from Propp, the best known of these are probably Claude Lévi-Strauss, Carl Jung, Sigmund Freud, and Joseph Campbell.

3. Even infants under six months of age show remarkable "scientific" abilities in their responses to psychologists' tasks that test memory, number, speech-sound recognition, and awareness of the properties of physical objects (Grunwald 1998).

4. In chapter 4 I suggest another consequence of general and computer literacy, namely, that when people learn about the world primarily by looking things up and retrieving information processed by others, they may be deprived of a valuable sort of intimate, agile, pragmatic knowledge and activity that is developed only in interaction with nature.

5. Walter Burkert's recent book, *Creation of the Sacred*, addresses the biological roots of religion. Although I deal in this chapter with the evolved human psychological need for "meaning," whereas Burkert is concerned with the origins of "religion," our subjects overlap in numerous important respects and our interpretations are complementary. (See also the discussion of religion at the beginning of chapter 5.) A chapter on meaning cannot help but be "about" religion.

6. Robert Boyd and Peter Richerson (1990) posit that humans have a genetically heritable capacity for "conformist"

cultural transmission. They base this hypothesis on two well-observed features of human psychology: (1) children faithfully copy the beliefs and values of adults in their society; (2) through individual learning, people tend to modify their beliefs in the direction of their own self-interest. I suggest that the evolved rhythms and modes of mutuality and belonging are part of this capacity, a psychophysiological means for instilling or transmitting the culture's beliefs and values (meanings). Boyd and Richerson point out that today's ethnic groups hold attitudes and beliefs that favor cooperation within the group and noncooperation toward members of other groups. The in-group sees its members as virtuous and superior (and those of the out-group as contemptible, immoral, and inferior). It sees its own standards as universal and intrinsically true, its own customs as original and centrally human (and those of the out-group as parochial, false, and derived). Members obey in-group authorities, disapprove of in-group killing, and are willing to fight and die for their group (and hold the reverse of these attitudes toward the out-group, whom they distrust, fear, and blame for in-group troubles [LeVine and Campbell 1972]). See also my discussion of identity in chapter 2.

4. "HANDS-ON" COMPETENCE

1. *Be* and *have* are auxiliaries; *say* implies speaking, although it can also be used for writing; *do* frequently, but not always, requires hands.

2. I have derived much of this section, sometimes with my own interpretations, from Trevarthen 1986.

3. Howard Gardner (1993b) has proposed that among the multiple "intelligences" of humans is a natural history intelligence. See also Mithen (1996, 123–24) and Wilson (1984).

4. Different methods of dating archaeological sites and artifacts (for example, thermoluminescence, optically stimulated luminescence, and accelerator mass spec-

trometry radiocarbon) and different techniques for interpreting these methods give different determinations of age. The proposed date of fifty-eight thousand to seventy-five thousand years before the present originally reported for Jinmium has recently been challenged (Roberts et al. 1998). Scientists associated with Jinmium, however, remind me that the debate concerns the deposit and not the cupules directly. Moreover, like hand stencils, cupules are a common form of visual representation that have been made over the globe at various times from tens of thousands of years ago until quite recently, and many northern Australian sites with cupules are notably early.

5. The images of animals and humans seem in many cases to have been *suggested by* the natural features of rock walls. Sylvia Fein (1993, 13) proposes that human non-representational scribbles, such as those drawn in the soft clay of the ceiling in the cave at Pech Merle, France, thirty to forty thousand years ago, may also have provided a source for later deliberate drawings of bodies and muzzles of animals that were subsequently "seen" in the tangle of lines.

6. It is popularly believed today that traditional societies have sacred attitudes to the natural world that restrain them from overusing their resources. Bobbi Low (1996), however, has surveyed the literature and concludes that the low ecological impact of many traditional societies results not from conscious conservation efforts but from varied combinations of low population density, inefficient techniques for extracting resources, and a lack of profitable markets for resources. She argues that resource practices are ecologically driven and do not appear to correlate with expressed attitudes, including sacred prohibition. In other words, need and opportunity overwhelm edict and expressed attitude.

7. It is also the case that *access* to acquiring these skills is limited—even for those who have innate verbal-analytic abil-

ity. Thus the "right" school (a material resource, bought with money like other commodities) and the "right" family (one that has sufficient purchasing power for the right school and other opportunities) are also important.

8. Indeed, TV-Free America and the A. C. Nielsen Company reported in 1996 that the average American watched television more than twenty-eight hours per week, or two months per year.

9. Wallace Stevens, *The Man Whose Pharynx Was Bad.*

5. ELABORATING

1. I am not saying here that other animals do not display any evidence of remembering or planning. Many animal mothers seem to grieve for and even "look for" dead or missing young, and their behavioral programs for, say, finding food look like "plans." The difference is one of degree of mental elaboration, memory, and foresight, not of kind.

2. Burkert (1996, 177) alludes to the existence of biological patterns of actions, reactions, and feelings activated and elaborated through ritual practice and verbalized teachings, but he does not specifically mention those developed in mother-infant engagement. He also discusses biological programs that religious and ritual behavior seems to address: escape (offerings), hierarchy (authority and submission; the strategy of praise), reciprocity (giving, exchange, sacrifice), and the human need to explain and avert evil and disaster (to assign causality and atone for guilt).

3. The Sanskrit word *alankara*, or ornamentation, as applied to the arts, carries these associations.

4. Such animal (and human) elaborations are also said to be indirect but genuine advertisements of superior fitness, since only the strongest can overcome the "handicap" of enormous antlers, long sweeping tails, or overlong exertion (e.g., Zahavi and Zahavi 1997).

5. Indeed, one can think of elaborations as supernormal stimuli (as described

near the end of chapter 4), where a feature of natural interest or attraction—a striking color, shape, sound, movement, entity, word, event, idea—is exaggerated or emphasized in order to become more interesting or attractive. See also chapter 6, and Aiken (1998, 56).

6. Humans may in some circumstances, where no other response is possible, also fight, flee, or freeze. Indeed, in developing her theory of how art evokes emotion, Aiken (1998, chapters 5–7) provides many examples of specific stimuli that affect this defensive capacity (fight, flight, and freeze) in humans. Certainly our mammalian heritage ensures that we react appropriately to threat. Nonetheless, compared with other animals, humans have a greater capacity to remember the past, anticipate the future, and control their environment—and this is my point. See also note 1, this chapter.

7. In the modern world we are rightly suspicious of an expressed "need for control," since we are victims as well as beneficiaries of an accelerated cultural disposition to control nature by immoderate and often unstoppable technological means. As described here, the ancestral need to affect the world can be understood less as a zealous drive to subjugate nature than as a psychological imperative to feel able to cope with the demands of life. Successful coping provides the healthy sense of competence described in chapter 4.

8. I reiterate here that rituals also can generate or manufacture anxiety by directing attention to matters of vital but problematic concern, but they then go on to resolve it.

9. Since then, I have found several archaeologists who report an increase in arts during stressful periods in human evolution. For example, Late Dorset peoples (A.D. 800–1500) in what is now northern Canada faced two growing threats—changing climatic conditions and Thule invaders from the west—which coincided with a dramatic increase in the production of Dorset art (Taçon 1983). Similarly,

J. J. Brody (1977, 210) has suggested that a crisis in food production stimulated not only the novel pottery style of the Mimbres people of the American Southwest but also a variety of innovative rituals. Steven Mithen (1996, 157) states that "Stone Age art is not a product of comfortable circumstances; it was most often created when people were living in conditions of severe stress." Historian William McNeill (1995, 89) notes that "preaching and song combined with rhythmic muscular movement" are conspicuous "in times of trouble and among distressed populations." See also Taçon and Brockwell 1995 and Taçon, Wilson, and Chippindale 1996 for prehistoric Arnhem Land, Australia.

Brian Hayden (1993), however, points out that abundance of game leading to surpluses promotes the need for status display or prestige items such as ornaments or fine garments. Elsewhere (Hayden 1987) he recognizes that scarce and fluctuating resources make sharing and cooperative alliances imperative for long-term and short-term survival and that ecstatic states, facilitated by stress, sensory deprivation, rhythmic drama, shock, or certain types of sounds, were means toward the forming of emotional bonds between members in different bands.

10. Joseph LeDoux, a specialist in the neurobiology of emotion, has investigated the amygdala, a region of the brain that is important in appraising the emotional significance of sensory stimuli. He suggests that the amygdala may contribute (through its connections with basal ganglia), along with cognitive systems in the cortex, to voluntary instrumental emotional and behavioral responses that are emitted in an effort to cope with the involuntary reactions that emotional information produces (LeDoux 1994, 218–19). I suggest that controlled movements such as regularization and repetition are among these voluntary coping behaviors.

11. Again, ritual can also *generate* or manufacture anxiety, insofar as it points to areas of uncertainty that require attention and then resolve this anxiety.

12. See notes 1 and 6, this chapter.

13. A temporary increase in stress hormones (and associated neuropeptides) allows the body to respond effectively to changing environmental conditions and enhances activity in localized areas of the brain for short periods, hence improving cognitive processes for responding to challenges (Flinn et al. 1996, 127–28). Novelty itself stimulates stress response in a linear fashion (Sapolsky 1992, 313); the effects can range from mild curiosity to active investigation and creative activity, or to confusion and mental disorganization, depending on the source of the novelty and one's ability to deal with it. When provoked for relatively brief periods in response to physical stressors, stress responses are obviously adaptive. When activated for too long or too frequently, or for no physiological reason (that is, by prolonged psychological or social anxiety), they can compromise a wide range of associated somatic functions, including energy release, immune system activity, mental activity, digestion, growth and tissue repair, and reproductive physiology and behavior. An individual's perceived sense of control over the provoking situation affects the degree of severity of the response and hence influences whether or not a stress disorder occurs (Sapolsky 1992, 324).

14. William H. McNeill (1995) notes the euphoria of "muscular bonding," which in his stimulating and original book refers to moving together in time, especially in dancing and military drill. He does not discuss the emotion that attends anticipating and responding to slight deviations from a steady beat.

15. In December 1994, near Avignon in southeastern France, a limestone cave containing more than three hundred painted images of animals was discovered. The paintings in this site (named "Chauvet" after one of its discoverers) have been dated to 30,000–32,000 B.P., which makes them at present the oldest known cave paintings. This is nearly twice as old as the images in Lascaux, perhaps the most famous Paleolithic painted gallery. Before

Chauvet was discovered, Cosquer cave (discovered in 1991 by Henri Cosquer, a professional diver, while exploring underwater grottoes near Marseilles) held the record for early wall markings: stenciled handprints from 26,500–27,800 B.P., along with later paintings from the time of Lascaux.

16. In his informative survey of the Ice Age, Paul Bahn reports numerous early human sites (dating from one hundred twenty-five thousand to perhaps more than eight hundred thousand years before the present) in which ocher of various colors has been found, although he cautions that we cannot know the purposes for which it was used (Bahn and Vertut 1997, 23–24).

17. Poem published in the *Times Literary Supplement* (London), August 16, 1996, 25, and reprinted by permission of the poet, John Gohorry.

18. Power Boothe, who, among other things, is a set designer, reminds me that some of these characteristics of *mbari* are inherent in modern theater productions. Many hands participate and more work occurs than is ever paid for. And when it is over, the sets are discarded and the cast disperses.

6. TAKING THE ARTS SERIOUSLY

1. For example, Plato famously banished poets from his Republic and claimed that artists and musicians were deceivers insofar as they added embellishments and other sensory seductions that could distract us from or mislead us in our understanding of true or ideal reality.

2. Many artists from the time at least of the Impressionists until the 1950s have chosen to suffer in order to make their art. As Modernism has given way to Postmodernism, this has come to seem less noble or necessary, although artists are still torn between the van Gogh model (all guts and heart, no sales) and the Warhol model (promotion and market strategy placed before personal engagement) (Jones 1996).

3. The antisocial, dangerous excesses

of persons who run amok or of berserkers seem to contradict this conclusion. Perhaps these persons' frenzy and seeming invulnerability convince observers of mighty but accessible powers that lie dormant below the surface of their worldview and thereby reinforce belief in its truth and efficacy.

4. Even art history majors are preponderantly females, although enrollment in studio art subjects is roughly equal in males and females.

5. "Nonfunctionality" is a serious liability to many in a society like ours that sacrifices the achievement of communal integrity and well-being to the bottom line.

6. Thomas Crow (1996, 213) reminds us that visuality has been withdrawn and the beholder suppressed from much contemporary art (for example, in conceptual, aleatory, transitory, and replicative art). He reports that as a field, visual culture studies replaces the myth of the pursuit of knowledge for its own sake (inherent in the discipline of art history as it developed) with an interdisciplinary dialogue that admits its concern with the relevance of contemporary values for academic study.

7. Perception, emotion/motivation, and cognition are of course also bodily, inseparable from intentional motor activity.

8. An interesting report by David Henley (1992) describes "pre-art and proto-artistic behavior" of apes, elephants, and dolphins, as revealed both in practice and in field observations with these animals. As an art therapist, Henley is interested in the aesthetic outcomes of these animals' behavior, since he has found that severely retarded, psychotic, autistic, and very young humans, who have no apparent aesthetic intention, may nevertheless produce powerful aesthetic imagery. Henley's discussion of the question of animal art and human response to it is both sophisticated and sensitive and repays reading.

9. Thomas Crow (1996) calls for a more publicly available, world-referencing, and nonironic conceptual art and mentions several contemporary artists who, he suggests, have "transformed conceptual art from something cold and impersonal into a drama of lives driven onto treacherous emotional shoals." This may well be desirable within the art world, but it would seem even more publicly relevant to advocate that people in general—children, patients, adults of all types—be encouraged to transform their own lives and emotions—that is, to make connections, make special, make art—as a means to reference and value their worlds.

10. Seymour Simmons III (1998) reviews some current approaches to building community through the arts, as described in recent surveys and assessments of such programs by two university research projects.

11. For nearly thirty years the Touchstone Center in New York City, founded and directed by Richard Lewis, has shown in numerous programs and activities how the natural world can be used to engage children's imaginations.

12. The Getty Education Institute for the Arts has distributed over twenty-five thousand copies of this supplement, free of charge, to interested persons who request it.

13. In a book about the life of Friedrich Froebel, the nineteenth-century German educator who "invented" kindergarten, Norman Brosterman (1997) suggests that the widespread use of Froebel's educational toys, some of which taught the repetitive use of geometrical forms as the building blocks of all design, shaped the abstract renderings of early-twentieth-century architects and artists (such as Frank Lloyd Wright and Picasso, who were schooled during Froebel's most influential period). If this is so, the direction of influence stated in the text was originally reversed.

14. For a cornucopia of information about the arts in education and their relationship to human needs and abilities, see the publication lists of the National Art

Education Association, the Getty Education Institute for the Arts, and the recent National Endowment for the Arts publication *American Canvas* (Larson 1997). See also note 12, this chapter, and Carroll 1993 and London 1994.

15. To say that "human beings are simply incarnated vocabularies" or "nothing more than the presence or absence of dispositions toward the use of sentences phrased in some historically conditioned vocabulary" (Rorty 1989, 88) is to disregard half a million years of human existence and experience. The multiplicity and sensuality of the meanings of the arts cannot be confined to or exhausted by verbal description.

16. I do not refer here to such well-known bittersweet humor as that of the central Europeans' mordant responses to the bleakness of life behind the Iron Curtain but to the stock-in-trade of "sick" comedy, shock radio, and the like.

17. This is not to say that hunter-gatherer life is unfailingly sunny and conflict-free but to make the point that many of today's distressing social problems are symptoms of the way we live and were rarer and less problematic in ancestral times. I find it difficult to imagine hunter-gatherers with bulimia, anorexia, or attention deficit disorder.

18. Peter London (1989) gives a differently worded but similar list of "the earlier, more profound functions of art, which have always had to do with personal and collective empowerment, personal growth, communion with this world, and the search for what lies beneath and above this world." When compiling my list, I had not read his, which includes renewing and reaffirming the covenants between humankind and nature and between man and God; grappling with the ephemeral qualities of life and with our own mortality; marking significant times, places, and events; celebrating the gifts of life; fulfilling individual potentialities and collective possibilities; discovering the actual range of human possibilities; and awakening us to higher levels of consciousness.

19. From an after-dinner speech at the Plaza Hotel, published in the *New Yorker*, 27 May 1996, pp. 33–34.

APPENDIX: TOWARD A
NATURALISTIC AESTHETICS

1. With regard to understanding the most heightened or transcendent states, evolutionists are largely silent (although see Oubré 1997 on "numinous experience").

2. Much of the formulation in this section was developed in conversations and correspondence with Joel Schiff.

3. Although Thornhill and his colleagues do not specifically discuss aesthetic quality, they sometimes write (e.g., Thornhill 1998) as if "beauty" preferences for signs of health and fecundity in prospective mates—low female waist-to-hip ratios by males, or symmetrical body features by both sexes—are meaningful contributions, as they stand, to understanding human art.

4. Although Turner (1991) considers beauty as a "precultural, neurobiological phenomenon," his study goes far beyond that of evolutionary psychology and claims that beauty is an emergent property at every level of the universe.

5. Around 400,000 B.P., *Homo erectus* transported gem-quality rock crystal from a distance, for unknown reasons (Kenneth Oakley, personal communication).

6. An analogous "modal" progression from dark and dull to light and brilliant also occurs in the content of Yolngu songs and song sequences and in their dances, where a shimmering sense of movement again carries both emotional and cognitive meaning of conferred sacredness (Morphy 1992, 197–98).

7. Taçon (1991, 204) proposes that a symbolic complex may have emerged about six thousand years ago in western Arnhem Land that encompassed quartzite stone tools and polychrome rock paintings in which iridescence was shown through cross-hatched, hatched, and X-ray infill. Between three thousand years ago and the present, a correspondence

between powerfully bright and dazzling substances and the potency of ancestral beings, and the relationship of these to cycles of human and animal life, became entrenched in the Aboriginal belief system. Cross-hatched designs are likened by Aboriginal people today to the shimmering effect of the sun on water and are also said to represent the essence of rainbow color and life itself. The rainbow serpent, one of the most widespread and powerful ancestral beings, is associated with and often resides in water. Taçon, Wilson, and Chippindale (1995, 103) argue that cross-hatching denoting an element of sacredness originated with early rainbow serpent depictions. (See also Coss 1990 for a study investigating the association of visual gloss and glitter with water.)

8. Poudjougou also said that the difference between a creation that was "magical" and one that was not was a combination of pleasure for the eyes, efficacy in its intended use, and "something else that was not for words" (Hoffman 1995).

9. Dutton (1994) finds the example of Kominimung shields to illustrate the "crucial social binding function of art," an interpretation with which I agree. This is evident in the examples cited in the present book, as in the rhythms and modes of Temiar healing ceremonies which create in their participants a feeling of overflow and conjoinment that they interpret as spiritual transformation and healing.

10. One could add the loss of one's home in a natural disaster, a serious injury, or the loss of employment.

11. Sexual selection theory proposes that females choose a mate on the basis of qualitative differences in males' color, pattern, or performance. In humans, this would correspond to qualitative differences in accessibility and strikingness, and perhaps tangible relevance, but probably not to evocative resonance, as I discuss shortly.

12. Aiken's four-part diagram of aesthetic response (Aiken 1998, 16) includes universal reactions, cultural and personal associations, and recognition of skill or originality, which would all be subsumable under my first three levels. Joseph Carroll's (1995) three levels of analysis of literary works—universal, cultural, and individual—also correspond roughly to my levels one through three.

13. For an example of such inseparability of moral and aesthetic matters, what the Igbo call *ndu oma* ("the good life") denotes not simply pleasure (*la dolce vita*) but also beauty and incorporates ideals of good health, strength, abundance, wealth, children, communal feasting, and enjoyment (Willis 1989). All these things are biologically relevant and all are sustained by adherence to customary laws. As in other traditional societies, what is morally good is expected to display valued aesthetic qualities, and what displays valued aesthetic qualities is expected to be morally good: life and art are reflections of each other.

14. To be sure, there are arcane matters in small-scale societies, as in our own, which only the adept know. But I do not consider this to be superiority or elitism as in modern stratified societies.

15. According to Karl Heider (1979), the Dani "rarely expend energy to add beauty to a thing," and Cora Dubois (1944) reported that the people of Alor had a slovenly and perfunctory attitude toward their rituals.

16. Certainly acid indigestion, insomnia, and obesity are serious and real concerns, but pills and liposuction are hardly fundamental solutions. Friendly offers of postponed payment for purchases do not address subsistence needs when consumers' credit is already overextended.

17. Of course, in every traditional society, periodic "unserious" festivals and holidays have been welcome and important, but such enjoyment and leisure provided diversion and replenishment to subsistence lives, not additional distraction and indulgence to already frenetic and fractionated ones.

References Cited

Abu-Lughod, Lila. 1986. *Veiled Sentiments: Honor and Poetry in a Bedouin Society.* Berkeley: University of California Press.

Agee, James. 1941. *Let Us Now Praise Famous Men.* Boston: Houghton Mifflin.

Aiken, Nancy E. 1998. *The Biological Origins of Art.* Westport, Conn.: Praeger.

Ainsworth, Mary D. Salter. 1967. *Infancy in Uganda: Infant Care and the Growth of Love.* Baltimore: Johns Hopkins University Press.

Aitken, Kenneth J., and Colwyn Trevarthen. 1997. Self/other organization in human psychological development. *Development and Psychopathology* 9: 653–77.

Alland, Alexander. 1983. *Playing with Form.* New York: Columbia University Press.

Alonso, Marcelo. 1995. The challenge of the information society. Plenary address, Twentieth International Conference on the Unity of the Sciences, Seoul, Korea.

Alpers, Svetlana. 1988. *Rembrandt's Enterprise.* Chicago: University of Chicago Press.

Appleton, Jay. 1975. *The Experience of Landscape.* New York: Wiley.

———. 1990. *The Symbolism of Habitat.* Seattle: University of Washington Press.

Arenz, Tré. 1995. Artist statement. *Borderline Clay* (annual publication of the National Council on Education for the Ceramic Arts), 70–71.

Bahn, Paul G., and Jean Vertut. 1997. *Journey through the Ice Age.* Berkeley: University of California Press.

Bailey, Kent. 1996. Mismatch theory 1: Basic principles. *ASCAP (Across Species Comparison and Psychopathology) Newsletter* 9(2). Galveston: University of Texas Medical Branch.

Bal, Mieke. 1994. Dead flesh, or the smell of painting. In *Visual Culture: Images and Interpretations,* N. Bryson, M. A. Holly, and K. Moxey, eds., 365–83. Hanover: University Press of New England (Wesleyan University Press).

Barber, Benjamin. 1995. *Jihad vs. McWorld.* New York: Times Books.

Baron-Cohen, Simon. 1995. *Mindblindness: An Essay on Autism and Theory of Mind.* Cambridge, Mass.: MIT Press.

Basso, Ellen B. 1985. *A Musical View of the Universe: Kalapalo Myth and Ritual Performances*. Philadelphia: University of Pennsylvania Press.

Beahrs, John O. 1990. The evolution of post-traumatic behavior: Three hypotheses. *Dissociation* 3(1): 15–21.

———. 1992. Hypnotic transactions and the evolution of psychological structure. *Psychiatric Medicine* 10(1): 25–39.

Beebe, Beatrice. 1986. Mother-infant mutual influence and precursors of self- and object-representations. In *Empirical Studies of Psychoanalytic Theories*, vol. 2, J. Masling, ed., 27–48. Hillsdale, N.J.: Erlbaum.

Beebe, Beatrice, and Louis Gerstman. 1984. A method of defining "packages" of maternal stimulation and their functional significance for the infant with mother and stranger. *International Journal of Behavioral Development* 7: 423–40.

Beebe, Beatrice, and Frank M. Lachmann. 1988. The contribution of mother-infant mutual influence to the origins of self- and object-representations. *Psychoanalytic Psychology* 5(4): 305–37.

Begley, Sharon. 1998. Your child's brain. *Child Growth and Development 97/98*, 53–58. Guilford, Conn.: Dushkin (Annual Editions from the Public Press).

Birket-Smith, Kaj. 1950 [1927]. *The Eskimos*. London: Methuen.

Blurton-Jones, Nicholas. 1993. The lives of hunter-gatherer children: Effects of parental behavior and parental reproductive strategy. In *Juvenile Primates: Life History, Development, and Behavior*, M. E. Pereira and L. A. Fairbanks, eds., 309–26. New York: Oxford University Press.

Bonami, Francesco. 1996. *Il Villaggio a Spirale/The Spiral Village*. Campo 6, Galleria Civica d'Arte Moderna e Contemporanea, Torino. Milan: Skira.

Boothe, Power. 1996. Notes on Abstract/Meaning. *American Abstract Artists Journal* 1: n.p. New York: American Abstract Artists.

Bourguignon, Erika. 1972. Dreams and altered states of consciousness in anthropological research. In *Psychological Anthropology*, 2d ed., F.L.K. Hsu, ed., 403–34. Cambridge, Mass.: Schenkman.

Bowers, C. A. n.d. *Let Them Eat Data: The Ecological and Educational Consequences of Globalizing Computer Culture*. In preparation.

Bowlby, John. 1969–80. *Attachment and Loss*. 3 vols. New York: Basic Books.

Boyd, Robert, and Peter J. Richerson. 1990. Culture and cooperation. In *Beyond Self-Interest*, J. J. Mansbridge, ed., 111–32. Chicago: University of Chicago Press.

Brain, Robert. 1980. The Ibo Mbari. In his *Art and Society in Africa*, 250–58. London: Longman.

Brazelton, T. Berry. 1977. Implications of infant development among the Mayan Indians of Mexico. In *Culture and Infancy*, P. H. Leiderman, S. R. Tulkin, and A. Rosenfeld, eds., 151–87. New York: Academic Press.

Brody, J. J. 1977. *Mimbres Painted Pottery*. Albuquerque: University of New Mexico Press.

Brosterman, Norman. 1997. *Inventing Kindergarten*. New York: Abrams.

Brothers, Leslie. 1992. Perception of social acts in primates: Cognition and neurobiology. *Seminars in the Neurosciences* 4: 409–14.

Brothers, L., and B. Ring. 1992. A neuroethological framework for the representation of minds. *Journal of Cognitive Neuroscience* 4: 107–18.

Brothers, L., B. Ring, and A. Kling. 1990. Response of neurons in the macaque amygdala to complex social stimulation. *Behavioural Brain Research* 57: 53–61.

Burford, Bronwen. 1988. Action cycles: Rhythmic actions for engagement with children and young adults with profound mental handicap. *European*

Journal of Special Needs Education 3(4): 189–206.

Burkert, Walter. 1996. *Creation of the Sacred: Tracks of Biology in Early Religions.* Cambridge, Mass.: Harvard University Press.

Callaghan, John W. 1981. A comparison of Anglo, Hopi, and Navajo mothers and infants. In *Culture and Early Interactions*, T. M. Field, A. M. Sostek, P. Vietze, and P. H. Leiderman, eds., 115–31. Hillsdale, N.J.: Erlbaum.

Carritt, E. F., ed. 1931. *Philosophies of Beauty.* Oxford: Clarendon.

Carroll, Joseph. 1995. *Evolution and Literary Theory.* Columbia: University of Missouri Press.

———. 1999. The deep structure of literary representations. *Evolution and Human Behavior* 20(3): 159–73.

Carroll, Karen Lee. 1993. Taking responsiblity: Higher education's opportunity to affect the future of the arts in the schools. *Arts Education Policy Review* 95(1): 17–22.

———. 1997. Cultivating artistic behaviors. In *Creating Meaning through Art*, J. Simpson, J. Delaney, K. L. Carroll, et al., eds., 75–114. Columbus, Ohio: Prentice Hall.

Chalmers, F. Graeme. 1996. *Celebrating Pluralism: Art, Education, and Cultural Diversity.* Los Angeles: Getty Education Institute for the Arts, Occasional Paper Series 5.

Chisholm, James. 1983. *Navajo Infancy: An Ethological Study of Child Development.* New York: Aldine.

Clore, Gerald L. 1994. Why emotions vary in intensity. In *The Nature of Emotion: Fundamental Questions*, P. Ekman and R. J. Davidson, eds., 386–93. New York: Oxford University Press.

Coe, Kathryn. 1992. Art: The replicable unit—an inquiry into the possible origin of art as a social behavior. *Journal of Social and Evolutionary Systems* 15(2): 217–34.

———. 1995. Visual art as ancestral lectures: Toward a definition of art and theory of its social function. Unpublished conference paper.

Coe, Kathryn, and Lyle B. Steadman. 1995. The human breast and the ancestral reproductive cycle: A preliminary inquiry into breast cancer etiology. *Human Nature* 6(3): 197–220.

Cole, Herbert. 1969a. Mbari is life. *African Arts* 2(30).

———. 1969b. Mbari is a dance. *African Arts* 2(4).

———. 1982. *Mbari: Art and Life among the Owerri Igbo.* Bloomington: Indiana University Press.

———. 1989. *Icons: Ideals and Power in the Arts of Africa.* Washington, D.C.: Smithsonian Insitution Press.

Coote, Jeremy. 1992. 'Marvels of everyday vision': The anthropology of aesthetics and the cattle-keeping Nilotes. In *Anthropology, Art, and Aesthetics*, J. Coote and A. Shelton, eds., 245–73. Oxford: Clarendon.

Coss, Richard G. 1990. All that glistens: Water connotations in surface finishes. *Ecological Psychology* 2(4): 367–80.

Courtwright, David T. 1996. *Violent Land: Single Men and Social Disorder from the Frontier to the Inner City.* Cambridge, Mass.: Harvard University Press.

Cousins, Norman. 1979. *Anatomy of an Illness as Perceived by the Patient.* New York: Norton.

———. 1983. *The Healing Heart: Antidotes to Panic and Helplessness.* New York: Norton.

Covarrubias, M. 1937. *Island of Bali.* New York: Knopf.

Crosby, Alfred W. 1997. *The Measure of Reality: Quantification and Western Society.* Cambridge: Cambridge University Press.

Crow, Thomas. 1996. *Modern Art in the Common Culture.* New Haven, Conn.: Yale University Press.

Csikszentmihalyi, Mihaly. 1990. *Flow: The Psychology of Optimal Experience.* New York: Harper and Row.

Cubbs, Joanne. 1994. Rebels, mystics, and

outcasts: The romantic artist as outsider. In *The Artist Outsider: Creativity and the Boundaries of Culture*, M. D. Hall and E. W. Metcalf, Jr., eds., 76–93. Washington, D.C.: Smithsonian Institution Press.

Daly, Martin, and Margo Wilson. 1995. Discriminative parental solicitude and the relevance of evolutionary models to the analysis of motivational systems. In *The Cognitive Neurosciences*, M. S. Gazzaniga, ed., 1269–86. Cambridge, Mass.: MIT Press.

Daniel, Vesta A. H. 1995. The Kwanzaa playground: A culturally transferable model of art education as a community act. Presentation at 1995 INSEA-Asian Regional Congress, November 10–15, Taiwan, R.O.C.

Danto, Arthur C. 1997. *After the End of Art: Contemporary Art and the Pale of History*. Princeton, N.J.: Princeton University Press.

DeCasper, A. J., and W. P. Fifer. 1980. Of human bonding: Newborns prefer their mothers' voices. *Science* 208: 1174–76.

Deren, Maya. 1970. *Divine Horsemen: The Living Gods of Haiti*. New York: Chelsea House.

de Waal, Frans. 1989. *Peacemaking among Primates*. Cambridge, Mass.: Harvard University Press.

Diamond, Stanley. 1974. *In Search of the Primitive*. New Brunswick, N.J.: Transaction.

Dissanayake, Ellen. 1988. *What Is Art For?* Seattle: University of Washington Press.

———. 1992. *Homo Aestheticus: Where Art Comes From and Why*. Seattle: University of Washington Press.

———. 1995. Chimera, spandrel, or adaptation: Conceptualizing art in human evolution. *Human Nature* 6(2): 99–117.

———. 1998. Komar and Melamid discover Pleistocene taste. *Philosophy and Literature* 22(2): 486–96.

———. 1999. Antecedents of musical meaning in the mother-infant dyad. In *Biopoetics: Evolutionary Explorations in the Arts*, L. B. Cooke and F. Turner, eds., 367–97. New York: Paragon House.

Dixon, Suzanne, E. Tronick, C. Keefer, and T. B. Brazelton. 1981. Mother-infant interaction among the Gusii of Kenya. In *Culture and Early Interactions*, T. M. Field, A. M. Sostek, P. Vietze, and P. H. Leiderman, eds., 149–68. Hillsdale, N.J.: Erlbaum.

Donald, Merlin. 1991. *Origins of the Modern Mind: Three Stages in the Evolution of Culture and Cognition*. Cambridge, Mass.: Harvard University Press.

Dubois, Cora. 1944. *The People of Alor*. Minneapolis: University of Minnesota Press.

Dunning, Joan. 1994. *Secrets of the Nest: The Family Life of North American Birds*. Boston: Houghton Mifflin.

Dutton, Denis. 1994. Authenticity in the art of traditional societies. *Pacific Arts* 9–10: 1–9.

———. 1991. On Price and Torgovnick (book review). *Philosophy and Literature* 15: 377–90.

Eibl-Eibesfeldt, I. 1989. *Human Ethology*. Translated by Pauline Wiessner-Larsen and Anette Heunemann. New York: Aldine de Gruyter.

Eimas, P. D. 1984. Infant competence and the acquisition of language. In *Biological Perspectives on Language*, D. Caplan, A. Roch Lecours, and A. Smith, eds., 109–29. Cambridge, Mass.: MIT Press.

Eiseley, Loren. 1979. *The Star Thrower*. New York: Harcourt Brace Jovanovich.

Eisenstein, Elizabeth. 1993. *The Printing Revolution in Early Modern Europe*. Cambridge: Cambridge University Press.

Eisner, Elliot W. 1995. Aesthetic forms of thinking in the arts and the sciences. Presentation at 1995 INSEA-Asian

Regional Congress, November 10–15, Taiwan, R.O.C.

Ekman, Paul. 1992. Facial expressions of emotion: An old controversy and new findings. *Philosophical Transactions of the Royal Society of London* 335: 63–70.

———. 1994. Antecedent events and emotion metaphors. In *The Nature of Emotion: Fundamental Questions*, P. Ekman and R. J. Davidson, eds., 146–49. New York: Oxford University Press.

Ekman, Paul, and R. J. Davidson. 1994. Afterword: What is the function of emotions? In *The Nature of Emotion: Fundamental Questions*, P. Ekman and R. J. Davidson, eds., 137–39. New York: Oxford University Press.

Ekman, Paul, R. J. Davidson, and W. V. Friesen. 1990. Emotional expression and brain physiology: II. The Duchenne smile. *Journal of Personality and Social Psychology* 58: 342–53.

Ekman, Paul, R. W. Levenson, and W. V. Friesen. 1983. Autonomic nervous system activity distinguishes among emotions. *Science* 218: 1208–10.

Ellsworth, Phoebe. 1994a. Some reasons to expect universal antecedents of emotions. In *The Nature of Emotion: Fundamental Questions*, P. Ekman and R. J. Davidson, eds., 150–54. New York: Oxford University Press.

———. 1994b. Levels of thought and levels of emotion. In *The Nature of Emotion: Fundamental Questions*, P. Ekman and R. J. Davidson, eds., 192–96. New York: Oxford University Press.

Evans-Pritchard, E. E. 1940. *The Nuer: A Description of a Nilotic People*. Oxford: Clarendon.

Fajado, Barbara F., and Daniel G. Freedman. 1981. Maternal rhythmicity in three American cultures. In *Culture and Early Interactions*, T. M. Field, A. M. Sostek, P. Vietze, and P. H. Leiderman, eds., 133–47. Hillsdale, N.J.: Erlbaum.

Falick, Melanie. 1996. *Knitting in America*. New York: Artisan.

Fein, Sylvia. 1993. *First Drawings: Genesis of Visual Thinking*. Pleasant Hill, Calif.: Exelrod Press.

Feiring, Candice, and Michael Lewis. 1981. Middle-class differences in the mother-child interaction and the child's cognitive development. In *Culture and Early Interactions*, T. M. Field, A. M. Sostek, P. Vietze, and P. H. Leiderman, eds., 63–91. Hillsdale, N.J.: Erlbaum.

Feld, Steven. 1982. *Sound and Sentiment: Birds, Weeping, Poetics, and Song in Kaluli Expression*. Philadelphia: University of Pennsylvania Press.

Fernald, Anne. 1992. Human maternal vocalizations to infants as biologically relevant signals: An evolutionary perspective. In *The Adapted Mind: Evolutionary Psychology and the Generation of Culture*, J. H. Barkow, L. Cosmides, and J. Tooby, eds., 391–428. New York: Oxford University Press.

Fernandez, James. 1972. *Tabernanthe Iboga*: Narcotic ecstasies and the work of the ancestors. In *Flesh of the Gods: The Ritual Use of Hallucinogens*, P. T. Furst, ed., 237–60. London: George Allen and Unwin.

Field, Tiffany M., and Susan M. Widmayer. 1981. Mother-infant interactions among lower SES Black, Cuban, Puerto Rican, and South American immigrants. In *Culture and Early Interactions*, T. M. Field, A. M. Sostek, P. Vietze, and P. H. Leiderman, eds., 41–62. Hillsdale, N.J.: Erlbaum.

Flinn, Mark V., Robert Quinlan, Mark Turner, Seamus A. Decker, and Barry G. England. 1996. Male-female differences in effects of parental absence on glucocorticoid stress response. *Human Nature* 7(2): 125–62.

Freeman, Walter. 1995. *Societies of Brains*. Hillsdale, N.J.: Erlbaum.

Freud, Sigmund. 1979 [1921]. *Group Psychology and the Analysis of the Ego*. Translated and edited by J. Strachey. New York: Norton.

Friedrich, Otto. 1990. What do babies know? In *Human Development 89/90*, H. E. Fitzgerald and M. G. Walraven, eds., 40–45. Guilford, Conn.: Dushkin (Annual Editions from the Public Press).

Frijda, Nico H. 1994. Emotions are functional, most of the time. In *The Nature of Emotion: Fundamental Questions*, P. Ekman and R. J. Davidson, eds., 112–22. New York: Oxford University Press.

Fullagar, R.L.K., D. M. Price, and L. M. Head. 1996. Early human occupation of northern Australia: Archaeology and thermoluminescence dating of Jinmium rock-shelter, Northern Territory. *Antiquity* 70(270): 751–73.

Gambrell, Jamey. 1994. Sarajevo: Art in extremis. *Art in America* (May), 100–105.

Gardner, Howard. 1973. *The Arts and Human Development*. New York: Wiley. Reprint, Basic Books, 1994.

———. 1993a. *Creating Minds: An Anatomy of Creativity*. New York: Basic Books.

———. 1993b. *Multiple Intelligences: The Theory in Practice*. New York: Basic Books.

Gardner, Russell, Jr. 1996. Psychiatry needs a basic science titled sociophysiology. *ASCAP (Across Species Comparison and Psychopathology) Newsletter* 9(2): 15–16. Galveston: University of Texas Medical Branch.

Gell, Alfred. 1992. The technology of enchantment and the enchantment of technology. In *Anthropology, Art, and Aesthetics*, J. Coote and A. Shelton, eds., 40–63. Oxford: Clarendon.

Gennep, Arnold van. 1960 [1908]. *The Rites of Passage*. London: Routledge and Kegan Paul.

Glaze, Anita J. 1981. *Art and Death in a Senufo Village*. Bloomington: Indiana University Press.

Goldman, Irving. 1964. The structure of ritual in the northwest Amazon. In *Process and Pattern in Culture*, R. A. Manners, ed., 111–22. Chicago: Aldine.

Goldstein, Harriet, and Vetta Goldstein. 1926. *Art in Every Day Life*. New York: Macmillan.

Gorman, Albertus. 1995. Celebration of renewal. *Visual Art Review* (Louisville Visual Art Association) 7: 18–19.

Gorman, Carma R. 1997. The "period eye" and design and costume of the 1920s and 1930s. Paper presented at the annual meeting of the College Art Association, February 14, New York, N.Y.

Grant, E. C. 1968. An ethological description of nonverbal behavior during interviews. *British Journal of Medical Psychology* 41: 177–83.

———. 1972. Nonverbal communication in the mentally ill. In *Non-Verbal Communication*, R. Hinde, ed., 349–58. Cambridge: Cambridge University Press.

Greenspan, Stanley I. 1997. *The Growth of the Mind and the Endangered Origins of Intelligence*. Reading, Mass.: Addison Wesley.

Grunwald, Lisa. 1998. The amazing minds of infants. *Child Growth and Development 1997/98*, 44–48. Guilford, Conn.: Dushkin (Annual Editions from the Public Press).

Guss, David M. 1989. *To Weave and Sing: Art, Symbol and Narrative in the South American Rain Forest*. Berkeley: University of California Press.

Haith, M., T. Bergman, and M. Moore. 1997. Eye contact and face scanning in early infancy. *Science* 198: 855–65.

Hamilton, Annette. 1981. *Nature and Nurture: Aboriginal Child-Rearing in North-Central Arnhem Land*. Canberra: Australian Institute of Aboriginal Studies.

Hansen, Brian. 1991. *Theatre: The Dynamics of the Art*. 2d ed. Englewood Cliffs, N.J.: Prentice-Hall.

Harlow, H. F. 1958. The nature of love. *American Psychologist* 13: 673–85.

Harlow, H. F., and R. R. Zimmermann.

1959. Affectional responses in the infant monkey. *Science* 130: 421–32.

Hauser, Marc D. 1996. *The Evolution of Communication*. Cambridge, Mass.: MIT Press.

Hayden, Brian. 1987. Alliances and ritual ecstasy: Human responses to resource stress. *Journal for the Scientific Study of Religion* 26(1): 81–91.

———. 1993. *Archaeology: The Science of Once and Future Things*. New York: W. H. Freeman.

Heidegger, Martin. 1971. The origin of the work of art. In *Poetry, Language, Thought*, translated by Albert Hofstadter, 17–87. New York: Harper and Row.

Heider, Karl G. 1979. *Grand Valley Dani: Peaceful Warriors*. New York: Holt, Rinehart and Winston.

Henley, David R. 1992. Facilitating artistic expression in captive mammals: Implications for art therapy and art empathicism. *Art Therapy* 9(4): 178–92.

Hesketh, Phoebe. 1994. *The Leave Train: New and Selected Poems*. London: Enitharmon Press.

Hewlett, Barry S. 1991. *Intimate Fathers: The Nature and Context of Aka Pygmy Paternal Infant Care*. Ann Arbor: University of Michigan Press.

Hildebrand, Grant. 1991. *The Wright Space*. Seattle: University of Washington Press.

Hillman, James. 1989. Back to beyond: On cosmology. In *Archetypal Process: Self and Divine in Whitehead, Jung, and Hillman*, D. R. Griffin, ed., 213–31. Evanston, Ill.: Northwestern University Press.

Himmelheber, Hans. 1993 [1938]. *Eskimo Artists (Fieldwork in Alaska, June 1936 until April 1937)*. Fairbanks: University of Alaska Press. (Originally published in German.)

Hofer, M. A. 1990. Early symbolic processes: Hard evidence from a soft place. In *Pleasure beyond the Pleasure Principle*, R. A. Glick and S. Bones,

eds., 55–78. New Haven, Conn.: Yale University Press.

Hoffman, Rachel. 1995. Objects and acts. *African Arts* (Summer), 56–59.

van Hooff, Jan A.R.A.M. 1989. Laughter and humour, and the 'duo-in-uno' of nature and culture. In *The Nature of Culture*, W. A. Koch, ed. Proceedings of the International and Interdisciplinary Symposium, October 7–11, 1986. Bochum, Germany: N. Brockmeyer.

Huxley, Aldous. 1923. *Antic Hay*. New York: Doran.

Imberty, Michel. 1997. Trends of developmental psychology in music. Paper presented at the Florentine Workshops in Biomusicology 1: The Origins of Music, May 29–June 2, Fiesole, Italy.

James, William. 1941 [1902]. *The Varieties of Religious Experience*. New York: Longmans, Green.

Jones, Caroline. 1996. *The Machine in the Studio*. Chicago: University of Chicago Press.

Kalma, Akko. 1986. Uncertainty reduction: A fundamental concept in understanding a number of psychological theories. In *Essays in Human Sociobiology*, J. Wind and V. Reynolds, eds., 213–41. Brussels: V.U.B. Study Series, 26.

Kapferer, Bruce. 1983. *A Celebration of Demons: Exorcism and the Aesthetics of Healing in Sri Lanka*. Bloomington: Indiana University Press.

Kaplan, Stephen. 1992. Environmental preference in a knowledge-seeking, knowledge-using organism. In *The Adapted Mind: Evolutionary Psychology and the Generation of Culture*, J. H. Barkow, L. Cosmides, and J. Tooby, eds., 581–98. New York: Oxford University Press.

Kartomi, Margaret J. 1991. Musical improvisations of children at play. *World of Music* 33(3): 53–65.

Katz, Richard. 1982. *Boiling Energy: Community Healing among the Kalahari*

!Kung. Cambridge, Mass.: Harvard University Press.

Kivy, Peter. 1990. *Sound Sentiment: An Essay on the Musical Emotions.* Philadelphia: Temple University Press.

Klaus, Marshall H., and John H. Kennell. 1976. *Parent-Infant Bonding.* St. Louis, Mo.: Mosby.

Knight, Chris, Camilla Power, and Ian Watts. 1995. The human symbolic revolution: A Darwinian account. *Cambridge Archaeological Journal* 5: 75–114.

Kobasa, S. C. 1979. Stressful life events, personality and health: An inquiry into hardiness. *Journal of Personality and Social Psychology* 37(1): 1–11.

Komar, Vitaly, and Alexander Melamid. 1997. *Painting by Numbers: Komar and Melamid's Scientific Guide to Art,* JoAnn Wypijewski, ed. New York: Farrar, Straus and Giroux.

Konner, Melvin. 1977. Infancy among the Kalahari Desert San. In *Culture and Infancy,* P. H. Leiderman, S. R. Tulkin, and A. Rosenfeld, eds., 287–328. New York: Academic Press.

Kugiumutzakis, G. 1993. Intersubjective vocal imitation in early mother-infant interaction. In *New Perspectives in Early Communicative Development,* J. Nadel and L. Camaioni, eds., 23–47. London: Routledge.

Kuhl, P. K., J. E. Andruski, I. A. Chistovich, L. A. Chistovich, E. V. Kozhevnikova, V. L. Ryskina, E. I. Stolyarova, U. Sundberg, and F. Lacerda. 1997. Cross-language analysis of phonetic units in language addressed to infants. *Science* 277: 684–86.

Lakeman, James. 1997. Review. *Times Literary Supplement* (London), June 13, 4915: 28.

Lancaster, Jane B. 1978. Carrying and sharing in human evolution. *Human Nature* 1(2): 82–89.

Langer, Susanne. 1953. *Feeling and Form.* New York: Charles Scribner's Sons.

Larson, Gary O. 1997. *American Canvas.* Washington, D.C.: National Endowment for the Arts.

Laski, Marghanita. 1961. *Ecstasy: A Study of Some Secular and Religious Experiences.* London: Cresset.

Lau, Beverly, Bonnie A. B. Blackwell, Henry P. Schwarcz, Ivan Turk, and Joel I. Blickstein. 1997. Dating a flautist? Using ESR (electron spin resonance) in the Mousterian cave deposits at Divje Babe I, Slovenia. *Geoarchaeology* 12(6): 507–36.

Laughlin, Charles D., John McManus, Jr., and Eugene G. d'Aquili. 1990. Mature contemplation. In *Brain, Symbol and Experience: Toward a Neurophenomenology of Human Consciousness,* 296–333. Boston, Mass.: Shambhala.

Lawal, Babatunde. 1996. *The Gèlèdé Spectacle: Art, Gender, and Social Harmony in an African Culture.* Seattle: University of Washington Press.

Lazarus, Richard. 1994. The past and present in emotion. In *The Nature of Emotion: Fundamental Questions,* P. Ekman and R. J. Davidson, eds., 306–10. New York: Oxford University Press.

Leakey, Richard. 1994. *The Origin of Humankind.* New York: Basic Books.

LeDoux, Joseph E. 1994. Cognitive-emotional interactions in the brain. In *The Nature of Emotion: Fundamental Questions,* P. Ekman and R. J. Davidson, eds., 216–23. New York: Oxford University Press.

LeVine, R. A., and D. T. Campbell. 1972. *Ethnocentrism: Theories of Conflict, Ethnic Attitudes, and Group Behavior.* New York: Wiley.

Lévi-Strauss, Claude. 1969. *The Raw and the Cooked.* Translated by John and Doreen Weightman. New York: Harper and Row.

Lewis, Michael, and Peggy Ban. 1977. Variance and invariance in the mother-infant interaction: A cross-cultural study. In *Culture and Infancy,* P. H. Leiderman, S. R. Tulkin, and A. Rosenfeld, eds., 329–55. New York: Academic Press.

Lewis-Williams, J. D. 1995. Seeing and construing: The making and meaning of a southern African rock art motif. *Cambridge Archaeological Journal* 5(1): 3–23.

Lewis-Williams, J. D., and Thomas A. Dowson. 1988. The signs of all times: Entopic phenomena and Upper Palaeolithic art. *Current Anthropology* 29(2): 201–45.

Lewkowicz, D. J., and G. Turkewitz. 1980. Cross-modal equivalence in early infancy: Auditory-visual intensity matching. *Developmental Psychology* 16(6): 597–607.

Leys, Simon. 1996. Review. *New York Review of Books* 43: 28–31.

Lippard, Lucy R. 1994. Crossing into uncommon ground. In *The Artist Outsider: Creativity and the Boundaries of Culture*, M. D. Hall and E. W. Metcalf, Jr., eds., 2–18. Washington, D.C.: Smithsonian Institution Press.

Locke, John L. 1993. *The Child's Path to Spoken Language*. Cambridge, Mass.: Harvard University Press.

London, Peter. 1989. *No More Second-Hand Art: Awakening the Artist Within*. Boston: Shambhala.

———. 1994. *Step Outside: Community-Based Art Education*. Portsmouth, N.H.: Heinemann.

Lopreato, Joseph. 1984. *Human Nature and Biocultural Evolution*. Boston: Allen and Unwin.

Lorenz, Konrad. 1966. *On Aggression*. London: Methuen.

Low, Bobbi S. 1996. Behavioral ecology of conservation in traditional societies. *Human Nature* 7(4): 353–79.

Lynch, M. P., D. Kimbrough-Oller, M. L. Steffens, and E. H. Buder. 1995. Phrasing in prelinguistic vocalizations. *Developmental Psychobiology* 28(1): 3–25.

MacCarthy, Fiona. 1994. *William Morris: A Life for Our Time*. London: Faber and Faber.

Maddock, Kenneth. 1973. *The Australian Aborigines: A Portrait of Their Society*. London: Allen Lane, Penguin Press.

Marks, Lawrence E., Robin J. Hammeal, and Marc H. Bornstein. 1987. Perceiving similarity and comprehending metaphor. *Monographs of the Society for Research in Child Development* 52(1): 1–92.

Martin, R. D. 1990. *Primate Origins and Evolution: A Phylogenetic Reconstruction*. Princeton, N.J.: Princeton University Press.

Martini, Mary, and John Kirkpatrick. 1991. Early interactions in the Marquesa Islands. In *Culture and Early Interactions*, T. M. Field, A. M. Sostek, P. Vietze, and P. H. Leiderman, eds., 189–213. Hillsdale, N.J.: Erlbaum.

Masataka, Nobuo. 1996. Perception of motherese in a signed language by 6-month-old deaf infants. *Developmental Psychology* 32(5): 874–79.

McGuire, M. T., and A. Troisi. 1987. Physiological regulation-deregulation and psychiatric disorders. *Ethology and Sociobiology* 8: 9S–26S.

McLuhan, T. C. 1971. *Touch the Earth: A Self-Portrait of Indian Existence*. Toronto: New Press.

McNeill, William H. 1995. *Keeping Together in Time: Dance and Drill in Human History*. Cambridge, Mass.: Harvard University Press.

Mealey, Linda. 1995. The sociobiology of sociopathy: An integrated evolutionary model. *Behavioral and Brain Sciences* 18(3): 523–99.

Meltzoff, A. N., and M. H. Moore. 1977. Imitation of facial and manual gestures by human neonates. *Science* 219: 1347–49.

Miller, Geoffrey. 1998. How mate choice shaped human nature: A review of sexual selection in human evolution. In *Handbook of Evolutionary Psychology: Ideas, Issues, and Applications*, C. Crawford, and D. L. Krebs, eds., 87–130. Mahwah, N.J.: Erlbaum.

Mithen, Steven. 1996. *The Prehistory of the Mind: The Cognitive Origins of Art, Religion and Science*. London: Thames and Hudson.

Morgan, Elaine. 1995. *The Descent of the*

Child: Human Evolution from a New Perspective. Oxford: Oxford University Press.

Morphy, Howard. 1992. From dull to brilliant: The aesthetics of spiritual power among the Yolngu. In *Anthropology, Art, and Aesthetics*, J. Coote and A. Shelton, eds., 181–208. Oxford: Clarendon.

Morris, William. 1886–87. *A Dream of John Ball*. Serialized in *The Commonweal* (London).

Morton, E. S., and J. Page. 1992. *Animal Talk: Science and the Voices of Nature*. New York: Random House.

Murray, Lynne, and Colwyn Trevarthen. 1985. Emotional regulation of interactions between two-month-olds and their mothers. In *Social Perception in Infants*, Tiffany Field and Nathan Fox, eds., 177–98. Norwood, N.J.: Ablex.

Nakano, Shigeru. 1996. Heart-to-heart (inter-*jo*) resonance: A concept of intersubjectivity in Japanese everyday life. *Annual Report* 19, Research and Clinical Center for Child Development, Faculty of Education, Hokkaido University, Sapporo, Japan.

Nemerowicz, Gloria, and Eugene Rosi. 1997. *Education for Leadership and Social Responsibility*. London: Falmer Press.

Nunley, John. 1996. The beat goes on: Recycling and improvisation in the steel bands of Trinidad and Tobago. In *Recycled, Re-Seen: Folk Art from the Global Scrap Heap*, C. Cerny and S. Seriff, eds., 130–39. New York: Abrams.

Oakley, Kenneth. 1981. The emergence of higher thought 3.0–0.2 Ma B.P. In *The Emergence of Man*, Philosophical Transactions of the Royal Society of London, B 292: 205–11.

O'Hanlon, Michael. 1989. *Reading the Skin: Adornment, Display, and Society among the Wahgi*. London: British Museum Publications.

Olson, Janet L. 1997. Encouraging visual storytelling. In *Creating Meaning through Art*, J. Simpson, J. Delaney, K. L. Carroll et al., eds., 163–205. Columbus, Ohio: Prentice Hall.

Orians, Gordon H., and Judith H. Heerwagen. 1992. Evolved responses to landscapes. In *The Adapted Mind: Evolutionary Psychology and the Generation of Culture*, J. H. Barkow, L. Cosmides, and J. Tooby, eds., 555–79. New York: Oxford University Press.

Osborne, Nigel. 1994. Playing at the very edge. *The Independent* (London), Weekend, 2 April, p. 31.

Oubré, Alondra. 1997. *Instinct and Revelation: Reflections on the Origins of Numinous Perception*. Amsterdam: Gordon and Breach.

Papousek, H., M. Papousek, and L. S. Koester. 1982. Sharing emotionality and sharing knowledge: A microanalytic approach to parent-infant communication. In *Measuring Emotions in Infants and Children*, vol. 2, C. E. Izard and P. B. Read, eds., 93–123. New York: Cambridge University Press.

Pickstone, Charles. 1996. *For Fear of the Angels: How Sex Has Usurped Religion*. London: Hodder and Stoughton.

Pinker, Steven. 1994. *The Language Instinct: How the Mind Creates Language*. New York: Morrow.

———. 1997. Evolutionary psychology: An exchange. *New York Review of Books* 44(15) (October 9): 55–56.

Pitcairn, T. K., and M. Schleidt. 1976. Dance and decision: An analysis of a courtship dance of the Medlpa, New Guinea. *Behaviour* 58: 298–316.

Portmann, A. 1941. Die Tragzeit der Primaten und die Dauer der Schwangerschaft beim Menschen: Ein Problem der vergleichende Biologie. *Revue Suisse de Zoologie* 48: 511–18.

Postman, Neil. 1993. *Technopoly: The Surrender of Culture to Technology*. New York: Vintage Books.

Propp, Vladimir. 1968. *Morphology of the Folktale*. 2d ed. Austin: University of Texas Press.

Radcliffe-Brown, A. R. 1948 [1922]. *The Andaman Islanders.* Glencoe, Ill.: Free Press.

Randal, Jonathan. 1995. "No child's play for boy soldiers." *Washington Post,* June 12: A12.

Rauscher, Frances H., Gordon L. Shaw, and Katherine N. Ky. 1993. Music and spatial task performance. *Nature* 365 (14 October): 611.

Rauscher, Frances H., Gordon L. Shaw, Linda J. Levine, Eric L. Wright, Wendy R. Dennis, and Robert L. Newcomb. 1997. Music training causes long-term enhancement of preschool children's spatial-temporal reasoning. *Neurological Research* 19: 208.

Reichel-Dolmatoff, Gerardo. 1972. The cultural context of an aboriginal hallucinogen: *Banisteriopsis caapi.* In *Flesh of the Gods: The Ritual Use of Hallucinogens,* P. T. Furst, ed., 84–113. London: George Allen and Unwin.

Reynolds, Vernon. 1975. *The Biology of Human Action.* San Francisco: W. H. Freeman.

Roberts, Richard, Michael Bird, Jon Olley, Rex Galbraith, Ewan Lawson, Geoff Laslett, Hiroyuki Yoshida, Rhys Jones, Richard Fullager, Geraldine Jacobsen, and Quan Hua. 1998. Optical and radiocarbon dating at Jinmium rock shelter in northern Australia. *Nature* 393: 358–62.

Rorty, Richard. 1989. *Contingency, Irony, and Solidarity.* New York: Cambridge University Press.

Roseman, Marina. 1984. The social structuring of sound: The Temiar of peninsular Malaysia. *Ethnomusicology* 28(3): 411–45.

———. 1991. *Healing Sounds of the Malaysian Rainforest.* Berkeley: University of California Press.

Ruskin, John. 1851. *The Stones of Venice,* vol. 2. New York: American Publishing Corporation.

Sapolsky, Robert M. 1992. Neuroendocrinology of the stress-response. In *Behavioral Endocrinology,* Jill R. Becker, S. Marc Breedlove, and David Crews, eds., 287–324. Cambridge, Mass.: MIT Press.

Sarno, Louis. 1993. *Song from the Forest: My Life among the Ba-Benjellé Pygmies.* Boston: Houghton Mifflin.

Schelde, Tyge, and Mogens Hertz. 1994. Ethology and psychotherapy. *Ethology and Sociobiology* 15(5–6): 383–92.

Scheper-Hughes, Nancy. 1987. The cultural politics of child survival. In *Child Survival: Anthropological Perspectives on the Treatment and Maltreatment of Children,* N. Scheper-Hughes, ed., 1–29. Boston: Reidel.

Schieffelin, Bambi B. 1990. *The Give and Take of Everyday Life: Language Socialization of Kaluli Children.* Cambridge: Cambridge University Press.

Schieffelin, Edward. 1976. *The Sorrow of the Lonely and the Burning of the Dancers.* New York: St. Martin's.

Schore, A. N. 1994. *Affect Regulation and the Origin of the Self: The Neurobiology of Emotional Development.* Hillsdale, N.J.: Erlbaum.

Seelig, Warren. 1992. Craft and the impulse to abstract. *Haystack Institute 1992,* 11–16. Deer Isle, Me.: Haystack Mountain School of Crafts.

Simmons, Seymour, III. 1998. Creating community through art: Two research project reviews. *Journal of Social Theory in Art Education* 18: 59–76.

Simpson, J., J. Delaney, K. L. Carroll, C. Hamilton, S. Kay, M. Kerlavage, and J. Olson. 1997. *Creating Meaning through Art.* Columbus, Ohio: Prentice Hall.

Smidt, Dirk. 1990. Kominimung sacred woodcarvings. In *The Language of Things: Studies in Ethnocommunication,* P. ter Keurs and D. Smidt, eds., 77–111. Mededelingen van het Rijksmuseum voor Volkenkunde, no. 25. Leiden: Rijksmuseum voor Volkenkunde.

Sostek, A. M. 1981. Social context in caregiver-infant interaction: A film study of Fais and the United States. In *Culture and Early Interactions*, T. M. Field, A. M. Sostek, P. Vietze, and P. H. Leiderman, eds., 21–37. Hillsdale, N.J.: Erlbaum.

Stanford, Craig B. 1996. The hunting ecology of wild chimpanzees: Implications for the evolutionary ecology of Pliocene hominids. *American Anthropologist* 98(1): 96–113.

Stern, Daniel. 1985. *The Interpersonal World of the Infant*. New York: Basic Books.

———. 1995. *The Motherhood Constellation: A Unified View of Parent-Infant Psychotherapy*. New York: Basic Books.

Storey, Robert. 1996. *Mimesis and the Human Animal: On the Biogenetic Foundations of Literary Representation*. Evanston, Ill.: Northwestern University Press.

Storr, Anthony. 1992. *Music and the Mind*. New York: Free Press.

Stroh, Katrin, and Thelma Robinson. 1993. *Learning and Communication: Functional Learning Programmes for Young Developmentally Delayed Children* (handbook and video). Suffolk, England: Concord Video and Film Council Ltd.

Taçon, Paul S. C. 1983. Dorset art in relation to prehistoric culture stress. *Etudes Inuit/Inuit Studies* 7(1): 41–65.

———. 1991. The power of stone: Symbolic aspects of stone use and tool development in western Arnhem Land, Australia. *Antiquity* 54: 192–207.

Taçon, Paul S. C., and Sally Brockwell. 1995. Arnhem Land prehistory in landscape, stone, and paint. *Antiquity* 69: 676–95.

Taçon, Paul S. C., Richard Fullagar, Sven Ouzman, and Ken Mulvaney. 1997. Cupule engravings from Jinmium-Granilpi (northern Australia) and beyond: Exploration of a widespread and enigmatic class of rock markings. *Antiquity* 71: 942–65.

Taçon, Paul S. C., Meredith Wilson, and Christopher Chippindale. 1996. Birth of the rainbow serpent in Arnhem Land rock art and oral history. *Archaeology Oceania* 31: 103–24.

Talbot, Margaret. 1998. Attachment theory: The ultimate experiment. *New York Times Magazine*, May 24: 24–30, 38, 46, 50, 54.

Thomas, Nicholas. 1995. *Oceanic Art*. London: Thames and Hudson.

Thompson, Laura. 1945. Logico-aesthetic integration in Hopi culture. *American Anthropologist* 47: 450–53.

Thornhill, Randy. 1998. Darwinian aesthetics. In *Handbook of Evolutionary Psychology: Ideas, Issues, and Applications*, C. Crawford and D. L. Krebs, eds., 543–72. Mahwah, N.J.: Erlbaum.

Tiger, Lionel. 1969. *Men in Groups*. New York: Random House.

Tizon, Alex. 1995. A new start in Seattle. *Seattle Times*, July 23: A1, 8.

Tolbert, Elizabeth. 1990. Women cry with words: Symbolization of affect in the Karelian lament. *Yearbook for Traditional Music* 22: 80–105.

Tooby, John, and Leda Cosmides. 1992. The psychological foundations of culture. In *The Adapted Mind: Evolutionary Psychology and the Generation of Culture*, J. H. Barkow, L. Cosmides, and J. Tooby, eds., 19–136. New York: Oxford University Press.

Townsend, J. M., J. Kline, and T. H. Wasserman. 1995. Low-investment copulation: Sex differences in motivations and emotional reactions. *Ethology and Sociobiology* 16: 25–51.

Trevarthen, C. 1979. Communication and cooperation in early infancy: A description of primary intersubjectivity. In *Before Speech: The Beginning of Human Communication*, M. Bullowa, ed., 321–47. Cambridge: Cambridge University Press.

———. 1984. Emotions in infancy: Regulators of contact and relationship with persons. In *Approaches to Emotion*, K. Scherer and P. Ekman, eds., 129–57. Hillsdale, N.J.: Erlbaum.

———. 1986. Form, significance and psychological potential of hand gestures of infants. In *The Biological Foundations of Gestures: Motor and Semiotic Aspects*, J.-L. Nespoulous, P. Perron, and A. Roch Lecours, eds., 149–202. Hillsdale, N.J.: Erlbaum.

———. 1987. Brain development. In *The Oxford Companion to the Mind*, R. L. Gregory and O. L. Zangwill, eds., 101–10. Oxford: Oxford University Press.

———. 1990. Growth and education in the hemispheres. In *Brain Circuits and Functions of the Mind*, C. Trevarthen, ed., 334–63. Cambridge: Cambridge University Press.

———. 1993. The function of emotions in early infant communication and development. In *New Perspectives in Early Communicative Development*, J. Nadel and L. Camaioni, eds., 48–81. London: Routledge.

———. 1997. Fetal and neonatal psychology: Intrinsic motives and learning behavior. In *Advances in Perinatal Medicine*, Proceedings of the Fifteenth European Congress of Perinatal Medicine, Forrester Cockburn, ed., 282–91. New York: Parthenon.

———. 1998. The concept and foundations of infant intersubjectivity. In *Intersubjective Communication and Emotion in Early Ontogeny*, S. Bråten, ed., 15–46. Cambridge: Cambridge University Press.

Trevarthen, C., and K. J. Aitken. 1994. Brain development, infant communication, and empathy disorders: Intrinsic factors in child mental health. *Development and Psychopathology* 6: 597–633.

Trevarthen, C., T. Kokkinaki, and G. A. Fiamenghi, Jr. 1999. What infants' imitations communicate: With mothers, with fathers, and with peers. In *Imitation in Infancy*, J. Nadel and G. Butterworth, eds., 127–85. Cambridge: Cambridge University Press. In press.

Trinkaus, E. 1983. *The Shanidar Neandertals*. New York: Academic Press.

Trivers, Robert. 1974. Parent-offspring conflict. *American Zoologist* 14: 249–64.

Tronick, Edward Z., Gilda A. Morelli, and Steve Winn. 1987. Multiple caretaking of Efe (pygmy) infants. *American Anthropologist* 89(1): 96–106.

Turnbull, Colin. 1961. *The Forest People*. London: Chatto and Windus.

Turner, Frederick. 1985. The neural lyre: Poetic meter, the brain, and time. In *Natural Classicism*, 61–108. Charlottesville: University Press of Virginia.

———. 1991. *Beauty: The Value of Values*. Charlottesville: University Press of Virginia.

———. 1995. *The Culture of Hope: A New Birth of the Classical Spirit*. New York: Free Press.

Turner, Victor. 1969. *The Ritual Process*. London: Routledge and Kegan Paul.

Üher, Johanna. 1991. On zigzag designs: Three levels of meaning. *Current Anthropology* 32: 437–39.

Wagner, S., E. Winner, D. Cicchetti, and H. Gardner. 1981. 'Metaphorical' mapping in human infants. *Child Development* 52: 728–31.

Watson, David, and Lee Anna Clark. 1994. The vicissitudes of mood: A schematic model. In *The Nature of Emotion: Fundamental Questions*, P. Ekman and R. J. Davidson, eds., 400–405. New York: Oxford University Press.

Watson-Gegeo, Karen A., and D. W. Gegeo. 1986. Calling-out and repeating routines in Kwaia'ae children's language socialization. In *Language Socialization across Cultures*, B. B. Schieffelin and E. Ochs, eds., 17–50. Cambridge: Cambridge University Press.

White, Randall. 1989. Production complexity and standardization in early Aurignacian bead and pendant manufacture: Evolutionary implications. In *The Human Revolution*, P. Mellars and C. Stringer, eds., 366–90. Edinburgh: Edinburgh University Press.

———. 1993. Technological and social dimensions of 'Aurignacian Age' body ornaments across Europe. In *Before Lascaux: The Complex Record of the Early Upper Palaeolithic*, H. Knecht, A. Pike-Tay, and R. White, eds., 247–99. Boca Raton, Fla.: CRC Press.

Whitley, David S. 1994. Shamanism, natural modeling, and the rock art of far western North American hunter-gatherers. In *Shamanism and Rock Art in North America*, S. Turpin, ed., 1–43. Special Publication 1. San Antonio, Texas: Rock Art Foundation.

Williams, K., E. Kramer, D. Henley, and L. Gerity. 1997. Art therapy and the seductive environment. *American Journal of Art Therapy* 35: 106–17.

Willis, Liz. 1989. *Uli* painting and the Igbo world view. *African Arts* 23(1): 62–67.

Wilson, Brent. 1997. *The Quiet Evolution: Changing the Face of Arts Education*. Los Angeles: Getty Education Institute for the Arts.

Wilson, E. O. 1984. *Biophilia*. Cambridge, Mass.: Harvard University Press.

———. 1998. *Consilience: The Unity of Knowledge*. New York: Knopf.

Winner, Ellen. 1994. Some thoughts on the genesis of art. In *The Arts in Their Infancy: A Symposium*, A. Hurwitz, ed., 13–26. Maryland Institute, College of Art.

Zahavi, Amotz, and Avishag Zahavi. 1997. *The Handicap Principle: A Missing Piece of Darwin's Puzzle*. New York: Oxford University Press.

Zajonc, R. B. 1985. Emotion and facial efference: A theory reclaimed. *Science* 228: 15–22.

Zemp, Hugo. 1971. *Musique Dan: La musique dans la pensée et la vie sociale d'une société africaine*. Paris: Mouton.

Index of Names

Index of Subjects

Page numbers in italic type indicate illustrations.

www.ingramcontent.com/pod-product-compliance
Lightning Source LLC
Chambersburg PA
CBHW020856180526
45163CB00007B/2524